Poisonous Snakes

Poisonous Snakes

Tony Phelps

BLANDFORD PRESS
Poole   Dorset

First published in the UK in 1981

Copyright © 1981 Blandford Press Ltd.
Link House, West Street
Poole, Dorset BH15 1LL

Reprinted 1983

British Library Cataloguing in Publication Data

Phelps, Tony
  Poisonous snakes
  1 Poisonous snakes
  598.1'2'0469   QL666.06

ISBN 0 7137 0877 8 (hardback)
     0 7137 1433 6 (paperback)

Set in 10 on 12½ pt Monophoto Plantin
and printed and bound
by Butler & Tanner Ltd,
Frome and London

Contents

Author's Preface

The subject of snakes is often an emotive one. It is a topic that at once fills many people with fear and loathing and these are feelings that are very real; a phobia that is caused by very few other animals with the possible exception of spiders. This situation is further enhanced when it is known that many of these creatures, that move so mysteriously without the aid of limbs, can also deliver a fatal bite.

Although it is a medical fact that people do have phobias about snakes, the majority of prejudice is a result of plain ignorance and misunderstanding. This book does not profess to convert such people towards a kinder outlook on snakes, but to state the facts as they really are. This is achieved by exposing some of the myths that surround these creatures. I have also tried to be realistic and point out situations where venomous snakes are a hazard to man.

The primary function of this book, and indeed most books, is for the reader to gain from the author's experience and the knowledge gathered as a result of that experience. Many of us are specialists in our own particular fields and I have been lucky enough to have been able to study snakes in both wild and captive conditions.

Past literature on the subject has mainly dealt with identification and anatomy. In other words, we may know what a certain snake looks like and how its body functions, but to a much lesser extent do we know how it lives and how it functions within the environment where it occurs. Similarly, the care and handling of venomous snakes appears to have almost been a trade secret in the past, and this is highlighted by the fact that many of the world's authorities on the subject have been almost entirely self taught with regard to the actual problem of the 'first restrain your snake' type of situation.

It can be appreciated that the many and varied types of venomous snakes require different techniques when it comes to handling. This book can therefore be regarded essentially as a practical guide to both field study, and husbandry and handling. However, such important aspects as distribution, and relationships with man, have not been ignored. Descriptions of species have been kept to a minimum and I am indebted to such specialist knowledge that I have deemed fit to lean on.

Acknowledgements

Preparing a book about any group of animals is not without difficulty and is certainly not achieved by a completely lone effort. Therefore, I am indebted to the following for their help and understanding:

Dr E. N. Arnold, James Ashe, D. Ball, Prof. Angus D'A. Bellairs, J. Coborn, J. Foden, Susan Goebels, Herbert S. Harris Jr, J. Hoofien, Prof. Elazar Kochva, John Murphy, Ray Parker, D. Reid, Dr H. Alistair Reid, N. Shaefer, Dr Garth Underwood, Prof. André De' Vries, Dr D. Worrell, Eric Worrell.

I also wish to thank the publishers for their tolerance and understanding during the preparation of this manuscript.

Tony E. Phelps
Poole, 1980

Picture Credits

Thanks are due to the following for colour photographs:

Ardea Photographics/Adrian Warren (Pl. 4), S. C. Bisserot (Pl. 18), Joe F. Blossom (Pl. 1), H. G. Cogger (Pls 11, 12, 13), Bruce Coleman/Jean & Des Bartlett (Pl. 27), Bruce Coleman/S. C. Bisserot (Pl. 16), Bruce Coleman/C. B. Firth (Pls 3, 5), Bruce Coleman/ Bill Wood (Pl. 14), M. Jaeger (Pl. 29), John Murphy (Pls 23, 26, 28, 30, 31, 32, 33), Tony Phelps (Pls 2, 6, 7, 9, 10, 15, 17, 19, 20, 21, 22, 24, 25), N. Shaeffer (Pl. 8);

for black and white photographs:

S. C. Bisserot (Figs 14, 22, 24, 28, 30, 31, 33, 35, 46, 47, 48, 52, 53, 54, 65), H. G. Cogger (Figs 20, 32), Evening Post-Echo Limited (Fig. 61), W. Gillespie (Fig. 34), John Murray (Figs 42, 43, 44, 45), Tony Phelps (Figs 1, 15, 16, 17, 23, 25, 26, 29, 41, 51, 66), Mike Pollard, Evening Mail Ltd (Fig. 62), N. Schaeffer (Fig. 63), Philip T. Smith (Figs 56, 64, 69), Syndication International (Figs 68, 70), D. A. Warrell (Figs 57, 58, 59, 60), Eric Worrell (Figs 18, 19, 21, 55);

and for line drawings:

Admen (Figs 39, 40, 49), Michael Clark (Figs 2, 3, 4, 5, 6), Helen Downton (Fig. 67), D.W. Graphics (Figs 7, 8, 9, 10, 11, 12, 13), Tell Hicks (Figs 36, 37, 38, 71), Tony Phelps (Figs 27, 50).

1
Introduction

Reptiles are the remnants of a bygone age and all the groups that remain today are familiar to most people. The crocodiles, turtles, lizards and snakes that inhabit the earth are just a small reminder of the great age of reptiles when *Triceratops* and *Iguanodon* roamed the humid swamps; an age that lasted 120 million years.

The lizards and snakes form the majority of contemporary reptiles, each group having about three thousand species.

The snakes represent many diverse forms and are distributed throughout the world with the exception of the polar regions. One group, the sea snakes, have successfully colonised the open sea.

Front-fanged venomous snakes constitute about 15 per cent of the total number of snake species, and only a comparatively small number of these are considered dangerous to man. Venomous snakes are further represented by the majority group of snakes, the colubrids, which contain many genera of rear-fanged snakes of which only two or three species offer any threat to man.

Before describing venomous snakes in particular it is necessary to have some understanding of what snakes are: their anatomy, bodily functions, how they feed and, quite simply, how they move.

Anatomy

Snakes evolved from lizard-like ancestors and as a result of the slow process of evolution the elongate flexible body underwent considerable changes both externally and internally. The most obvious change is the complete lack of limbs; the boas and pythons and several other small groups, have vestigial remains of hind limbs in the form of small spurs. Internally, with the exception of those mentioned, no snakes have any traces of any skeletal features relating to limbs. All snakes have well-formed vertebrae and ribs which vary in number from species to species but usually in the region of between 140–160. Notable modification of the vertebrae can be seen in such groups as the sea snakes where the tail is laterally compressed and oar-like.

The internal organs have also become adapted to accommodate an elongate form. Most snakes possess only one lung; only some primitive species have retained both lungs. The heart is simple and consists of a left and right auricle and a single ventricle.

Most snakes feed on large prey which they swallow whole, and for this reason the gullet is capable of great distension to allow the passage of large items of food. Similarly, the long tubular stomach has the capability of accommodating large food items.

Snakes do not possess a single penis but a paired organ which is joined at the base and is called the hemipenis. This organ when not erected lies in the anterior part of the tail close to the vent. Each penis is employed quite independently of the other. The hemipenis of snakes varies, but is generally a stubby organ covered with soft spines. These spines prevent the penis from being dislodged from the female. Snakes pair for long periods and withdrawal is eventually effected by a retractor muscle. Snakes will often expose the hemipenis when handled or in pain.

Senses

Snakes have no external ear and as such cannot perceive airborne sounds. However, snakes are perceptive to ground vibrations which are picked up via the jaw and quadrate bone. Snakes are particularly perceptive to changes in the surface on which they lie, whether it be vibration or temperature change, and it is possible that some of the internal organs play a major role in detecting these changes.

Situated in the palate is the remarkable organ known as the organ of Jacobson, which is the snake's main means of perceiving smell. The constant flickering of the tongue of a snake is familiar and in fact the tongue is passing scent particles to the Jacobson's organ.

Snakes do not have eyelids and the eye is capable of only limited

FIG. I The false water cobra, *Cyclagras gigas*, a colubrid snake of the New World which resembles some of the Old World elapids in appearance. Note the prominent hood.

movement. This does not involve even partially closing the eye. The covering of the eye is a watch-glass affair called the brille, which in fact is part of the skin and is shed periodically each time the snake moults. Many snakes, notably the burrowing types, are virtually blind while others have fairly good vision and can spot irregularities on the horizon for some distance. However, sight can be regarded as a secondary sense, particularly when considering the fact that during the post-moulting period the eye covering is opaque, rendering the snake blind for several days.

Other senses include a susceptibility to temperature changes which must be paramount for a creature that is dependent on the immediate surrounding temperature.

Heat detection is perfected by one group of venomous snakes known as the pit vipers. The term, pit viper, refers to an organ, the 'loreal pit', which is situated just below the eye and is used for locating warm-blooded prey.

It is true to summarise by stating that snakes are poorly equipped for perceiving distant stimuli but much better adapted for close contact conditions.

Feeding

The majority of snakes do not feed every day but usually about once each week. Snakes cannot chew or tear their food and so they are

3

obliged to swallow food whole. The jaws, however, are not rigidly hinged and are capable of expanding to allow prey of a larger girth than the snake to be swallowed. Swallowing is effected by literally 'walking' the jaws over the prey. This is seen to full effect with the vipers, which use the large fangs alternately to pull the food into the throat. The skin of a snake exhibits great elasticity and can accommodate seemingly impossible large prey.

Locomotion

It is at once obvious that the lack of limbs is no handicap to a snake's life style. Although the movements are extremely graceful it is this ease of motion, without the apparent aid of limbs, that repels many people.

Snakes have adopted several modes of locomotion, the most common of which is what is termed as 'lateral undulatory'. This means simply that the snake progresses with a side-to-side movement. There is no magic in the way a snake moves; a snake is supersensitive to its bodily contact with the ground and takes advantage of every irregularity on the surface. Place a snake on a polished surface, such as glass, and it is virtually helpless.

Other legless animals such as eels and some species of lizard move by actually wriggling, but the movement of a snake is a pure muscular action co-ordinated through the vertebrae as the snake progresses.

When in a restricted space, such as a burrow, snakes adopt a concertina movement. Large heavy snakes such as the large rattlesnakes and puff adders usually use this concertina movement in normal conditions, but can employ a lateral undulatory movement when in a hurry.

Desert species employ what is known as 'sidewinding', and one species, the small desert-living rattlesnake, *Crotalus cerastes*, is called the sidewinder. However, other small desert-living vipers employ this mode of locomotion in various parts of the world. This mode of locomotion is very effective over loose sand and is effected by lifting the body, leaving only two points of the body in contact with ground at either end. The snake then moves in a sideways fashion with astonishing speed and appears to move in a series of little jumps.

Skin shedding

The renewal of the outer layer of skin in vertebrates is obligatory; in man, for example, it is a continuous process which goes almost unnoticed. Snakes shed the skin in one piece and adults may shed two or three times each year. Immature snakes, which grow rapidly, shed the skin much more often.

Several weeks prior to shedding a snake becomes dull in colour and the eyes become cloudy until just a few days before the moult, when the eyes clear and the snake resumes almost normal coloration.

The snake then rubs the jaws against a stone, branch or some other rough object, until the skin becomes loosened. When the head becomes free of the old skin the snake literally crawls slowly out of its skin, turning it inside out as we would a sock. The skin when shed is quite fragile but retains a faithful image of the pattern of its old owner.

Periods of inactivity

The term hibernation has been deliberately avoided as it is often misleading and is better applied to mammals. Snakes that occur throughout the temperate zones of the world are obliged to spend the winter months in a state of torpor. Similarly, snakes that occur in the warmer regions are inactive for varying amounts of time during periods of excessive heat. In either case a critical factor is exhibited at each end of the temperature scale. This aspect is dealt with later when considering individual species and at this point it is sufficient to state that climate is the one major influence which determines a snake's annual cycle.

These then are the basic functions which govern the lives of snakes, be they venomous or otherwise. In addition many of the diverse species have particular requirements with regard to habitat and food while others show remarkable degrees of adaptability, even to the point of sharing our houses.

2
Classification and Distribution

The first snakes probably appeared on this earth during the Cretaceous period, some seventy to eighty million years ago. Fossil records of snakes are virtually non-existent, and the main clues to their origins are to be found by the examination of the reptile forms that exist today.

Several hypotheses exist which offer differing views as to the origins of snakes. One popular theory is that the early snakes were fossorial, or burrowing forms.

Examples of burrowing snakes exist today—the blind snakes (Typhlopidae) are typical burrowers, as are the shield tails (Uropeltidae). The primitive characteristics of contemporary burrowing snakes vary in degree; for example, some groups possess important characters of skull and lung structure, and this is an indication that these groups have evolved a stage further. However, while it is true that these fossorial snakes exhibit various stages of evolution, they differ very little in their actual habits. Some may burrow deeper than others, some may almost be considered as surface dwellers. There exists also some variation in size, but the bodily form of all these species suggests a snake that is adapted to a subterranean way of life. The most obvious external characteristics found in burrowing forms are the reduced eyes and the reduction, or absence, of the ventral plates (gastroteges).

If all snakes possess a common burrowing ancestor, then it follows that many adaptations have been achieved, both in bodily form, and in the way that snakes have colonised the various habitats. This is made

6

apparent by the diversity of forms that exist today. The evolution of the eye is a notable example of just one of these achievements.

As the Viperinae can be regarded as a more advanced, or recent, group, the removal of the mole vipers, *Atractaspis*, a burrowing form, from this sub-family to the colubrid sub-family Aparallactinae has certainly given support to the theory of a common burrowing ancestor. It is now true to say that no exclusively burrowing form of viper exists today, though at least two genera, *Azemiops* and *Causus*, possess other primitive characteristics.

The reptiles probably started branching out into their respective diverse groups as early as the Upper Carboniferous period, that is to say, the stem reptiles were beginning to form into different lines, and it is likely that one group of stem reptiles (Captorhinomorpha) was the common ancestor to all contemporary reptiles.

The present-day order, the Squamata, embraces both the lizards and snakes. Both are closely allied to one another, possessing many similar characteristics. This appears most superficially obvious in the legless lizards such as *Anguis* and *Ophisaurus*, and other lizards where the body is elongate and the limbs degenerate, e.g. *Lerista*. However, the monitor lizards, *Varanus spp.*, and the tegus, *Tupinambis*, possess a forked tongue and not a notched tongue as is found in other lizard species. In addition, those who are familiar with these reptiles will know that they are very serpent-like in their manner.

We know that snakes evolved from lizards, and it has been mentioned that the first snakes were probably burrowing forms. Some authorities have suggested that the common ancestor of the snakes was a lizard type with a surviving form that exists as a single species which is referred to as the earless monitor, *Lanthanotus borneensis*, which occurs in Borneo. It is interesting to note that the earless monitor is a burrowing form, measuring about 360 mm. But more interesting still is the fact that this lizard utilises the head only when digging, although it has well-developed limbs. Obviously, if it is accepted that *Lanthanotus* is related, this also gives support to the theory of a common burrowing snake ancestor. However, it is still largely a matter of conjecture and mystery, especially if other aspects such as parallel evolution and adaptive radiation are considered. This is best exemplified by the knowledge that burrowing colubrids exist, which means that these snakes at some stage have reverted to a burrowing existence.

Although some explanations of snake evolution have been

7

mentioned, it is equally likely that the ancestral stock of snakes has no living representative.

Snakes have evolved into efficient predators that have successfully colonised the varied habitat forms found in most parts of the world with the exception of the polar regions and the depths of the seas and lakes. Poisonous snakes probably represent the more advanced forms, but it does not follow that they are the more successful or efficient of the world's snake species. The lightning strike of a rattlesnake, for example, is quite spectacular, but many non-poisonous snakes obtain their food with an equal lack of effort. This applies when it is not necessary to subdue large and active prey which otherwise may present some danger to the predator. For example, some snakes of the genus *Natrix* prey on fish, and burrowing forms such as *Typhlops* prey exclusively on invertebrates.

Snakes that constrict comparatively large and active prey are always at risk from bites, or injury, received from prey species during the early stages of constriction. To subdue prey efficiently a constricting snake must first seize the prey in the right place. Even large constrictors such as pythons are often injured because the head of the prey is left free to bite the aggressor.

The rear-fanged snakes are somewhat variable in the use of their venom, and the front-fanged snakes have an obvious advantage in that they can deliver a quick lethal bite then retreat. This also means that in many cases front-fanged snakes are able to prey on larger animals and therefore feed less often than, say, a colubrid snake of similar size.

Before listing the groups of poisonous snakes that exist today it is necessary to state that, in presenting a classification, I have not allied it to any one particular authority, but have derived a system from a 'melting pot' which represents a mixture of opinion that exists within present-day literature.

Obviously, the system of Romer, and the work of Garth Underwood and others, have played an important part in the research for this section of the book. However, it has been impossible to ignore the work of H. Cogger on Australian snakes, and for this reason the reader may be surprised to find certain genera of Australian elapids absent, and perhaps even more surprised to find new genera! Another consequence of Cogger's work is that many of the species of Papua New Guinea will now need revising, especially when considering such genera as *Demansia*.

8

The classification of contemporary snakes is constantly under revision, and this must be applauded as there are groups and species of snakes that are in urgent need of reassessment. Amateur herpetologists often accuse the taxonomists of being over-zealous in their efforts to juggle the world's herpetofauna. However, to be fair, much of the present-day classification of reptiles is unsatisfactory, and current taxonomic work will eventually rectify and probably simplify matters to the satisfaction of all concerned.

One group that is currently undergoing revision is the important sub-family Viperinae. Three prominent European species which belong to this sub-family—the adder, *Vipera berus*, the asp viper, *V. aspis*, and the long-nosed viper, *V. ammodytes*—have for a long while all been allocated sub-species. However, the wide variety that exists between individuals of the same species would appear to render the designation of sub-species in some instances somewhat artificial.

The concept of sub-species is essentially geographical, and when considering mainland sub-species their validity is often contradicted by the fact that sometimes large areas of overlapping range exist which may have resulted in intergrade forms, and this can cause some confusion. However, many specialists insist that intergradation is an accepted part of the concept of sub-specific rank.

Island races, and mainland sub-species that have well-defined and perhaps localised boundaries of distribution, do not suffer from the problems of intergradation. In some cases specific rank has been given to island forms; for example, the rattlesnakes, *Crotalus tortugensis* and *C. exsul*, are both island forms that have been designated specific rank, although the criteria for determining this has more to do with the divergence from their nearest mainland counterparts. In this particular instance the degree of divergence is quite small, and Klauber, in his treatise of the rattlesnakes, has stated that *C. exsul* is perhaps a borderline case and might be referred to as a sub-species of *C. ruber*. It is obvious that opinions vary regarding the designation of sub-species, and apart from the divergence from specific forms, it seems that there are differing views regarding the aspect of intergradation.

If we gloss over these arguments, and even accept the validity of possible intergradation, then obviously many current sub-specific forms must be considered as valid, although the judgement is subjective unless a breeding barrier is demonstrated.

Although I have not included sub-species in the list of species and

9

their distribution, many readers would expect to find reference to sub-species, and for this reason I have included reference to sub-specific forms throughout the remainder of the text. The nine sub-species of *Naja naja* are obvious examples, and these all represent regional variation throughout the range for the species. The rattlesnakes have already been mentioned, and these are prolific in sub-species.

There are also examples where genera have been removed entirely from a family. This usually occurs when snakes are thought to have been wrongly placed in the first instance, but certain aspects of their characteristics have allied them to a particular family. A recent example, which has already been mentioned, is the mole viper, *Atractaspis*, a burrowing genus, which bears little resemblance to the typical vipers, but possesses greatly enlarged folding fangs. Recent work on the cranial mechanics of this genus has revealed that the fangs, although canaliculated, have a somewhat different structure from those of the true vipers, e.g. puff adder, carpet viper, etc.

The genus *Atractaspis* is now thought to be closely allied to the Aparallactinae, all of which are colubrid burrowing forms with well-developed venom apparatus and enlarged rear fangs, and occur throughout most of Africa and just reach the Middle East.

Fea's viper, *Azemiops fea*, a somewhat rare snake from upper Burma and southern China, bears some resemblance to a colubrid snake. However, this species, the only member of the genus, is still considered to be a true viper, but is now contained in a separated sub-family, the Azemiopinae. Fea's viper and the Malayan pit viper, *Agkistrodon rhodostoma*, are the only members of the Viperidae which possess smooth scales. At least one authority has claimed that the Malayan pit viper is placed in the genus *Agkistrodon* somewhat artificially. Apart from the smooth scales, the claim was supported by evidence of significant differences in skull structure, and in fact, if this criterion is followed, then all the Old World representatives of this genus could be subject to revision.

The other group of Old World pit vipers, *Trimeresurus*, have been extended by some authorities to include in the past the New World genus, *Bothrops*. This merger represents a total of about eighty species, and many herpetologists would prefer to have the New World and Old World forms separated as before, if only just for convenience!

In fact, it must be true to say that convenience plays a large part when considering the classification of the many and varied reptile species, and whether or not the various criteria used are subject to any degree of criticism is largely a matter of taste. The actual criteria used to separate groups, or families, of snakes are varied and include scalation (squamation), skull and bone structure, shape and form of hemipenes, and dentition (Figs 2–7). These all serve a major role in present-day classification. Colour and pattern are obvious guides to identification, but variation amongst individuals of the same species renders this an unreliable single method of accurate assessment.

Although all the major groups are now more or less well defined, we have seen that even at this stage of modern taxonomy it is still possible for a species to be re-allocated to an entirely different group (e.g. *Atractaspis*). However, in this instance, it was not too surprising as this species has long been a 'thorn' in the side of the systematists.

In addition to the revised classification of various species and genera, the main groups, or sub-families, have also undergone some changes. The Aparallactinae have been separated from the Colubrinae to form a distinct sub-family. Therefore the family Colubridae can now be considered as containing three sub-families of poisonous snakes, the Colubrinae, the Aparallactinae and the Homalapsinae.

Similarly, the Elapidae also contain three sub-families, the sea snakes form two of these, and current opinion does not regard these marine reptiles to be sufficiently dissimilar as to warrant the designation of a separate family (formerly Hydrophidae, sub-family Laticaudinae).

The Viperidae have also been subject to some changes. Fea's viper, *Azemiops*, has already been mentioned, and the Azemiopinae is now a separate sub-family, which, together with the Viperinae and the Crotalinae, form three sub-families in the Viperidae. There are, however, still some authorities that give the pit vipers family status, i.e. Crotalidae, but some species contained within the sub-family Viperinae would appear to show some similarity to the pit vipers. Certain species of *Bitis* and *Vipera*, for example, may have some affinity to the pit vipers due to certain subtle characteristics pertaining to the sense organs which seem to go some way towards the loreal pit present in all members of the Crotalinae. It would seem then that to draw a distinct line between the two groups, the true vipers and the pit vipers, may not be such a simple matter.

Finally, mention must be made of the fact that until quite recently, the rear-fanged snakes were all grouped into one sub-family: the Boiginae. Very few taxonomists today, however, accept this, and this is

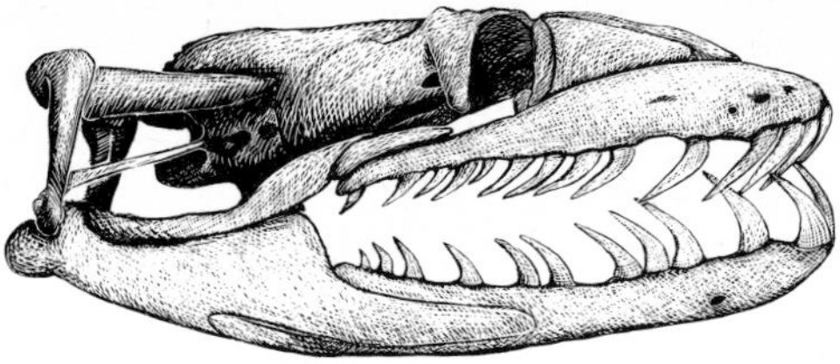

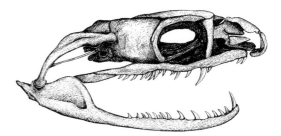

Fig. 2   African rock python, *Python sebae* (aglyphous).

Fig. 3   African sand snake, *Psammophis sibilans* (opistoglyphous).

Fig. 4   Black mamba, *Dendroaspis polylepis* (proteroglyphous).

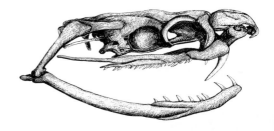

Fig. 5   Egyptian cobra, *Naja haje* (proteroglyphous).

12

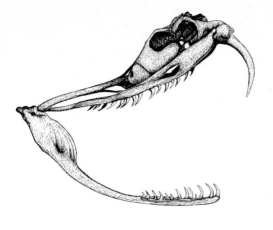

Fig. 6   Gaboon viper, *Bitis gabonica* (solenoglyphous).

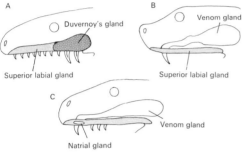

A

Duvernoy's gland

Superior labial gland

B

Venom gland

Superior labial gland

C

Venom gland

Natrial gland

Fig. 7   Venom-conducting apparatus of: A, rear-fanged colubrid; B, viperid C, elapid.

made fully apparent by the diversity of forms represented by the three existing sub-families of rear-fanged colubrids.

Numerically, the present-day classification of poisonous snakes conveniently tells us that there are three venomous families, each containing three sub-families.

The origins of the present-day distribution of snakes is another topic which is full of speculation, and again, contemporary species give us vital clues as to how worldwide snake distribution came about.

Firstly, one must visualise the world during the time that various land bridges existed which offered avenues of dispersal for the many species of mammals and other creatures, in addition to reptiles. The great diversity of reptile life is found in the warmer parts of the world, but there were obvious periods during the early history of snakes when suitable conditions for a wide variety of forms were much more widespread. Fossil records of cobras have been found in France; and Africa, the present-day headquarters for the group, was probably the centre of distribution. Today, the cobras are widespread, and are represented throughout Africa, and across Asia including Indonesia and the Philippines.

The most important land bridge that existed was the land mass that once connected the Old World and the New World, situated across the Bering Sea. The movement of species from east to west was a slow process and subject to interruption, due to changes brought about by several geographical and climatical eras and possible changes in flow. In addition, when climatical conditions were at an optimum, it is highly probable that this land mass was occupied by many species for considerable lengths of time. For these reasons it would be incorrect to describe this movement as a migration as this immediately conjures up visions of a massive, continuous and purposeful flow of species, rather than an extremely slow process.

The pit vipers evolved from the true vipers in Asia where they are represented today by two genera, *Agkistrodon* and *Trimeresurus*. The pit viper that crossed into the New World probably resembled *Agkistrodon*, where it is today represented by three species. Therefore there is little doubt that the rattlesnakes evolved from this early representative of *Agkistrodon*, probably during the Oligocene, although there is no strict evidence for this.

Although *Bothrops* and *Trimeresurus* can be regarded as one genus, it is likely that this is a result of parallel development in New and Old World respectively.

Other avenues of dispersal were available via the Panama land bridge and the faunal exchange between Africa and the Oriental region. Problematical areas are highlighted by such distinctiveness to be found amongst the species of the Australasian area.

Island species pose some interesting possibilities when considering the initial means by which these various islands were occupied. It is likely that some are the remnants of mainland species that were present when separation occurred, and most island species have similar mainland counterparts. Other island species may have been transferred physically on rafts of weed and driftwood, or else they reached these islands just simply by swimming.

On reaching their island destinations, by whatever means, some species underwent some changes and became endemic, but still retaining the similar characteristics to the mainland forms to varied degrees.

14

However, the elapid *Ogmodon vitianus* occurs only on Fiji, a thousand miles from the nearest mainland, and there is some speculation as to its origins. It seems unlikely that this species reached Fiji by physical means, and it is more probable that it evolved as a separate species, but from what, is a mystery.

There are no snakes in New Zealand, and it is not certain that snakes ever existed there. The lack of snakes in Ireland is due to the fact that Ireland became separated from the rest of Britain during the period when Britain was still attached to Europe, when the snakes were still spreading northwards. Alas they did not reach Ireland in time.

It would seem that on a general scale the world's snake distribution is fairly settled. On a local scale, man's intervention has meant that many species have had to adapt to quite sudden changes in their environment, and some species appear to manage this quite effectively.

Major changes in the world's snake distribution are unlikely, but at least one species, the sea snake, *Pelamis platurus*, has been offered scope for extending its range on a somewhat large scale. This species of sea snake is truly pelagic, and part of its range includes the south western seaboard of America, and it is possible that this species could colonise the Caribbean via the Panama Canal.

Classification of venomous snakes

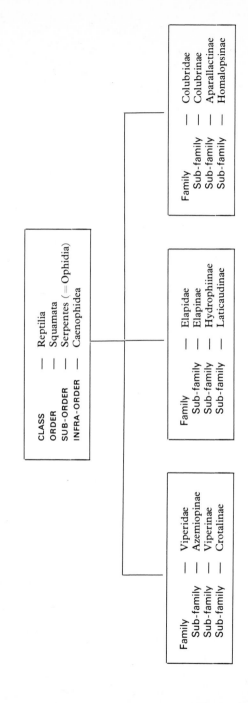

CLASS	— Reptilia
ORDER	— Squamata
SUB-ORDER	— Serpentes (= Ophidia)
INFRA-ORDER	— Caenophidea

Family	—	Viperidae
Sub-family	—	Azemiopinae
Sub-family	—	Viperinae
Sub-family	—	Crotalinae

Family	—	Elapidae
Sub-family	—	Elapinae
Sub-family	—	Hydrophiinae
Sub-family	—	Laticaudinae

Family	—	Colubridae
Sub-family	—	Colubrinae
Sub-family	—	Aparallactinae
Sub-family	—	Homalopsinae

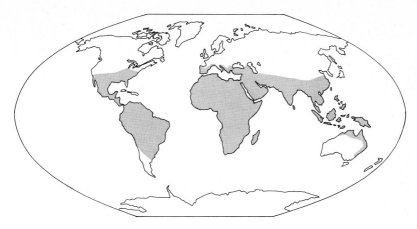

Fig. 8   Distribution of the rear-fanged colubrids.

The genera and distribution of the rear-fanged snakes (Opistoglyphs) (Fig. 8)

SUB-FAMILY COLUBRINAE	DISTRIBUTION
Ahaetulla	Southern Asia
Alluadina	Malagasy
Amplorhinus	Africa
Apostolepis	South America
Boiga	Africa, southern Asia, Papua New Guinea, northern Australia
Chamaetortus	Africa
Chrysopelea	Southern Asia, East Indies
Clelia	Central and South America
Conophis	Central and South America
Crotaphopeltis	Africa
Diaphorolepis	South America
Dipsadoboa	Africa
Dispholidus	Africa
Ditypophis	Socotra Island (Indian Ocean)
Dromophis	Africa
Dryophiops	Southern Asia
Elapomojus	South America

SUB-FAMILY COLUBRINAE	DISTRIBUTION
Erythrolamprus	North and South America
Geodipsas	Malagasy
Hemirhagerrhis	Africa
Heteroloidon	Malagasy
Hologerrhum	Philippines
Hypsiglena	North and South America
Ialtris	West Indies
Imantodes	South America
Ithycyphus	Malagasy
Langaha	Malagasy
Lycodryas	Malagasy
Macroprotodon	Southern Europe, northern Africa
Malpolon	Southern Europe, northern Africa, western Asia
Mimophis	Malagasy
Oxybelis	South and Central America, North America (S. Arizona)
Philodryas	South America
Platyinion	South America
Psammodynastes	Southern Asia, East Indies
Psammophis	Africa, western Asia
Psammophylax	Africa
Pseudablabes	South America
Pseudotomodon	South America
Pythonodipsas	Africa
Rhabdophis	Asia
Rhachidelus	South America
Rhamphiophis	Africa
Rhinobothryum	South America
Rhinocalamus	Africa
Rhinostoma	South America
Stenophis	Malagasy
Stenorhina	South America
Tachymenis	South America
Tantilla	North and South America
Telescopus	Southern Europe, Africa, western Asia

SUB-FAMILY COLUBRINAE	DISTRIBUTION
Thamnodynastes	South America
Thelotornis	Africa
Tomodon	South America
Trimorphodon	North, Central and South America
Tripanurgos	South America

SUB-FAMILY
APARALLACTINAE

Amblyodipsas = *Calamelaps*	Africa
Aparallactus	Africa
*Atractaspis	Africa, Middle East
Brachyophis	Africa
Chilorhinophis	Africa
Choristocalamus	Africa
Cynodantophis	Africa
Elapocalamus	Africa
Elapotinus	Africa
Hypoptophis	Africa
Macrelaps	Africa
Melanocalamus	Africa
Micrelaps	Africa
Miodon	Africa
Polemon	Africa
Xenocalamus	Africa

SUB-FAMILY
HOMALOPSINAE

Bitia	Southern Asia
Cantoria	Southern Asia
Cerberus	Southern Asia, northern Australia
Enhydris	Southern Asia, northern Australia
Erpeton	Southern Asia
Fordonia	Southern Asia, northern Australia

---

* Formerly *Viperinae*, i.e. mole vipers.

SUB-FAMILY

HOMALOPSINAE	DISTRIBUTION
Gerarda	Southern Asia
Heurnia	Southern Asia
Homalopsis	Southern Asia
Myron	Southern Asia, northern Australia

★ ★ ★

Species and distribution of the front-fanged snakes (Proteroglyphs and Solenoglyphs)

SUB-FAMILY

ELAPINAE (Fig. 9)	DISTRIBUTION
Acanthophis antarcticus	Australia, New Guinea
Acanthophis pyrrhus	Central Australia
Apistocalamus grandis	Papua New Guinea
Apistocalamus lamingtoni	Papua New Guinea
Apistocalamus loennbergii	Papua New Guinea
Apistocalamus loriae	Papua New Guinea
Apistocalamus pratti	Papua New Guinea
Aspidelaps lubricus	Southern Africa
Aspidelaps scutatus	Southern Africa
Aspidomorphus christieanus	Northern Australia
Aspidomorphus diadema	Southern Australia

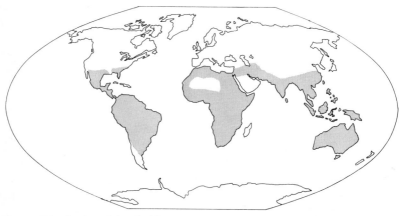

Fig. 9   Distribution of the elapids.

SUB-FAMILY ELAPINAE	DISTRIBUTION
Aspidomorphus minutus	South eastern Australia
Austrelaps superbus	South eastern Australia
Boulengerina annulata	Eastern and western Africa
Boulengerina christyi	Kinshasa, Zaire
Bungarus bungaroides	India, Nepal, Bhutan
Bungarus caeruleus	Pakistan, India, Sri Lanka
Bungarus candidus	South East Asia
Bungarus ceylonicus	Sri Lanka
Bungarus fasciatus	India, Bangladesh, southern China, South East Asia
Bungarus flaviceps	South East Asia
Bungarus javanicus	Java
Bungarus lividus	Eastern India, Bangladesh
Bungarus magnimaculatus	Burma
Bungarus multicinctus	Southern China, Taiwan
Bungarus niger	North eastern India
Bungarus walli	Eastern India
Cacophis harrietae	Eastern Australia
Cacophis krefftii	Eastern Australia
Cacophis muellerii	Papua New Guinea
Cacophis schlegelii	Papua New Guinea
Cacophis squamulosus	Eastern Australia
Calliophis beddomei	Southern India
Calliophis bibroni	Southern India
Calliophis boettgeri	Ryukyu Island
Calliophis calligaster	Philippines
Calliophis gracilis	South East Asia
Calliophis iwasakii	Ryukyu Island
Calliophis kelloggii	Southern China, Vietnam
Calliophis macclellandii	North eastern India, Nepal, South East Asia, Vietnam, Taiwan
Calliophis maculiceps	South East Asia
Calliophis melanurus	India, Sri Lanka
Calliophis nigrescens	India
Calliophis sauteri	Taiwan
Cryptophis nigrescens	Eastern Australia

SUB-FAMILY
ELAPINAE   DISTRIBUTION

Cryptophis pallidiceps	Central northern Australia
Demansia atra	Eastern and northern Australia
Demansia olivacea	Northern Australia, New Guinea
Demansia psammophis	Widespread non-tropical Australia
Demansia torquata	North eastern Australia
Dendroaspis angusticeps	Eastern and southern Africa
Dendroaspis jamesoni	Central and eastern Africa
Dendroaspis polylepis	Central, eastern and southern Africa
Dendroaspis viridis	Western Africa
Denisonia boschmai	Southern Papua New Guinea
Denisonia devisii	Eastern Australia
Denisonia fasciata	Western Australia
Denisonia maculata	Eastern Queensland
Denisonia punctata	The drier parts of north central and Western Australia
Drysdalia coronata	South western Australia
Drysdalia coronoides	NSW Australia
Drysdalia mastersi	South eastern Australia
Echiopsis curta	Southern Australia
Elapognathus minor	South western Australia
Elaps dorsalis	Southern Africa
Elaps lacteus	Southern Africa
Elapsoidea guntheri	Angola, Zambia, Zimbabwe
Elapsoidea laticincta	Central Africa
Elapsoidea loveridgei	Eastern Africa
Elapsoidea nigra	Tanzania
Elapsoidea semiannulatus	Western, central, eastern and southern Africa
Elapsoidea sundevallii	Eastern, western and southern Africa
Furina diadema	Widespread Australia, except extreme south
Glyphodon barnardi	North eastern Australia
Glyphodon dunmalli	South eastern Queensland
Glyphodon tristis	North eastern Australia and south eastern New Guinea
Hemachatus haemachatus	Southern Africa

SUB-FAMILY
ELAPINAE   DISTRIBUTION

Hoplocephalus bitorquatus	Eastern Australia
Hoplocephalus bungaroides	South eastern Australia
Hoplocephalus stephensi	South eastern Australia
Leptomicrurus collaris	Northern South America
Leptomicrurus narduccii	North western South America
Maticora bivirgata	South East Asia
Maticora intestinalis	South East Asia
Micruroides euryxanthus	Arizona, northern Mexico
Micrurus albicinctus	Central Brazil
Micrurus alleni	Central America
Micrurus ancoralis	Panama, north western South America
Micrurus annellatus	North western South America
Micrurus averyi	Surinam
Micrurus balzani	Eastern Bolivia
Micrurus bernadi	Western Mexico
Micrurus bocourti	Northern Colombia, western Equador
Micrurus browni	Southern Mexico, Guatemala
Micrurus carinicauda	Colombia, Venezuela, Equador
Micrurus circinalis	Venezuela, Trinidad
Micrurus clarki	Costa Rica, Panama
Micrurus corallinus	Eastern Brazil, northern Argentina
Micrurus decoratus	Eastern Brazil
Micrurus diastema	Eastern Mexico, Honduras, eastern Guatemala
Micrurus dissoleucus	Southern Panama, Colombia, Venezuela
Micrurus distans	Western Mexico
Micrurus dumerilii	Colombia
Micrurus elegans	Eastern Mexico, Guatemala
Micrurus ephippifer	Western Mexico
Micrurus filiformis	Colombia, northern Brazil, Peru, Equador
Micrurus fitzingeri	Eastern Mexico
Micrurus frontalis	Southern Brazil, Bolivia, Paraguay, Uruguay, northern Argentina

SUB-FAMILY ELAPINAE	DISTRIBUTION
Micrurus fulvius	Southern North America, north eastern Mexico
Micrurus hemprichii	Northern South America
Micrurus ibiboboca	North eastern Brazil
Micrurus isozonus	Colombia, northern Venezuela
Micrurus langsdorffi	Colombia, central Brazil, Peru, Equador
Micrurus laticollaris	South western Mexico
Micrurus latifasciatus	Southern Mexico, southern Guatemala
Micrurus lemniscatus	Northern South America, central Brazil, Bolivia, Trinidad
Micrurus mertensi	North western Peru, south western Equador
Micrurus mipartitus	Southern Central America, Colombia, Venezuela, Peru, Equador
Micrurus nigrocinctus	Central America, north western Colombia
Micrurus nuchalis	Southern Mexico
Micrurus ornatissimus	Peru, Equador
Micrurus peruvianus	Peru
Micrurus psyches	Northern South America
Micrurus putumayensis	Peru
Micrurus pyrrhocryptus	Bolivia, Argentina
Micrurus ruatanus	Honduras
Micrurus spixii	Widespread northern half of South America
Micrurus spurelli	Colombia
Micrurus stewarti	Panama
Micrurus surinamensis	Venezuela, Guyana, Brazil, Bolivia, Peru, Equador
Micrurus tschudii	Southern Colombia, southern Venezuela, Bolivia, Peru, Equador
Naja haje	Central, eastern and southern Africa, Middle East
Naja melanoleuca	Widespread Africa

SUB-FAMILY ELAPINAE	DISTRIBUTION
Naja mossambica	Southern Africa
Naja naja	Iran, Afghanistan, India, Pakistan, South East Asia, Philippines, Taiwan
Naja nigricollis	Widespread Africa except south of the Zambesi
Naja nivea	South western Africa
Neelaps bimaculatus	South western Australia
Neelaps calonotus	South western Australia
Notechis ater	Tasmania and patchy distribution in southern Australia
Notechis scutatus	South eastern Australia
Ogmodon vitianus	Fiji
Ophiophagus hannah	India, Bangladesh, South East Asia, Philippines
Oxyuranus scutellatus	Northern Australia, Papua New Guinea
Parademansia microlepidota	Central eastern Australia
Paranaja multifasciata	Cameroon, Congo Republic
Parapistocalamus hedigeri	Solomon Islands
Pseudapistocalamus nymanni	Papua New Guinea
Pseudechis australis	Widespread Australia
Pseudechis colletti	Central Queensland
Pseudechis guttatus	Eastern Australia
Pseudechis papuanis	South eastern Papua New Guinea
Pseudechis porphyriacus	Eastern Australia
Pseudohaje goldii	Western Africa, Uganda, Kenya
Pseudohaje nigra	Western Africa
Pseudonaja affinis	South western Australia
Pseudonaja guttata	Central Queensland
Pseudonaja ingrami	Northern Queensland
Pseudonaja modesta	Central and western Australia
Pseudonaja nuchalis	Widespread Australia except south east, east and north east
Pseudonaja textilis	Eastern Australia
Rhinoplocephalus bicolor	South western Australia

SUB-FAMILY
ELAPINAE   DISTRIBUTION

Simoselaps australis	Southern Queensland, NSW
Simoselaps bertholdi	Western Australia
Simoselaps fasciolatus	South western Australia and arid regions of NSW and Queensland
Simoselaps incinctus	Central Australia
Simoselaps semifasciatus	Western and north eastern Australia
Simoselaps warro	North eastern Australia
Suta suta	Widespread eastern two-thirds of Australia
Toxicocalamus longissimus	Eastern Papua New Guinea
Toxicocalamus stanleyanus	Papua New Guinea
Tropidechis carinatus	Eastern Australia
Unechis brevicaudus	Localised southern Australia
Unechis carpentariae	Eastern Queensland
Unechis flagellum	South eastern Australia
Unechis gouldii	Southern Australia
Unechis monachus	South western Australia
Unechis nigrostriatus	North eastern Australia
Vermicella annulata	North western Australia, widespread rest of Australia except extreme south east
Vermicella multifasciata	Northern Australia
Walterinnesia aegyptia	Northern Africa, Middle East, western Asia.

SUB-FAMILY
HYDROPHIINAE (Fig. 10)

Acalyptophis peronii	Gulf of Siam, Arufura Sea, Gulf of Carpentaria, Coral Sea
Astrotia stokesii	Arabian Sea, Bay of Bengal, Gulf of Siam, South China Sea, Timor Sea, Java and Flores Sea, Arufura Sea, Gulf of Carpentaria, Coral Sea
Enhydrina schistosa	Arabian Sea, Bay of Bengal, Andaman Sea, Gulf of Siam, South China Sea, Timor Sea, Java and Flores

SUB-FAMILY
HYDROPHIINAE DISTRIBUTION

	Sea, Banda Sea, Molucca Sea, Arufura Sea, Gulf of Carpentaria, Coral Sea
Ephalophis greyi	Timor Sea
Hydrelaps darwiniensis	Timor Sea, Arafura Sea
Hydrophis belcheri	Java and Flores Sea, Molucca Sea, Celebes Sea, Arafura Sea, Philippine Sea, south western Pacific
Hydrophis bituberculatus	Bay of Bengal
Hydrophis brookei	Andaman Sea, Gulf of Siam, South China Sea, Java and Flores Sea
Hydrophis caerulescens	Arabian Sea, Bay of Bengal, Andaman Sea, Gulf of Siam, South China Sea, Java and Flores Sea, Molucca Sea
Hydrophis cyanocinctus	Persian Gulf, Arabian Sea, Andaman Sea, Gulf of Siam, South China Sea, East China and Yellow Sea, Sulu Sea, Java and Flores Sea

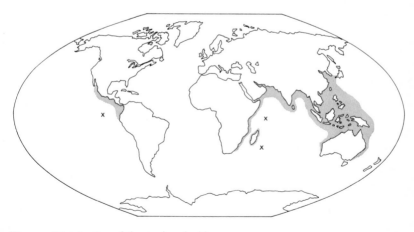

Fig. 10   Distribution of the marine elapids.

SUB-FAMILY
HYDROPHIINAE

DISTRIBUTION

Hydrophis elegans	Timor Sea, Arafura Sea, Gulf of Carpentaria, Coral Sea, Tasman Sea
Hydrophis fasciatus	Bay of Bengal, Andaman Sea, Gulf of Siam, South China Sea, Timor Sea, Sulu Sea, Java and Flores Sea
Hydrophis kingii	Timor Sea, Arafura Sea, Gulf of Carpentaria
Hydrophis klossi	Andaman Sea, Gulf of Siam
Hydrophis lapemoides	Persian Gulf, Arabian Sea
Hydrophis major	Timor Sea, Arafura Sea, Gulf of Carpentaria
Hydrophis mamillaris	Arabian Sea, Bay of Bengal
Hydrophis melanosoma	South China Sea, Java and Flores Sea
Hydrophis mertoni	Arafura Sea
Hydrophis nigrocinctus	Bay of Bengal
Hydrophis obscurus	Bay of Bengal
Hydrophis ornatus	Bay of Bengal, Adaman Sea, Gulf of Siam, South China Sea, East China and Yellow Sea, Timor Sea, Java and Flores Sea, Arafura Sea, Gulf of Carpentaria, Coral Sea, south western and central Pacific
Hydrophis parviceps	South China Sea
Hydrophis semperi	Lake Taal, Philippines
Hydrophis spiralis	Persian Gulf, Arabian Sea, Bay of Bengal, Andaman Sea, South China Sea, Java and Flores Sea
Hydrophis stricticollis	Bay of Bengal
Hydrophis torquatus	Andaman Sea, South China Sea, Gulf of Siam, Java and Flores Sea
Kerilia jerdonii	Bay of Bengal, Andaman Sea, Gulf of Siam, South China Sea
Kolpophis annandalei	Gulf of Siam, South China Sea

SUB-FAMILY HYDROPHIINAE	DISTRIBUTION
Lapemis hardwickii	Gulf of Siam, South China Sea, East China and Yellow Sea, Sulu Sea, Java and Flores Sea, Banda Sea
Microcephalophis cantoris	Arabian Sea, Bay of Bengal
Microcephalophis gracilis	Persian Gulf, Arabian Sea, Bay of Bengal, Andaman Sea, Gulf of Siam, South China Sea, Java and Flores Sea
Pelamis platurus	Occurs over all known sea snake distribution plus western and southern Indian Ocean, also along eastern Pacific coast from California to Equador
Praescutata viperina	Persian Gulf, Arabian Sea, Bay of Bengal, Andaman Sea, Gulf of Siam, South China Sea, Java and Flores Sea
Thalassophis anomalus	Gulf of Siam, South China Sea, Sulu Sea, Java and Flores Sea

SUB-FAMILY LATICAUDINAE	
Aipysurus apraefrontalis	Timor Sea
Aipysurus duboisii	Timor Sea, Arafura Sea, Gulf of Carpentaria
Aipysurus eydouxi	Gulf of Siam, South China Sea, Timor Sea, Java and Flores Sea, Arafura Sea, Gulf of Carpentaria
Aipysurus foliosquama	Timor Sea
Aipysurus fuscus	Timor Sea
Aipysurus laevis	Timor Sea, Arafura Sea, Gulf of Carpentaria, Coral Sea
Emydocephalus annulatus	East China and Yellow Sea, Timor Sea, Arafura Sea, Philippine Sea

29

SUB-FAMILY LATICAUDINAE	DISTRIBUTION
Laticauda colubrina	Andaman Sea, South and East China Sea, Yellow Sea, Gulf of Siam, Timor Sea, Sulu Sea, Java and Flores Sea, Banda Sea, Molucca Sea, Celebes Sea, Arafura Sea, Gulf of Carpentaria, Philippine Sea, Coral Sea, Tasman Sea, south west Pacific
Laticauda crockeri	Lake Tongano, Solomon Islands
Laticauda laticaudata	South and East China Sea, Yellow Sea, Timor Sea, Sulu Sea, Java and Flores Sea, Banda Sea, Molucca Sea, Celebes Sea, Arafura Sea, Gulf of Carpentaria, Philippine Sea, Coral Sea, south west Pacific
Laticauda semifasciata	South and East China Sea, Yellow Sea, Sulu Sea, Java and Flores Sea, Banda Sea, Molucca Sea, Celebes Sea, Philippine Sea, south western Pacific

SUB-FAMILY
AZEMIOPINAE

Azemiops feae	Southern Tibet, northern Burma, northern Vietnam

SUB-FAMILY
VIPERINAE (Fig. 11)

Adenorhinos barbouri	Tanzania
Atheris ceratophorus	Central Africa, Tanzania
Atheris chlorechis	Western Africa
Atheris hindii	Aberdare Mountains (Kenya)
Atheris hispida	Central and eastern Africa
Atheris katangensis	Congo Republic
Atheris nitschei	Central and eastern Africa
Atheris squamiger	Cameroon, central and eastern Africa

30

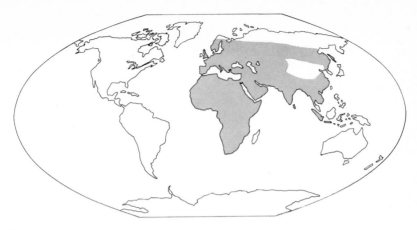

Fig. 11   Distribution of the Old World vipers.

SUB-FAMILY VIPERINAE	DISTRIBUTION
★Atheris superciliaris	Southern Tanzania, Mozambique
Bitis arietans	Widespread Africa except Libya and Tunisia, also occurs in Arab Republic, Lebanon, Jordan
Bitis atropos	Southern Africa
Bitis caudalis	Southern Africa
Bitis cornuta	Namibia
Bitis gabonica	Western Africa, central Africa, eastern Africa, extra-limital southern Sudan, northern Zululand
Bitis heraldica	Angola
Bitis nasicornis	Western Africa, central Africa, eastern Africa
Bitis peringueyi	Angola, Namibia
Bitis schneideri	Orange River, South Africa
Bitis worthingtoni	Kenya
Bitis xeropaga	Localised southern Africa
Causus bilineatus	Angola, Zambia, Katanga, western and central Africa

★ Problematical form, formerly, *Vipera*, but now thought to be terrestrial form of *Atheris*.

SUB-FAMILY
VIPERINAE   DISTRIBUTION

Causus defilippii	Central, eastern and southern Africa
Causus lichtensteinii	Western, central and eastern Africa
Causus maculatus	Western and central Africa
Causus resimus	Tropical Africa
Causus rhombeatus	Widespread Africa
Cerastes cerastes	Northern Africa, Middle East
Cerastes vipera	Northern Africa, southern Israel
Echis carinatus	Extensive range, Africa north of the Equator, Middle East across to India
Echis coloratus	Arab Republic, Israel, Jordan, Saudi Arabia, the Yemen
Eristicophis macmahonii	Southern Iran, southern Afghanistan, northern Pakistan
Pseudocerastes persicus	Middle East, Pakistan
Vipera ammodytes	Southern Austria, northern Italy, Yugoslavia, Greece, Bulgaria, Romania, southern European Russia
Vipera aspis	North west Spain, across Central Europe to Switzerland and Italy
Vipera berus	Most widespread poisonous snake; British Isles (except Ireland), most of Europe except southern Italy, extending across the Balkans and Russia to the Pacific coast
Vipera kaznakovi	South western European Russia
Vipera latasti	Spain, Portugal, northern Tunisia, Morocco
Vipera lebetina	Northern Africa, Middle East, Cyclades, northern Pakistan, southern Kashmir
Vipero palaestinae	Middle East
Vipera russelli	Bangladesh, across India into South East Asia
Vipera ursinii	Southern Austria, south eastern France, Hungary, Italy, Bulgaria,

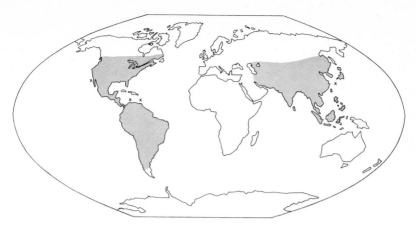

Fig. 12 Distribution of the pit vipers.

SUB-FAMILY VIPERINAE	DISTRIBUTION
	Yugoslavia, Romania, European Turkey
Vipera xanthina	Middle East, Turkey

SUB-FAMILY
CROTALINAE

Agkistrodon acutus	South eastern China, Vietnam, Taiwan
Agkistrodon bilineatus	Mexico and Central America
Agkistrodon contortrix	Eastern and southern North America
Agkistrodon halys	Eastern European Russia, eastern Middle East, northern Kashmir and Northern Yunnan, Japan, eastern China, Korea, Siberia and eastern Asian Russia
Agkistrodon himalayanus	Pakistan, north western India, Nepal, Kashmir, Tibet
Agkistrodon hypnale	Southern India, Sri Lanka
Agkistrodon monticola	Southern China
Agkistrodon nepa	Sri Lanka
Agkistrodon piscivorous	Eastern and southern North America

33

SUB-FAMILY
CROTALINAE   DISTRIBUTION

Agkistrodon rhodostoma	South East Asia
Agkistrodon strauchi	Western China, Tibet, Kashmir
Bothrops albocarinatus	Equador
Bothrops alternatus	Southern Brazil, Paraguay, Uruguay, northern Argentina
Bothrops alticola	Equador
* *Bothrops ammodytoides*	Argentina
Bothrops andianus	Peru
Bothrops atrox	Mexico, Central America, Trinidad, Tobago, Venezuela, Surinam, Guyana, northern Brazil, northern Bolivia, Peru, Equador
Bothrops barbouri	South western Mexico
Bothrops barnetti	Northern Peru
Bothrops bicolor	Southern Mexico, southern Guatemala
Bothrops bilineatus	Brazil, northern South America
Bothrops caribbaeus	Saint Lucia
Bothrops castelnaudi	Northern Brazil, eastern Peru, Equador
Bothrops cotiara	Southern Brazil, northern Argentina
Bothrops dunni	Southern Mexico
Bothrops erythromelas	Eastern Brazil
Bothrops fonsecai	Southern Brazil
Bothrops godmanni	Southern Mexico, Central America
Bothrops hyoprorus	Southern Colombia, Peru, eastern Equador, western Brazil
Bothrops iglesiasi	Eastern Brazil
Bothrops insularis	Queimada Grande Island (Brazil)
Bothrops itapetiningae	Southern Brazil
Bothrops jararaca	Southern Brazil, northern Paraguay, northern Argentina
Bothrops jararacussu	Southern Brazil, eastern Bolivia, Paraguay, northern Argentina

---

* Poisonous snake with the most southerly distribution.

34

SUB-FAMILY
CROTALINAE   DISTRIBUTION

Bothrops lanceolatus	Martinique
Bothrops lansbergii	Southern Mexico, Central America, Colombia, northern Venezuela
Bothrops lateralis	Costa Rica, eastern Panama
Bothrops lichenosus	Venezuela
Bothrops lojanus	Equador
Bothrops medusa	Venezuela
Bothrops melanurus	Southern Mexico
Bothrops microphthalmus	Colombia, Peru, Equador
Bothrops nasutus	Eastern Mexico, Central America, Colombia, Equador
Bothrops neglectus	Colombia, Venezuela, Surinam, Brazil
Bothrops neuwiedi	Southern Brazil, eastern Bolivia, Paraguay, northern Argentina
Bothrops nigroviridis	Southern Mexico, Central America
Bothrops nummifer	South eastern Mexico, Central America
Bothrops peruvianus	Southern Peru
Bothrops picadoi	Costa Rica
Bothrops pictus	Peru
Bothrops pifanoi	Northern Venezuela
Bothrops pirajai	Eastern Brazil
Bothrops pulcher	Eastern Peru, eastern Equador
Bothrops punctatus	Panama, Colombia, western Equador
Bothrops roedingeri	Western Peru
Bothrops schlegelii	Southern Mexico, Central America, Venezuela, Colombia, Equador
Bothrops sphenophrys	Southern Mexico
Bothrops undulatus	Eastern Mexico
Bothrops xanthogrammus	Equador
Crotalus adamanteus	South eastern North America
Crotalus atrox	California, Nevada, Texas, Kansas, Arizona, northern Mexico
Crotalus basiliscus	Western Mexico
Crotalus catalinensis	North western Mexico (Catalina Island)

SUB-FAMILY CROTALINAE	DISTRIBUTION
Crotalus cerastes	Arizona, New Mexico, southern California and Nevada, western Mexico
Crotalus durissus	Southern Mexico, Central America, Colombia, Venezuela, Guyana, Surinam, Brazil, Paraguay, Uruguay, eastern Bolivia, northern Argentina
Crotalus enyo	North west Mexico
Crotalus exsul	North west Mexico (Cedros Island)
Crotalus horridus	Central, southern and eastern North America
Crotalus intermedius	Southern Mexico
Crotalus lannomi	South western Mexico (Autlan)
Crotalus lepidus	South western Texas, southern Arizona and New Mexico, northern Mexico
Crotalus mitchellii	Western Arizona and New Mexico, southern California and Nevada, north western Mexico
Crotalus molussus	Western Texas, Arizona, New Mexico, Mexico
Crotalus polystictus	Western central Mexico
Crotalus pricei	Western Texas, Arizona, New Mexico, north western Mexico
Crotalus pusillus	South western Mexico
Crotalus ruber	South western California, north western Mexico
Crotalus scutulatus	South western Texas, western Arizona and New Mexico, south eastern California, Nevada, Mexico
Crotalus stejnegeri	North western Mexico
Crotalus tigris	South western Arizona and New Mexico, northern Mexico
Crotalus tortugensis	North western Mexico (Tortuga Island)

SUB-FAMILY
CROTALINAE   DISTRIBUTION

Crotalus transversus	Central Mexico
Crotalus triseriatus	Mexico
Crotalus unicolor	Venezuela (Aruba Island)
Crotalus vegrandis	Northern Venezuela
Crotalus viridis	Central and western North America, northern Mexico
Crotalus willardi	Southern Arizona, northern Mexico
Lachesis mutus	Southern Nicaragua, Costa Rica, Panama, northern half of South America, Trinidad
Sistrurus catenatus	New York, Pennsylvania, Illinois, Ontario, south west to Texas
Sistrurus miliarus	South eastern North America
Sistrurus ravus	Central Mexico
Trimeresurus albolabris	North eastern India, Bangladesh, Nepal, South East Asia
Trimeresurus cantori	Andaman and Nicobar Islands
Trimeresurus chaseni	Borneo
Trimeresurus convictus	Malaya
Trimeresurus cornutus	Vietnam
Trimeresurus elegans	Southern Ryukyu Islands
Trimeresurus erythrurus	North eastern India, Bangladesh, Nepal, Burma, Thailand
Trimeresurus fasciatus	Djampea Island
Trimeresurus flavomaculatus	Philippines
Trimeresurus flavoviridis	Ryukyu Islands
Trimeresurus gracilis	Taiwan
Trimeresurus gramineus	India, Bangladesh, Andaman and Nicobar Islands
Trimeresurus hageni	Sumatra
Trimeresurus huttoni	Southern India
Trimeresurus jerdonii	North eastern India, northern Bangladesh, southern Kashmir, eastern China, Burma, Vietnam
Trimeresurus kanburiensis	Southern Thailand
Trimeresurus kaulbacki	Northern Burma

37

SUB-FAMILY CROTALINAE	DISTRIBUTION
Trimeresurus labialis	Andaman and Nicobar Islands
Trimeresurus macrolepis	Southern India
Trimeresurus malabaricus	Southern India
Trimeresurus monticola	North eastern India, Nepal, South East Asia, east China, Taiwan
Trimeresurus mucrosquamatus	North eastern India, south eastern China, Taiwan, Burma, Vietnam
Trimeresurus okinavensis	Ryukyu Islands
Trimeresurus popeorum	North eastern India, South East Asia
Trimeresurus puniceus	South East Asia
Trimeresurus purpureomaculatus	Southern Bangladesh, Burma, South East Asia
Trimeresurus stejnegeri	North eastern India, Nepal, south eastern China, Burma, Thailand
Trimeresurus strigatus	Southern India
Trimeresurus sumatranus	Southern Thailand, Malaya, Sumatra, Borneo
Trimeresurus tonkinensis	Northern Vietnam
Trimeresurus trigonocephalus	Sri Lanka
Trimeresurus wagleri	Southern Thailand, Malaya, Borneo, Sumatra, Celebes, Philippines.

3
The Rear-fanged Colubrids

About 60 per cent of the world's snake species are colubrids, and this large group is represented by a wide variety of forms which are distributed throughout the temperate, tropical and desert regions of the world (Fig. 8).

This extensive family is well adapted to all modes of life styles and habitat occupation, having species that are terrestrial, many that are arboreal, some that are amphibious, and even those that are almost entirely aquatic. However, no colubrid has successfully colonised the open sea, and the only truly marine species are the sea snakes which belong to the family Elapidae (Hydrophinae).

It has been mentioned that the colubrids represent a wide variety of forms; however, the most important aspect which pertains to the theme of this book is the fact that approximately 30 per cent of the colubrid snakes can be described as technically venomous. In non-venomous colubrids, and indeed most snakes, there is a gland which is situated in the upper labial region on each side of the mouth (Fig. 7). This gland, the superior labial gland, is a mucus-producing gland which discharges into the roof of the mouth and on to the outer sides of the teeth, which in most species are sharp and recurved. The inferior labial gland is situated in the lower jaw and discharges mucus on to the lower teeth. It can be appreciated that for an animal that swallows its prey whole a copious supply of mucus is essential. However, for the purpose of defining a venomous snake, only the glands situated in the upper jaw need to be considered.

The saliva of some so-called non-venomous species is said to have a paralysing effect on prey (e.g. *Natrix spp.* and *Thamnophis spp.*). In such cases the saliva enters the prey via the many puncture wounds caused by the sharp teeth. When considering such events it becomes even more apparent that the distinction between venomous and non-venomous is in reality ill defined.

The distinguishing characteristic of a venomous colubrid is found in the actual structure of the mucus-producing gland. In the rear-fanged snakes this gland also incorporates the Duvernoy's gland, sometimes called the parotid gland, which secretes the venom. This gland is situated to the rear of the superior labial gland and contains protein-secreting cells as opposed to just mucus-producing cells of the former (Fig. 7).

Some snakes that lack the Duvernoy's gland may still possess enlarged teeth. The North American hog-nosed snakes, *Heterodon spp.*, have enlarged rear teeth, which are probably efficiently utilised on toads on which the species largely feeds. Conversely, a number of snakes that possess the Duvernoy's gland may lack enlarged teeth.

The actual size and number of these enlarged teeth or fangs varies, and they may be grooved or ungrooved. The North American night snakes, *Hypsiglena spp.*, possess rudimentary ungrooved fangs but a venom that is quite effective on lizards on which it mainly feeds.

The composition of colubrid saliva and venom still requires a great deal of investigation, but it is obvious that the many species included in this family must represent a wide variation in toxicity, be it insignificant or otherwise. However toxic a snake's venom may be, it can only be considered as truly effective when it is injected efficiently and in adequate amounts. Even so, it is prudent to avoid where possible a bite from any snake. For example, many people who handle snakes regularly will know that a bite from even a small python will cause the wound to bleed copiously, suggesting an anti-coagulant faction in the saliva.

It is currently thought that only a very small number of rear-fanged snakes constitute any threat to man; the boomslang, *Dispholidus typus* (Pl. 1), and the African twig snake, *Thelotornis kirtlandi*, have both been known to inflict fatal bites. More recently, the current mystery surrounding the venom and bite of the rear-fanged snakes was highlighted by the serious clinical effects suffered after a bite by the rear-fanged Asiatic keelback, *Rhabdophis subminiatus* (Reid, 1978). Due to our current lack of knowledge with regard to the venom of the rear-fanged snakes it is probably wise to afford some respect to other members of this group, particularly for example large individuals belonging to the genera *Boiga, Psammophis* and *Malpolon*.

The efficiency with which the opistoglyphous snakes utilise their venom is variable; lizard-eaters such as the Central and South American genus *Conophis* use the fangs with great effect, and the venom of the boomslang can paralyse a bird within seconds. However, many of the smaller insectivorous species, such as the North American genus *Tantilla*, appear to have little scope or initiative to use the venom.

Some rear-fanged snakes possess a venom that is particularly toxic for the prey on which they feed. The mussurana, *Clelia clelia*, of Central and South America, is said to have a venom that quickly subdues other snakes, on which it largely feeds, including those of the highly venomous genus *Bothrops*. The mussurana also applies constriction when securing prey, and this combination of talents renders this snake a highly efficient predator. In his book *Snakes of the World*, the late Raymond Ditmars includes a vivid account of a mussurana overpowering a 1·2 m barba amarilla, *Bothrops atrox*.

The white-bellied water snake, *Fordonia leucobalia*, of the coastal regions of South East Asia, Papua New Guinea and northern Australia, has a venom that is particularly toxic for crabs on which it mainly feeds.

The rear-fanged snakes occur mainly in the warmer regions of the world. There are six genera of rear-fanged snakeʳ ⁱn North America, but only one, *Tantilla*, reaches northwards of the south western states. Similarly, the three genera to be found in Europe are restricted to the warmer areas of the south, and could be said to represent the northern range of a more widespread African and west Asian distribution.

Malpolon

Of the three European species, the most widespread is the montpellier snake, *Malpolon monspessulanus*, which occurs in Iberia, the south coast of France, Italy, the eastern Adriatic coast, southern Balkans and on some of the Greek islands. This snake can reach lengths of 200 cm, but adult lengths of between 100 cm and 150 cm are more usual. When handled the montpellier snake appears to have a certain rigidity of the body and seems to lack the supple quality usually found in most other snakes.

The coloration is usually uniform brownish or greyish, and there may be present a variable density of light or dark spots. The ventral surface is yellowish with dark mottled or blotched markings. The body scales are smooth with indistinct grooves, and there are 17–19 rows at mid body. The head of the montpellier snake is very distinctive; the large eyes, the ridged supraoculars, or 'eyebrows', and the prominent rostral scale give this snake a most fierce and penetrating expression. In fact, in this instance the snake's appearance is true to its nature. The montpellier snake is an aggressive creature and usually tries to bite if restrained or interfered with. The venom has a powerful effect on prey, which includes lizards, small mammals, birds and other snakes. Prey is usually held, enabling the fangs to be brought into position. The effect of the bite on man is said to produce immediate pain, stiffness and, in some cases, fever.

The montpellier snake is also found in north Africa and south west Asia and prefers warm dry habitats, and is also often found near the sea. Another member of the genus is *M. moilensis*, which occurs in Egypt.

Telescopus

The cat snake, *Telescopus fallax*, also occurs in north Africa and south west Asia, and its European range is restricted to the eastern Adriatic coast, southern Balkans and the Greek islands. It also occurs on Malta. Adults reach a length of 80 cm or more. The head is broad and flat and body is slender; the body scales are smooth and number 19–21 at mid body. The ground colour is buff, brownish or greyish, and there is a dark collar behind the head. The patten consists of a series of dark dorsal and lateral blotches which vary in density. The ventral surface is whitish or cream, and some individuals may exhibit a pinkish tinge.

The cat snake preys mainly on lizards which it kills with its venom. The genus *Telescopus* is represented by about ten species, and in southern Africa these snakes are usually referred to as tiger snakes. The common, or eastern, tiger snake, *T. semiannulatus*, grows to an average length of 80 cm and the ground colour is brownish with distinct cross bars or blotches.

A broad flat head very distinct from the neck is characteristic of this genus, and the eye can be large, as with the large-eyed cat snake, *T. dhara*, of eastern and northern Africa, which grows to 75 cm and is a uniform brownish in colour.

Macroprotodon

The false smooth snake, *Macroprotodon cucullatus*, derives its common name due to the superficial resemblance to the smooth snake, *Coronella austriaca*. It is of similar size to the smooth snake, growing to 65 cm, and like the smooth snake the scales are smooth. In Europe it is found only in southern Iberia; it is more widespread in northern Africa where it ranges eastwards into Israel.

The coloration is greyish or brownish with vague dark crossbars, and there is a dark streak which runs from beneath the eye. It is a secretive snake, often found under debris or stones, and it appears to prefer stony places, walls, etc. The false smooth snake feeds almost entirely on lizards. The genus *Macroprotodon* is represented by just the single species.

Boiga

The most widespread genus of rear-fanged snakes is *Boiga*, which is distributed in parts of Africa, throughout India, South East Asia, Indonesia, the Philippines, Papua New Guinea and northern Australia, representing a total of about thirty species.

Two species occur in Africa: *Boiga blandingii* and *B. pulverulenta*. Blanding's tree snake, *B. blandingii*, occurs in eastern, central and western Africa, and is a snake of the equatorial forest. It is a large handsome snake growing up to 250 cm; the head is large and very distinct from the neck. Colour varies from brown to black and immature individuals are vividly marked with brown or reddish blotches on the sides of the body. The ventral surface is whitish or cream and in many individuals the ventral scales are edged with black. The body scales are smooth and number 21–25 at mid body. Although large individuals appear to be robust, the body is usually slender, and an outstanding characterstic is the snake's general appearance, in that the body is laterally compressed. This is also characteristic of most other species of *Boiga*, but is most outstanding when seen in *B. blandingii*. Blandings tree snake is essentially an arboreal species, and is extremely agile in trees and bushes. Food consists mainly of birds and it occasionally takes chameleons. Bats are also included in the diet and it often enters the roofs of houses to dine on these mammals.

The blotched tree snake, *B. pulverulenta*, is also an arboreal species of the rain forest and occurs over much of the same range as *B. blandingii*, but also ranges as far south as Angola. It is a smaller species, adults reaching a length of 100 cm. The blotched tree snake, as its name implies, has a series of dark rhombic marks on the sides of the body, while on the dorsal surface there is a series of crossbars. The ground colour is reddish brown, and the ventral surface is whitish with dark mottling. Food consists of small mammals and birds.

Boiga is represented in Australia by just one species, the brown tree snake, *B. irregularis*, which is confined to the northern and eastern coastal regions; the species also occurs in Papua New Guinea, the Philippines and Indonesia. It is a large species, growing to 200 cm, and the body colour is reddish brown with dark crossbars, and many of the body scales are edged with black. The ventral surface is cream or pinkish. The scales are smooth and the body scales number 19–23 at mid body. Cogger, in his book *The Reptiles and Amphibians of Australia*, states that the Australian species never attain a large size and that there may be justification in warranting it as an endemic species (*B. fusca*).

Asia must be considered as the headquarters of the genus where it is represented by many variable forms. A matter of confusion regarding the use of common names arises here; in South East Asia, snakes of the genus *Boiga* are often referred to as cat snakes. This and other examples highlight the importance of the use of scientific names; for example, it has been mentioned that members of the genus *Telescopus* are referred to as both cat and tiger snakes in various parts of their range. No doubt, an Australian would find this confusing, as the Australian tiger snake, *Notechis scutatus* (Pl. 11), is one of the deadliest snakes in the world.

The yellow-ringed cat snake, *B. dendrophila* (Pl. 2), is more commonly known as the mangrove snake. It inhabits lowland jungle and mangrove swamps and is found in Malaya, Sumatra and the Philippines. The mangrove snake can grow to 240 cm, and is strikingly marked with vivid yellow bands on a glossy black ground colour. The yellow bands number between forty and fifty and vary in width. Some meet on the back while in some individuals the bands are restricted to the lateral surface. The labials are also vivid yellow, and are edged with black. The ventral surface is leaden grey, the scales are smooth and number 21–23 at mid body. The mangrove snake is highly arboreal and feeds on lizards, birds, bats and also other snakes. The body is notably laterally compressed, and as in other members of the genus this is an adaptation to arboreal life.

44

The Indian gamma, *B. trigonata*, is widespread in that continent and grows to 100 cm. The coloration is greyish brown or greyish olive with darker crossbars or spots. The scales are smooth and number 21 at mid body. The Indian gamma prefers dry regions and is often found in areas of human habitation.

It can be appreciated that many species of *Boiga* are very similar in appearance; the large distinctive head, the large eyes with elliptic pupils, the slender, compressed body, are all distinguishing characteristics of the genus. Other prominent members of the genus are: *B. multimaculatus*, which occurs throughout South East Asia, southern China and Vietnam. The dark-headed cat snake, *B. nigriceps*, is found in the Malay peninsula, Borneo and Java. The jasper cat snake, *B. jaspideus*, occurs throughout a similar range but is said to be somewhat rare.

Chrysopelea

The flying snakes, *Chrysopelea*, are represented by five species which occur throughout South East Asia, Indonesia, southern China, Sri Lanka, Assam and Bengal. The most widespread of the genus is *C. ornata*, which grows to 160 cm, and has a green body colour with each scale edged with black. The markings are more dense on the dorsal surface where they usually form distinct crossbars. The body scales are smooth and number 17 at mid body.

The paradise tree snake, *C. paradisi*, shares much of the same range as *C. ornata* in South East Asia. The ground colour of this strikingly marked snake is black with red and green markings. This species grows to 120 cm; the body scales are sometimes faintly keeled and number 17 at mid body.

The flying snakes in actual fact glide for short distances by flattening the body, presenting a concave surface, and by employing lateral undulations of the body. Other members of the genus include: *C. taprobanica*, which is only found in Sri Lanka, and *C. chrysochlora*, which is found in Burma, the Malay peninsula, Sumatra and Borneo. All the members of the genus *Chrysopelea* are highly arboreal, occur mainly in forest regions and feed largely on lizards.

Slender-bodied snakes

Many of the species described so far have either slender or moderately slender bodies. Slenderness and elongation of the body are exemplified

45

in the extreme by several genera found in both the New and Old World. In South East Asia the genus *Ahaetulla* is typified by extremely slender-bodied snakes with long narrow pointed heads. The eyes are large and, unlike most other snakes, the pupils are horizontal. This highly arboreal genus consists of about twenty species, and all of these are to be found in South East Asia. Some are bright green in colour with pale linear markings such as *A. mycterizans* and *A. prasinus*. Although green is a prominent form of coloration for the genus, equally common are brown, greyish and even yellowish white. To give some idea of the body proportions for this genus, a snake 150 cm in length would be no thicker than a man's thumb at mid body. In addition, the body scales only number 15 at the thickest part.

The genus *Oxybelis* of Central and South America resembles *Ahaetulla* in appearance. There are four recognised species and the vine snake, *O. aeneus*, is also found in extreme southern Arizona. The coloration of the vine snake is greyish or yellowish brown and there is a distinctive black eye stripe. The vine snake inhabits low bushes and its cryptic coloration makes it almost impossible to find. The vine snake is principally a lizard feeder, but it has been known to take birds and small mammals.

Another slender-bodied new world genus is *Imantodes*, sometimes referred to as the blunt-headed snakes. This nocturnal and highly arboreal genus is unusual in that it has a large number of ventral and subcaudal scales—up to four hundred—and in one species, *I. cenchoa*, the scales of the mid dorsal line are broader than long.

The African vine or twig snake, *Thelotornis kirtlandii*, is well known, and is another elongate and slender species with a narrow pointed head. The twig snake is found in rain forest, and the other remaining species, *T. capensis*, is typically found in savanna. The coloration of *T. kirtlandii* is greenish with a livid green on the top of the head.

The twig snake is highly arboreal and the cryptic coloration consists of a bark-like ground colour with alternate streaked silvery green markings. The genus is considered to be highly venomous although it is not of a savage disposition. The scales are feebly keeled and number 19 at mid body. Both species grow to 150 cm and feed on lizards and birds. Some authorities place *T. capensis* as a sub-species of *T. kirtlandii*, but the latter is typically a forest species of east, west and central Africa, and *T. capensis* is found on the savanna land of South Africa.

The boomslang, *Dispholidus typus* (Pl. 1), is an arboreal species widely distributed throughout Africa south of the Sahara. Prominent colours are brown or green, with or without some dark mottling. The skin between the body scales is black and is most apparent when the snake inflates the body. The body scales are overlapping and strongly keeled, and number 19 at mid body. The boomslang is a slender snake growing to 150 cm and there are records of individuals reaching 200 cm or more. The eyes are very large and prominent, and the rostral scale is visible from above, the head being short and somewhat pointed.

The boomslang is extremely agile and favours thorn bush and savanna. Although it is rated as one of Africa's most deadly snakes, it is in fact an inoffensive creature and will only bite if restrained or molested. The bite of this snake, however, is very dangerous indeed, and unlike most rear-fanged snakes the boomslang strikes with a quick stabbing motion, which is quite effective due to the wide gape and relatively forward position of the fangs.

Diet consists of birds and lizards which are quickly subdued by the powerful venom.

The species is monotypic, but several races exist which appear to be based on coloration.

The green tree snake, *Dipsadoboa unicolor*, is another arboreal and cryptically coloured species. This slender snake grows to around 100 cm, and occurs in western and central Africa and some parts of east Africa. The body colour is darkish green, sometimes brownish; the ventral surface is whitish or greenish white. The eyes are large and bulging and the head is heart-shaped. The body scales are smooth and number 17 at mid body. The green tree snake is a forest species and feeds on amphibians.

It will be noted that many of the rear-fanged snakes are inclined to be arboreal, some totally so; e.g. *Oxybelis*, *Ahaetulla* and *Imantodes*. Others can be described as snakes of the low bush, although essentially considered as terrestrial, e.g. *Telescopus*.

Psammophis

One genus that can be described as terrestrial but which is also commonly found in low bushes and scrub is *Psammophil*, which is a widespread African and west Asian genus, and contains a variety of species.

The hissing sand snake, *P. sibilans*, is widely distributed throughout Africa, outside the forest regions, and its range includes Mediterranean Egypt and Mauretania. Coloration is variable and individuals can be almost any shade of olive, brown or yellowish. Juveniles and immature sometimes have a streaked pattern, and in some adults there may be a dark dorsal line. It is a relatively slender species, but large individuals can be quite robust; the maximum size for the species is around 180 cm, and lengths of 150 cm are not uncommon. The hissing sand snake is frequently found in gardens and on arable land; it also occupies quite arid habitat and can seemingly tolerate quite high day temperatures. It is an extremely agile snake and moves with surprising speed, and this speed and agility must be considered as a partially successful defence against avian predation, to which this and other diurnal species are prone. The diet consists mainly of lizards and amphibians, and to a lesser extent other snakes and small mammals. The body scales are smooth and number 17 at mid body.

The stripe-bellied sand snake, *P. subtaeniatus*, is similar to *P. sibilans*, in habits and choice of habitat. However, it is a somewhat smaller species growing to 130 cm, and most individuals have distinct pale stripes on an olive or brown ground colour. This species occurs over a more easterly distribution and the most southerly range is eastern Zimbabwe.

The link-marked sand snake, *P. biseriatus*, is very similar to the preceding species, but the top of the head is usually coloured a vivid green. Maximum size for the species appears to be 100 cm, and the species is notably more arboreal than other members of the genus.

The Sind sand snake, *P. schokari*, occurs in the Middle East and eastwards to the Punjab. The body colour is variable and can be greyish, olive or reddish brown, with or without darker spotted or striped markings. This species grows to 120 cm, and the body scales are smooth and number 17 at mid body.

Other characteristics of the genus *Psammophis* are a narrow elongated head, and the smooth body scales that give the genus a polished appearance. In addition, this genus is similar to *Malpolon*, in that the body appears stiff and unyielding.

Rhamphiophis

Rear-fanged colubrids that lead a burrowing existence but seemingly lack any special adaptation to do so are exemplified by the genus *Rham-*

phiophis, commonly known as the beaked snakes. The genus is distributed throughout various parts of Africa, and the rufous-beaked snake, *R. oxyryhyncus*, occurs in west, central, east and South Africa. The term 'beaked snake' is very apt—the rostral is broad and prominent, and the tip of the snout is hooked. The coloration of *R. oxyryhyncus* is reddish brown and there is a distinctive black stripe which runs through the eye and terminates at the neck. The body scales are smooth and number 17 at mid body. It has a varied diet and will take lizards, other snakes, amphibians and small mammals.

The rufous-beaked snake prefers dry areas and is often found in termite mounds, where it burrows freely.

Other members of the genus include *R. acutus*, the western striped beaked snake which is a central and west African species which occurs in grassland savanna, and is also found often in the vicinity of marshy ground. This species grows to lengths of up to 70 cm, and the coloration consists of a brownish or olive brown ground colour with distinctive dark stripe on the edges of the ventrals. There may be a faint greyish line on the dorsal surface. The diet includes frogs, liqards and small mammals.

The red-spotted beaked snake, *R. rubropunctatus*, has a more easterly range and occurs in southern Sudan, Kenya and Tanzania, and also Zanzibar. This species attains a large size, growing to 200 cm or more. It is also more brightly marked than other members of the genus, and the pattern consists of white spots on a red brown ground colour.

Crotaphopeltis

The white-lipped or herald snake, *Crotaphopeltis hotamboeia*, is a small terrestrial species which grows to 70 cm, but lengths of 60 cm or less are more common. This irascible little snake is widespread throughout Africa, excluding the mountain and desert regions. When annoyed, the herald snake will adopt the typical striking attitude of a viper, flatten the anterior part of the body and strike repeatedly. The ground colour is greyish, olive or blackish with a variable degree of white stippling, which is usually heaviest on the lateral parts of the body. The herald snake occurs in damp or wet areas and feeds mainly on frogs and toads.

Degens water snake, *C. degeni*, is a somewhat smaller species, reaching a maximum length of 50 cm. This species lacks the light stippling of the herald snake, but the dark olive green, or blackish green, ground colour has an outstanding iridescence. This species is almost always found in the vicinity of water and feeds entirely on amphibians.

Rear-fanged snakes of the New World

The rear-fanged snakes are well represented in the New World and some have already been mentioned. The mussurana, *Clelia clelia*, is probably one of the better known of the New World rear-fanged snakes and occurs in both Central and South America. It is a large handsome species growing to around 180 cm with a robust glossy black body. The mussurana is a powerful snake and feeds largely on other snakes, including venomous *Bothrops spp.* which it overpowers by employing both envenomation and constriction.

Another snake-eating species is the Central American road guarder, *Conophis lineatus*, which derives its name from the fact that it is often encountered on the roadside and on the edge of tracks. It is a small species, growing to 80 cm, and is boldly marked with longitudinal stripes.

Rear-fanged snakes of Malagasy

There are eight genera of rear-fanged snakes to be found on Malagasy and seven of these are endemic. The remaining genus, *Geodipsas*, is also found on the mainland, although it is represented there by a different species.

Some of these Malagasy species are arboreal, and the most bizarre in appearance is the leaf-nosed snake, *Langaha intermedia*, where the female of the species has a broad leaflike appendage protruding from the snout. The male, however, has a simpler and smaller protruberance. The maximum size for the species appears to be 100 cm and the coloration is brownish.

Aparallactus

The sub-family Aparallactinae consists of seventeen genera, most of which are venomous. Nearly all the species belonging to this group are to some extent burrowing forms, some entirely so. All are found in Africa, and one genus, *Atractaspis*, also occurs in the Middle East.

The African centipede eaters, *Aparallactus*, are represented by about a dozen species and are slender fossorial snakes growing to 60 cm; however, sizes of between 30 cm and 40 cm are more common.

The blotched backed centipede eater, *A. lunulatus*, has an extensive range and is found throughout central, east and southern Africa. Coloration is variable; individuals with a uniform brown or olive ground colour are common, other variations include dark crossbars or blotches. Most individuals have a pale yellow or whitish collar. Lengths of up to 50 cm appear to be the maximum for the species, and the body is slender and the tail is short. As the name implies, centipedes are the main food species.

The forest centipede eater, *A. modestus*, is essentially a west and central African species, although it is also found in western Uganda. This species grows slightly larger than *A. lunulatus*, reaching lengths of around 60 cm. Coloration is usually uniform greyish or black with a pale yellow collar.

Miodon

The genus *Miodon* is usually referred to as the snake eaters, and being fossorial such snakes as *Typhlops spp.* are preyed upon. However, any snake of suitable size would be a potential prey species, and the eastern snake eater, *M. christy*, has been known to prey on the herald snake (Pitman, 1974).

This genus also contains some larger species of the Aparallactinae, and 80 cm is the average size for such species as *M. christy* and *M. collaris*. Both are moderately slender and uniformly coloured greyish or black, sometimes with some dark mottling on the lateral and dorsal surface. Both species occur throughout eastern, central and parts of western Africa.

Micrelaps

The genus *Micrelaps* contains three species, all of which are small, all within the 30–45 cm size range. *M. boetgeri* is found in eastern Africa and is uniform brown or grey in colour.

Chilorhinophis

The most brightly coloured of the Aparallactinae are found in the several species belonging to the genus *Chilorhinophis*. These are small slender snakes rarely exceeding 45 cm in length, and are often referred to as the two-headed snakes due to the habit that the snakes of this genus have of raising the tail and moving backwards.

C. butleri is a central and western African species with a black head and neck and three black longitudinal stripes on a yellow ground colour. The ventral surface is bright orange or pinkish. *C. gerardi* is similarly marked and is found in central Africa and as far south as northern Zimbabwe. Lengths of between 30 cm and 35 cm are average for both species.

Amblyodipsas

The genus *Amblyodipsas* contains seven species which are distributed throughout Africa south of the Sahara. One species, the purple-glossed snake, *A. unicolor*, is fairly unique in that the females are usually twice the size of the males, or even more in some cases. Whereas 50 cm appears to be the maximum size of males, the females grow to lengths of 110 cm. The colour of both sexes is uniform iridescent black, and the genus superficially resembles the related genus *Atractaspis*.

Atractaspis

The 'mole vipers', *Atractaspis*, are represented by sixteen species found throughout Africa with two species occurring in the Middle East. *A. bibroni* is a widespread species and is the only member of the genus to be found in South Africa. Other parts of its range are central and eastern Africa.

All members of this genus are uniformly coloured grey, black or brownish. Most are within the 60 cm size range, but one species, *A. microlepidota*, of east Africa has been reputed to reach lengths of 100 cm or more. This genus feeds mainly on lizards, other snakes and small mammals.

The fangs of *Atractaspis* are wholly out of proportion to the size of the head. These fangs are folded in the roof of the mouth and can be erected independently in the manner of the true vipers. The fangs can also be brought into use without the snake actually opening the mouth, and this may have obvious advantages when feeding takes place in such restricted places as rodent burrows.

A. engaddensis and *A. microlepidota* are found in the Middle East, the former species occupying Jordan and Israel, and the latter occurring in the Yemen and Aden. Both species are also found on the African continent; *A. engaddensis* in northern Egypt, and *A. microlepidota* having a much wider range, occurring in western, central and eastern Africa.

Enhydris

The Homalopsinae are stoutly built aquatic colubrids with the eyes and nostrils placed towards the top of the head. The ten genera are distributed from peninsular India to Australasia and occur in coastal areas and areas of lowland freshwater.

The genus *Enhydris* contains a total of twenty-six species, and these are distributed throughout the entire range of the Homalopsinae. *E. plumbea* occurs in Burma, southern China, Vietnam and South East Asia. This species is dark brown or olive in colour with dark spots on the dorsal surface and the average length is around 40 cm. *E. bocourti* occurs in South East Asia and is a much larger species than *E. plumbea*, growing to 120 cm and of a stout build. The coloration is dark brown with narrow yellowish crossbars and spots which sometimes form irregular series of lines along the body.

E. polyepis is found in Papua New Guinea and northern Queensland. Colour varies from dark olive brown to olive black and the lateral surfaces are speckled with yellowish white. This species grows to a length of 70 cm.

Monotypic species

The genus *Myron* is restricted to northern Australia where it is represented by the one species, *M. richardsoni*. This small snake grows to 60 cm and is usually dark brown with darker crossbands.

Other monotypic species are *Heurnia ventromaculatus* of northern New Guinea, *Bitia hydroides* of South East Asia, *Gerarda prevostiana* of India, Sri Lanka and Burma, and *Homalopsis buccata* of South East Asia.

The remaining monotypic species is the tentacled or fishing snake, *Erpeton tentaculatum*, of Thailand and Cochin China. This species is the most aquatic of the Homalopsinae and is almost helpless on land.

The fishing snake is equipped with a pair of fleshy protruberances which extend from the snout, and these 'tentacles' are used as a lure to catch fish.

Fordonia

The genus *Fordonia* contains two species and the more widespread is *F. leucobalia* which occurs in coastal areas and rivers of Burma, Cochin China, Malay Archipelago, Papua New Guinea and northern Australia. The white-bellied water snake, as it is more commonly known, grows to a maximum length of 100 cm, but lengths of around 60 cm are more usual. The coloration can be uniform glossy black, or else with an irregular density of whitish or cream spots. *F. papuensis* is restricted to one area near Katru, New Guinea.

Cerberus

The genus *Cerberus* is represented in Australia and Papua New Guinea by *C. rhynchops*. This species has an extensive range and also occurs in coastal and tidal areas of India, Sri Lanka, South East Asia and Vietnam. The coloration varies from light greyish to red brown with a series of darker crossbars, and sometimes there is a prominent dorsal stripe present. There is also a distinctive dark stripe running through the eye. The species grows to lengths of 100 cm.

Cantoria

The two species contained in the genus *Cantoria* are *C. annulata*, which is restricted to Papua New Guinea, and *C. violacea*, which has a wider distribution and is found in Burma and throughout South East Asia. It is a large but slender species reaching lengths of 120 cm. This species occurs in two-colour forms; one is blackish with yellow bands, and the other is brownish with whitish bands.

Conclusion

It can be appreciated that the venomous colubrids present a wide variety of form, and the many diverse species have successfully colonised the different habitat types.

We need to know much more about this group of snakes; apart from classification, which appears to be in a permanent state of flux, a great deal of work remains to be done on the composition of the venom.

Equally important is the continuing task of finding out just how these snakes live; in other words, as with all the reptile groups, a great deal of ecological information has yet to be unearthed.

4

The Elapids

The elapids are a large group of venomous snakes which are distributed over Africa, Asia, the southern parts of North America, Central and South America and Australasia (Fig. 9). The snake fauna of Australia is unique in that the elapids constitute the greater majority and also represent the widest variety of forms.

The two hundred and twenty species of elapid snakes are represented by sixty-two genera and in general appearance there is a resemblance to the colubrid snakes. The majority of elapids are either slender or moderately so; however, some species are distinctly robust. Such examples are the monotypic species of sea snake, *Astrotia stokesii*, and the Australian death adder, *Acanthophis antarcticus* (Pl. 13), which is typically viper-shaped in build.

In addition to similar body proportions some colubrid snakes bear a close resemblance to their venomous relatives with regard to coloration; the king snake, *Lampropeltis triangulum*, for example, could be confused with the coral snake, *Micrurus fulvius*, as both are banded and brightly coloured, and both occur in south eastern North America. Furthermore, some colubrids are successful mimics as regards behaviour; the pipe snake, *Cylindrophis rufus*, for example, displays the underside of the tail in the manner of the Asiatic coral snakes (*Maticora*).

It is obvious that many species of elapids are not readily distinguishable from colubrids; however, the main difference is that the elapids include some of the world's most dangerous snakes; the African mambas, the kraits and the cobras are obvious examples.

In fact, the elapids are often referred to as the cobra family although the genus *Naja* contains only six species and the other cobras are represented by a further six species contained within five genera, *Hemachatus*, *Boulengerina*, *Pseudohaje*, *Paranaja* and *Ophiophagus*. Although referred to as a cobra one genus, *Paranaja*, is hoodless, and another genus, *Pseudohaje*, has only a slight suggestion of a hood. Some elapids are small in size and as such are considered to represent no danger to man due to the small mouth which would not facilitate a proper bite. Such examples are the African genus, *Elaps*, and the Australian genus, *Vermicella*. However, it is as well to remember that these snakes possess a very potent venom and that even a scratch from a fang could well prove serious.

All the elapids possess fixed front fangs that are situated in the front of the upper jaw. The fangs are enclosed venom canals and not grooved as in the rear-fanged snakes. However, the fangs of the elapids are not without trace of join, and Fig. 13 shows the suture clearly visible. The forward position of the fangs of elapids varies. Figs 4 and 5 show this difference for two African species, the Egyptian cobra, *Naja haje*, and the black mamba, *Dendroaspis polyepis*. In fact, the fangs of all

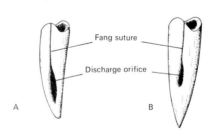

A   B

Fang suture

Discharge orifice

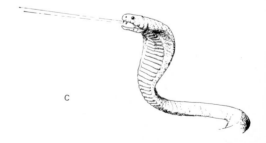

C

Fig. 13   How the spitting cobra 'spits'. The discharge orifice is situated just short of the tip of the fang in a forward position. Venom can be sprayed for a distance of up to eight feet, which covers an arc of some two feet in width.

56

Fig. 14   Mozambique spitting cobra, *Naja mossambica*, in typical alert posture.

the species of mamba are situated well forward in the upper jaw, almost directly beneath the snout, and it is one reason why extreme caution is required when handling this particular genus.

Although the fangs are fixed, there is some rotary movement which varies from species to species. The size and shape of the fangs are also variable, but all can be considered relatively short when compared with the huge fangs displayed by some of the viper family. Fangs that have been adapted to 'spit' venom are well exemplified in three African species, the black-necked cobra, *Naja nigricollis*, the Mozambique spitting cobra, *Naja mossambica* (Fig. 14), and the ringhals, *Hemachatus haemachatus*. These species have the ability to spray venom for a distance of up to 2·5 m. Other species of *Naja* also possess a 'spitting' ability, but are not so well adapted for the purpose.

The actual venom gland of the elapids is toughly encapsulated and is situated in most cases between the eye and the rear of the upper jaw. In one elapid genus, *Maticora*, the venom gland is elongated, reaching back over a third of the snake's length and displacing the

57

heart. Elongation of the venom gland occurs in three genera of venomous snakes.

No elapids occur in Europe, although it has been mentioned that fossil cobra remains dating back to the Miocene have been found in France.

The majority of the elapids are either terrestrial or aquatic; only two genera are truly arboreal, *Dendroaspis*, the mambas, and *Pseudohaje*, the tree cobras. However, one species of *Dendroaspis*, the black mamba, is mainly terrestrial. Many species of elapids will climb low bushes to feed or bask. Burrowing elapids are represented by several genera; the coral snakes of the New World, *Micrurus*, *Micruroides* and *Leptomicrurus*; these are all brightly coloured elapids with relatively short fangs. Other burrowers include the primitive genus *Apistocalamus* of Papua New Guinea. In this and some other primitive genera the fangs are just deeply grooved and of very small size.

The terminology of the common names of snakes is often misleading; the coral snakes of the New World have just been mentioned, but the term 'coral snake' equally applies to other species found in Africa and Asia. Similarly, the name 'garter snake' is well known in North America when referring to the genus *Thamnophis*, a harmless non-venomous species. However, the garter snakes of Africa include two genera of elapids, *Elaps* and *Elapsoidea*.

Elaps

It would be beyond the scope of this book to describe each and every species of elapid; the diversity of form ranges from the minute African garter snake, *Elaps dorsalis*, which only grows to 25 cm, to the massive King cobra, *Ophiophagus hannah* (Pl. 10), which can reach lengths of up to 550 cm, and is in fact the largest venomous snake in the world.

The South African dwarf garter snake, *Elaps lacteus*, is a fossorial species which is often found in termite hills where it feeds on the larvae and eggs; it also feeds on small lizards and blind snakes, *Typhlops*. This species grows somewhat larger than *E. dorsalis*, reaching a maximum length of 50 cm. Both species are restricted to southern Africa and the coloration of *E. dorsalis* is blackish brown above with a pale yellow stripe on the lateral surfaces.

E. lacteus occurs in both a speckled form and a barred form, and in the barred variety there is usually a reddish vertebral stripe.

58

Elapsoidea

The other African garter snakes are contained in the genus *Elapsoidea*. This genus is more widespread than the former and comprises six species which are distributed throughout central, east and southern Africa. *E. sundevallii* is a South African species which grows to 60 cm. Adults are usually glossy black and may have indistinct cross-bars; the young of this species are more distinctly marked with white bands. *E. loveridgei* is found in the western parts of east Africa and central Africa. This species is blackish and may be marked with fine white bands which may appear as indistinct markings, especially in individuals that are about to shed their skin. The Sudanese garter snake, *E. laticincta*, is very similar in appearance to that of *E. loveridgei*, but has a more pointed snout and fewer ventral scales. Lengths of around 65 cm would appear to be the maximum for the genus.

Aspidelaps

The species contained in the African genus *Aspidelaps* are somewhat larger than the garter snakes, and the two species, the coral snake, *A. lubricus*, and the shield-nosed snake, *A. scutatus*, are both restricted to southern Africa. Although 70 cm is the average length for *A. lubricus*, the body is robust. The coloration is usually reddish brown with conspicuous black bands. The shield-nosed snake, *A. scutatus*, is somewhat smaller than the coral snake, reaching lengths of 55 cm or a little more. The colour is a more uniform reddish brown with indistinct greyish blotches on the dorsal surface. The rostral scale is large and prominent and it is this feature that gives this species its common name.

Both species are capable of flattening the neck in the manner of a cobra, although the hood is far less pronounced than that of true cobras.

Maticora

The coral snakes of Asia are represented by two genera, *Maticora* and *Calliophis* (or *Callophis*). The genus *Maticora* does not occur on the Indian sub-continent and there are just two species, the long-glanded coral snake, *M. bivirgata*, and the banded coral snake, *M. intestinalis*. Both species have a number of recognised sub-species throughout their range, which extends from South East Asia to the Philippines.

M. bivirgata is dark blue or blackish in coloration with a pale band

59

on each side of the body and a dark stripe which runs below the paler markings. The most distinguishing feature is the coloration of the head and ventral surface, which is bright coral red. This species grows to around 150 cm.

The banded coral snake, *M. intestinalis*, is a much smaller species which reaches a length of 60 cm; the coloration is brownish with a red or orange dorsal stripe enclosed between two black stripes. Situated low on the lateral surfaces are pale or white stripes which are again enclosed within two black lines. The ventral surface is barred black and white with the exception of the tail, which is barred black and red.

Calliophis

The other Asiatic coral snakes are found in the genus *Calliophis*, represented by twelve species, and have a much wider distribution than that of *Maticora*, being found throughout India, Sri Lanka, South East Asia, southern China, Vietnam and the Philippines. Two species, *C. boettgeri* and *C. iwasakii*, are endemic to Ryukyu Island.

All the species in this genus are said to be uncommon, but this may be due to their secretive habits; they are usually found under logs or ground debris.

C. bibroni occurs only in south western India and grows to a length of 60 cm. The coloration ranges from red to purplish brown with a red ventral surface. Markings consist of black transverse bands which sometimes continue across the ventral surface.

C. macclellandii has a much wider distribution and is found in north east India, Nepal, South East Asia—with the exception of Malaya—Vietnam and Taiwan. This species is one of the largest of the genus, growing to 90 cm. It also exhibits the greatest variety of coloration. The ground colour is usually red or brown with black bands that vary in intensity. Some individuals may be blotched or else have a continuous vertebral stripe. The ventral surface is usually yellowish and the black bands continue across the belly.

Other members of the genus are *C. calligaster* of the Philippines, *C. sauteri* from Taiwan and *C. kelloggii* from southern China and Vietnam. *C. beddomei* is confined to southern India, and also to be found on the Indian continent are *C. nigrescens* and *C. melanurus*, the latter also being found in Sri Lanka. *C. maculiceps* (Pl. 3) is found throughout South East Asia but is said to be rare in many parts of its range. *C.*

gracilis is also found in South East Asia, but its distribution is confined to southern Thailand, Malaya and Sumatra.

Micruroides

The coral snakes of North and South America, *Micruroides*, *Leptomicrurus* and *Micrurus*, are in fact the only elapids to be found in the New World. All are small to medium sized snakes and are conspicuously marked with brightly coloured bands. The size and arrangement of bands vary from species to species but are represented by five basic colours: red, black, yellow, cream and white, the first three predominating. The New World coral snakes are fossorial species, often found under logs, leaf litter and other ground debris.

Coral snakes have accounted for a number of fatalities, although in parts of their range they are treated almost casually, often by children attracted by the bright coloration. Coral snake mimics have been mentioned earlier in this chapter; however, one subtle difference is that the black rings of the mimics usually occur in pairs, an occurrence never found in coral snakes. The other difference is that in the coral snakes the red bands, when present, are usually bordered in yellow, white or cream; in the mimics they are usually bordered in black.

The genus *Micruroides* is represented by just one species, *M. euryxanthus*, which occurs in southern Arizona and northern Mexico. The body is slender with a relatively short tail and the average length is around 50 cm. It is a strikingly coloured snake with broad alternating bands of red and black which are separated by bands of yellow or white. This species is found in fairly arid regions and is largely nocturnal. Food consists of small snakes and lizards.

Leptomicrurus

The slender, or thread coral snakes are found in the genus *Leptomicrurus* and all are restricted to the northern part of the South American mainland. Until recently only two species were recognised, *L. collaris* and *L. narduccii*. However, a third species, *L. schmidt*, is said to occur in north western Brazil. In fact, very little is known about this genus but they may reach a length of 75–80 cm which makes the genus potentially very dangerous, although there are no recorded bites from any of the three species mentioned. *Leptomicrurus* differ in appearance from the other coral snakes due to the fact that the bands are incomplete on the dorsal surface which is usually uniform black. The bands are best defined on the ventrals and appear on the lateral parts as triangles or as less well defined blotches which are usually red.

Micrurus

The majority of the coral snakes are contained in the genus *Micrurus* which embraces some forty-six species found in North, Central and South America. Most are of small size, but several species attain lengths of 100 cm or more. The North American representative of the genus is *M. fulvius*, which occurs from North Carolina across the southern states to west Texas; it also occurs in north eastern Mexico. This species is said to grow to lengths of up to 100 cm, but lengths of around 50 cm are more usual. The basic ground coloration is black with a regular series of red bands, a little narrower than the black, which are bordered with yellow rings. The red bands may be speckled black and in many individuals there are distinctive black spots on the red; the tail is black and the head is black in front with a distinctive yellow band on the nape. It seems to occur in both dry and wet situations and is mainly crepuscular in its habits. Food consists of lizards and snakes. Apart from the usual name, 'coral snake', in many parts of its range it is also called 'harlequin snake', 'candy-stick snake' and 'American cobra'. The venom is very toxic and several fatalities are attributed to this species.

Nineteen species of *Micrurus* occur in Mexico and Central America and four of these are also found in north western South America.

The most widespread is *M. nigrocinctus* which is found throughout Central America from southern Mexico to north western Colombia in South America. This species has broad red bands which alternate with single uniform black rings with narrow separating rings of yellow or white. Individuals of this species have been known to reach a size of 160 cm or more, but lengths of around 100 cm or less are more usual. This snake is a species of lowland rain forest.

On the South American mainland *Micrurus* is widely distributed as far south as northern Argentina; there are no coral snakes to be found in Chile. Two species, *M. circinalis* and *M. lemniscatus*, are also found in Trinidad. In fact, *M. lemniscatus* is one of the most widespread of the genus in South America, being found in nine countries.

The southern, or giant coral snake, *M. frontalis* (Pl. 4), is another large and widespread species which can attain sizes of up to 125 cm. This snake has caused a number of fatalities throughout its range, and the large size and wide distribution mark this species as the most dangerous of all the coral snakes. As with many species of *Micrurus* the red bands predominate and are separated by triads of black rings on white or yellowish. Many of the coral snakes belonging to the genus *Micrurus* have been allocated several sub-species; however, the validity of some of these is open to discussion. For example, *M. frontalis*, at some time or other, has been regarded as four different sub-species, and one of these, *M. f. pyrrocryptus*, is more usually awarded full specific rank, i.e. *M. pyrrocryptus*.

The giant of all the coral snakes is *M. spixii*, which has been known to attain the remarkable length of 150 cm. Although a widespread species, being found in nine countries, bites from this snake are almost unknown.

Most coral snakes are secretive in their habits and comparatively little is known about their life history, but they are probably more abundant than is thought.

Dendroaspis

Probably the most well known and feared group of elapids are the mambas, consisting of four species contained in the genus *Dendroaspis* which occur only in Africa south of the Sahara. Essentially arboreal, all of the mambas are extremely agile and a bite from any of the species is likely to prove fatal unless treated, and even then the chances would be limited for a bite from a large species such as the black mamba, *D. polylepis*.

However, it must be said that the mambas are generally timid in their disposition and will usually choose to flee from an intruder. The stories about mambas overtaking a man on a galloping horse are well known, but the black mamba, which is said to be the fastest moving snake in the world, is capable of speeds of up to 20 km/h. This is much less than attained by a horse, and snakes, being limbless, do give an illusion of speed, although they can only keep it up for comparatively short distances.

Three of the four species of mamba are predominantly green in colour and the most widespread of these is *D. angusticeps* (Pl. 7, Fig. 15), which occurs on the eastern side of Africa from Kenya in the north and southwards to southern Natal. This snake is highly arboreal and is a species of thick forest or bush. The coloration of adults is bright leaf green, often yellowish. Immature green mambas are usually bluish

63

Fig. 15   Green mamba, *Dendroaspis angusticeps*, a highly arboreal snake with a powerful neurotoxic venom but which possesses a fairly quiet disposition.

green, but the adults also adopt a bluish colour prior to skin shedding. Maximum length for the species is around 200 cm. A high percentage of food consists of birds and their eggs, but other tree-living animals such as chameleons and other lizards are included in the diet. Due to the green coloration green mambas are often confused with other green arboreal snake species such as the boomslang, and bush snakes of the genus *Philothamnus*.

Another 'green' mamba is jamesons mamba, *D. jamesoni* (Pl. 6), which is distributed in central Africa from western Kenya, Uganda, Rwanda, Burundi, the eastern part of the Congo Republic, Angola and Cameroon. The further occurrence of this species in western Africa is probably more widespread but confirmation is still needed. The ground colour is grass green, often yellowish in places, particularly in the neck region. The body scales are edged with black, and the head and tail are a darker shade of the general ground colour, effecting a velvety appearance. The average adult length for this species is again around 200 cm, although there are authentic records of this snake attaining lengths in excess of 300 cm. This is also a highly arboreal forest species, but it is encountered on the ground quite frequently. Small rodents and birds are the main items of food.

The western green mamba, *D. viridis*, occurs in the rain-forest regions of west Africa from Ghana to Senegal, it also is found on the Island of São Tome. This is a distinctive species and, although again green in colour, the body scales are unusually large and bordered with black. Little is known about the habits of the species, but average size is around 200 cm and the diet is probably similar to the other arboreal members of the genus.

The black mamba, *D. polylepis* (Fig. 16), is the largest member of the genus reaching lengths of 400 cm or even more. The black mamba is distributed throughout eastern and southern Africa and occurs westward as far as eastern Congo Republic. The term 'black' is something of a misnomer as most individuals are dark olive brown or else leaden grey. Although not adverse to climbing, the black mamba is usually more at home on the ground where it is found in open bush country or rocky terrain. This species is the most easily provoked of all the mambas, and the large size and uncertain temper make it a formidable

Fig. 16 Black mamba, *Dendroaspis polylepis*, a nervous and extremely agile elapid which is probably the most feared snake in Africa.

creature when aroused. When threatened, the black mamba will raise the forepart of the body from the ground and spread a neat and narrow hood. With mouth slightly agape this mamba may advance rapidly towards the intruder and in my own experience there is little of the bluff in these defensive actions that can be witnessed in the display of some of the cobra species. The head of the black mamba has been aptly described as coffin-shaped, and indeed the heads of all the mamba species have vertical sides. Although not conspicuously marked the black mamba looks exactly what it is, the malevolent expression alone seems to signify a highly dangerous animal. Food consists mainly of small rodents, but birds are also taken.

Naja

The cobras are another well-known group of elapids, the threatening attitude of a cobra reared with hood expanded is a familiar sight to most of us. The most widespread members of the group are contained in the genus *Naja* which embraces six species, five of which occur in Africa.

The Egyptian cobra, *N. haje* (Fig. 17), is the most widespread of the African cobras distributed throughout north Africa and southwards to central and east Africa to South Africa. The Egyptian cobra also occurs in parts of the Middle East. This is a large and somewhat robust species, adults reaching lengths in excess of 250 cm. The coloration is usually dull brown or greyish with pale brown or yellowish ventral surface. Some individuals have orange or pinkish tinges around the neck and tail region. Although usually uniformly coloured the Egyptian cobra is a handsome species, the body in freshly shed individuals has a velvet lustre. The spreading of the hood in cobras can be either a defensive or an inquisitive action and, as many snake handlers will know, the posture of a reared cobra is an indication of whether the snake is bluffing or not. The hood of the Egyptian cobra is prominent and wide, up to 15 cm, but when rearing it does not raise such a great portion of the body as in many other cobra species. The Egyptian cobra is a terrestrial species occurring in semi-arid or savanna type habitat and although largely nocturnal it is often seen basking by day at some permanent refuge.

A banded variety of the Egyptian cobra occurs in southern parts of Africa and many of these individuals that have been examined have been males. It is usually difficult to determine the sex of many elapids

Fig. 17 Egyptian cobra, *Naja haje*, a large and aggressive cobra of the African savanna.

and in many cases is only accurately accomplished by actually probing the anal opening.

When threatened, the Egyptian cobra is bold and aggressive, and it is also reputed to be the 'asp' that ended the life of Cleopatra.

The forest or black and white cobra, *N. melanoleuca* (Pl. 9), is another large African species which occurs principally in rain forest in western, central, eastern and southern Africa. It is a more slender species than the Egyptian cobra but matches it for length, growing in excess of 260 cm, and there are records of giants reaching over 300 cm. This species is readily distinguished from all other members of the genus by the intense glossy black body colour. The intensity of the black varies, and many individuals are distinctly brown or khaki around the head and forepart of the body. The hood of this cobra is also distinct, it is long and narrow and not saucer-shaped like the Egyptian cobra. In addition, this snake usually rears to a great height,

67

usually over two-thirds of the body are raised from the ground, an achievement not usually accomplished by other cobras. This means that an individual 240 cm in length can raise some 160 cm of its body when threatened!

The forest cobra is an excellent swimmer, and throughout many parts of its range it is at least semi-aquatic and fish and amphibians figure largely in its diet. However, this cobra is quite omnivorous and will take warm-blooded prey, and even quite large monitor lizards have been known to be taken.

An African cobra with a much more restricted range is the cape cobra, *N. nivea* (Pl. 8). The distribution of this cobra is confined to southern Africa from the southern Cape northwards to as far as the south western Transvaal. The average length for this species is around 150 cm, but it is said to attain sizes in excess of 200 cm. Another name for this snake is the yellow cobra; this can be misleading as although many individuals are yellow in colour the variety ranges from reddish, through brown to black, and speckled individuals are also quite common.

The Cape cobra is typically found in arid habitat but is equally at home around farms and homesteads where it can prove a hazard. Food consists mainly of small rodents, but lizards and other snakes are included in the diet.

The spitting cobras of Africa are well known and there are now two species which are recognised; the black-necked cobra, *N. nigricollis*, and the Mozambique spitting cobra, *N. mossambica* (Fig. 14). The two species were, until recently, regarded as one, the Mozambique spitting cobra being a sub-species of *N. nigricollis*, i.e. *N. n. mossambica*. However, they have now been shown to differ in colour, size and scalation, and it has also now been proved that the ranges of the two species overlap in some areas. In addition, both species have several recognised sub-species.

The average size for the black-necked cobra is around 160 cm, but much larger individuals have been recorded which compare with large specimens of the forest cobra. In my own experience, smaller, often immature, individuals are most in evidence during daylight, and large adults, which appear to be more nocturnal in their habits, usually lie up by day in burrows, tree roots or other retreats. In fact, all large individuals that I have caught during the daylight hours have involved actively digging them out; a process which often took several hours and was the result of someone spotting the snake entering the retreat perhaps the evening before. Many of the larger elapids tend to be very territorial in their habits and may occupy a relatively small area for a number of years.

An authentic account of the large size attained by this cobra was provided by the well-known African snake man the late C. J. P. Ionides. On a snake-catching trip to Baringo in Kenya, Ionides caught six very large spitting cobras; the largest of these was a male 225 cm in length with a body girth of 20 cm. It is of interest to note that on the same trip Ionides caught forty-six black mambas!

The body scales have a satiny effect and the colour is usually uniform brown, brownish grey or blackish. The ventral coloration is usually a near shade of the body colour. The hood of this species is neat and egg-shaped and the black band across the front of the hood is usually wide and prominent.

One race of this species, *N. n. pallida*, is quite distinct in that the coloration is reddish, pinkish or orange red.

The Mozambique spitting cobra is typically much smaller than the black-necked cobra and individuals in excess of 160 cm are rarely found. The coloration is also more restricted and consistent, being confined to a body colour of uniform slate, olive or brownish. The ventral surface is usually a dirty white or cream. This species is distributed essentially in southern Africa as far west as north eastern Namibia and as far north as south coastal Tanzania. *N. mossambica* and *N. nigricollis* are notably sympatric in eastern Zambia.

Both the black-necked and Mozambique spitting cobras inhabit arid areas of savanna and grassland, and are often found near water. The two species also represent the commonest cobras of Africa and are often found in and near areas of human habitation. A great variety of food is taken, including small mammals, amphibians especially toads, eggs, birds and other reptiles including snakes.

The remaining species of *Naja* is the Asiatic cobra, *N. naja*, which is widespread from west Asia through India, South East Asia, the Philippines and Taiwan. It occurs in ten distinct races which are listed in Table 1. One race, *N. n. sputatrix*, has some capability of spitting venom, but the fangs are not so well adapted for the purpose as are the African 'spitters'.

The most westerly of the races is *N. n. oxiana*, which also occurs in north east Iran and then eastwards to northern Pakistan. This race

Table 1

Distribution of *Naja naja* and sub-species

N. n. naja	India, Pakistan, Sri Lanka
N. n. atra	Southern China, Taiwan, Hainan
N. n. kaouthia	Bengal, Nepal, Burma, south western China
N. n. miolepis	Borneo, Palawan
N. n. oxiana	Afghanistan, Kashmir, Punjab
N. n. philippinensis	Luzon, Mindoro (Philippines)
N. n. sagitiffera	Andaman Islands
N. n. samarensis	Samar, Leyte, Bohol, Mindanao (Philippines)
N. n. sputatrix	Malayan Archipelago, Java, Bali, Lombok, Flores, Komodo, Celebes
N. n. sumatrana	Sumatra

has no hood markings and the body colour is brown, often with indistinct dark bars on the dorsal surface. In some parts of its range it is a montane species and can be found more than 2000 metres above sea level. Due to seasonal fluctuations in climate in parts of this species' range it is one of the few elapids that are obliged to spend a period of inactivity in the winter.

The cobra of India is the spectacled cobra, *N. n. naja*, which is distributed throughout the sub-continent except the extreme north west. It is also found in Sri Lanka. The spectacled marking on the back of the head is quite distinct, although it may be obscure in very dark individuals. The body colour may be uniform brown or blackish but equally may have a varied degree of speckling which may give an individual a banded appearance.

Another race with a distinct hood marking is the monocled cobra, *N. n. kaouthia*, which occurs in the lowlands from west Bengal through Bangladesh to South East Asia and south west China. The dorsal hood mark consists of a cream or whitish circle bordered with black enclosing up to three dark spots. The body colour again may be uniform brown or blackish with many individuals showing degrees of speckling which may form bands; sometimes these bands may be indistinct and only readily visible on a snake that has recently shed its skin.

The Chinese cobra, *N. n. atra*, is very similar to the monocled cobra and occurs in southern China, Thailand, eastwards to Vietnam, Hainan and Taiwan.

The Malayan cobra, *N. n. sputatrix*, occurs on the Malayan peninsula and most of the prominent islands of Indonesia. There are no definite markings on the body or hood and coloration is usually uniform brown, greyish or black. This cobra is able to discharge venom from the orifice of the fang, which is just short of the tip. It is said, however, to be less likely to include this habit in its repertoire than the African spitting cobras.

The Borneo cobra, *N. n. miolepis*, is another uniformly coloured cobra with no hood markings and with a body colour of black or dark brown. In addition to Borneo it also occurs in Palawan in the Philippines and is very similar to *N. n. samarensis*, which also occurs here. *N. n. philippinensis* also occurs in the Philippines in the regions of Luzon and Mindoro. However, it is quite distinctive from all the other races of *N. naja* in that it is the palest coloured, being light brown or olive.

The Asiatic cobra occurs in many different types of habitat, although there is a preference for flat grassland. It is also commonly found in and around rice fields and often enters houses either to search for prey or else to retreat from the heat. In the western part of its range the Asiatic cobra is generally diurnal, although it is not active during the hottest part of the day. Further east it tends to be more nocturnal and it is during this period, under the cover of darkness, that this cobra will seek a retreat in human habitation.

The average size of the Asiatic cobra is around 160 cm and some adults can be quite robust in build. This cobra is quite omnivorous and will take both warm and cold blooded prey including rodents, frogs, lizards and other snakes.

The king cobra, *Ophiophagus hannah* (Pl. 10), was once included in the genus *Naja*. This species is also known as the hamadryad and due to its large size stands out from all other cobras. Only the pythons exceed this species in length in Asia, although the keeled rat snake (*Zaocys*) can reach a length of 360 cm and could be confused with it.

This species is widespread but is nowhere common; it occurs in peninsular India to the Himalayan foothills, eastward across southern China, Vietnam and Cambodia. In Thailand and Malaya it is usually found in cultivated and more open areas. It also occurs in the Philippines and the larger islands of Indonesia.

A maximum size of 550 cm has been mentioned earlier, but individuals of around 300–400 cm are more common. The body colour is brown or olive, sometimes yellowish. The young of the species have prominent lighter coloured bold chevron markings, usually yellowish or white. Adult individuals from Burma and Thailand retain these chevrons, particularly on the posterior part of the body. The head scales of the king cobra are edged with black and the hood is not so pronounced as seen in the genus *Naja*, but it narrow and elongate.

Food consists almost entirely of other snakes, including other cobras and kraits (*Naja spp.* and *Bungarus spp.*), although lizards and amphibians may also be taken.

Other cobras

The remaining four genera of cobras occur again in Africa, and one of these, the rinkhals, or ringhals, *Hemachatus haemachatus*, is another spitting variety. It is greatly feared in southern Africa, where it occurs south of the Zambesi. The rinkhals attains a maximum size of 150 cm, but specimens of 100 cm and smaller are much more usual. The colour is variable; old adults may be uniform black, but many individuals are brown, grey, sometimes greenish, with bold crossbands of a lighter shade than the body colour.

Unlike cobras of the genus *Naja* the body scales of this species are strongly keeled; the hood is wide and prominent, and included in this snake's defensive behaviour is the ruse of shamming death by rolling over on its back with the tongue lolling out of the mouth. However, it is a 'spitting' species and the fangs, though short, are the most well adapted of the group for this purpose. Food consists mainly of small rodents. This cobra differs from other cobras also by the fact that it produces living young.

The water cobras, *Boulengerina*, are represented by two species confined to central Africa. *B. christyi* occurs only in western parts of the Congo Republic and little is known about its habits. *B. annulata* occurs in two distinct races, *B. a. annulata* in the west and *B. a. stormsi* in the eastern parts of its range.

The western race is distinguished by a series of narrow black bands on a glossy brown or reddish brown body. In the eastern race the bands are restricted to the neck region. The hood is very narrow and there is a narrow black band on the ventral surface. The water cobra can attain a large size, 250 cm or more, but lengths of up to 180 cm are more usual. As its common name implies, this cobra is very aquatic and is always found in and around water, its diet consisting almost entirely of fish. In southern parts of its distribution the eastern race is said to be quite common along some of the shores of Lake Tanganyika.

The burrowing cobra, *Paranaja multifasciata*, is an obscure little-known snake occurring only in the western parts of central Africa. It is virtually hoodless and only grows to around 60 cm.

The tree cobras, *Pseudohaje*, are represented by two species, and of one of these, *P. nigra*, virtually nothing is known except that it occurs in parts of west Africa as far as Sierra Leone and is rarely seen. Golds tree cobra, *P. goldii*, is also comparatively rare and is essentially a creature of the west African rain forests, but it also occurs in Angola and the northern border areas of Namibia and to the east in Uganda. It has also been recorded from the Kakamega forest region of western Kenya.

The tree cobra is a handsome snake, the body being a glossy black and the ventral surface yellow. The head is conspicuously barred on the lateral surfaces and the eye is large and prominent. This cobra, which is practically hoodless, can attain a size in excess of 250 cm and individuals of 200 cm are not uncommon. Diet consists almost wholly of amphibians and although essentially arboreal this species is said to be an expert swimmer.

Walterinnesia

The remaining African elapid is represented by one genus containing one species restricted to north Africa in the arid regions of Egypt to Iran. The desert black snake, *Walterinnesia aegyptia*, is a moderately robust species with a uniform black or dark brown shiny body colour. Maximum size is around 120 cm and food consists mainly of small rodents.

Bungarus

Although many of the elapids can be described as aggressive, some of the most venomous of the group can be described equally as timid or even docile. This is typical for one major group in particular, the kraits, *Bungarus*. All are restricted to Asia and there are twelve species distributed from India, across South East Asia to China, Vietnam, Cambodia and Indonesia. The kraits are often thought by many to be a group of small snakes, and in fact the common name is of Hindi origin and means 'small snake'. In fact, none of the kraits can be termed small, and at least two species reach 200 cm.

The Indian krait, *B. caeruleus*, is restricted to India and parts of Pakistan. The body colour is jet black with white or yellowish cross-bands which appear in pairs and may be indistinct on the anterior part of the body. This species grows to around 100 cm and is said to prefer dry open country.

The many-banded krait, *B. multicinctus*, is similar to the Indian krait, but the crossbands do not appear in pairs. It is also somewhat smaller, growing to an average length of 90 cm. In addition, this species is more often found near water, particularly in wooded areas; it is also said to be commonly encountered in rice paddies. It has the most eastern distribution of the genus, being found in southern China and Taiwan.

The banded krait, *B. fasciatus* (Pl. 5), is widespread from eastern India, through much of South East Asia and southern China. This species is probably the most docile of all the kraits and is often considered harmless over much of its range. This belief is further enhanced by the defensive attitude of tucking the head underneath the coiled body when annoyed. The coloration is quite striking, bright yellow bands on a black body colour. The bands of yellow are of almost equal width to those of the body colour and in some individuals may appear white or orange. This is one of larger kraits growing to 210 cm but averaging 150 cm.

The red-headed krait, *B. flaviceps*, occurs from the southern parts of Burma, through Malaya, Vietnam and the larger Indonesian islands. It is very striking in appearance with a bright red head and tail, the body being black with a pale bluish white stripe on the lateral surfaces. Habitat seems to be mainly mountain jungle and is somewhat rare. The average size is similar to that of the banded krait.

All the kraits are nocturnal and it is usually during the night that accidents occur. It is probable that the temperament of *Bungarus* differs greatly from its docile daytime behaviour and it must be remembered that this genus contains species with a very highly toxic venom. Food for all the species consists entirely of other snakes.

Australasian genera

Another elapid thought to be harmless is the obscure Fiji snake, *Ogmodon vitianus*, which occurs only on the island of Fiji and possibly on other small islands of the group. This is a small burrowing species growing to just 60 cm. It is said to be rare, so much so that many of the local inhabitants have never seen it. However, this is not an accurate guide to a snake's population density, for I know parts of Dorset in southern England where the adder, *Viper berus*, is very abundant indeed, and people living just a hundred metres or so away have never seen one. It has been mentioned earlier that such burrowing species as the coral snakes, *Micrurus* etc., may be more abundant than is known.

Australasia is unique in that the majority of the snakes are venomous, and all these, with the exception of the rear fanged species, are elapids. There are twenty-seven genera of elapids in the region, representing about seventy-five species. The majority of these are found in Australia and several in both Australia and Papua New Guinea; one genus, however, *Apistocalamus*, is endemic to Papua New Guinea and neighbouring islands. This number does not include the twelve genera of sea snakes which amount to an additional thirty or so species, making a grand total of thirty-nine genera of elapids in the region, representing around one hundred species!

Acanthophis

Although there are no vipers in Australasia one genus, *Acanthophis*, is typically viper-shaped in build and the two species, *A. antarcticus* and *A. pyrrhus*, can strike with lightning speed in true viper fashion. Both are small snakes, rarely exceeding 90 cm and usually much smaller. Although small, both are extremely dangerous and the common name of death adder is apparently well applied. Little is known about the habits of *A. pyrrhus*, and it is confined to the desert regions of central Australia. It is said to be more slender than the common death adder and have more strongly keeled scales. It is bright reddish brown in colour.

The common death adder, *A. antarcticus* (Pl. 13, Fig. 18), is much more widespread, being found throughout Australia with the exception of central desert regions and south eastern New South Wales. It also occurs in New Guinea, where it tolerates damper situations in rain-forest regions; throughout most of its range it is a creature of dry scrub. The body colour is varying shades of grey or brown with irregular dark crossbands. It is largely a nocturnal species and may often bury itself in loose sand during the day. This is when most bites are received as the death adder always seems to be on the alert and ready to strike even though it may appear sluggish at such times. The

Fig. 18   Death adder, *Acanthophis antarcticus*, a small but dangerous Australian elapid which closely resembles the vipers in bodily form and habits.

death adder is fairly omnivorous and will take a variety of small mammals, birds and reptiles.

Notechis

Many of the smaller elapids of Australia are thought to be innocuous to man; the species contained in the genera *Drysdalia*, *Elapognathus*, *Furina* and *Vermicella* are just a few examples. This is due to the fact that these and other genera are small secretive animals, many of which are burrowers. Furthermore, even some of the larger elapids of Australia are not considered dangerous due to their timid disposition.

However, this is not true of the genus *Notechis*, the tiger snakes, which, although not particularly aggressive, is a major hazard due to its abundance in south eastern Australia, where it is represented by *N. scutatus* (Pl. 11, Fig. 19)—often called the mainland tiger snake. The coloration is variable and ranges from grey, olive, brown and reddish, and some individuals may be very dark brown, almost black. Markings consist of narrow crossbands of yellow or creamish white. The tiger snake grows to around 120 cm.

The black tiger snake, *N. ater*, has a somewhat irregular distribution, being found in Tasmania and some of the surrounding islands. It is also found in the extreme south of South Australia and the south western parts of Western Australia. As the common name implies, the body colour is black or else very dark brown with light crossbands

Fig. 19   Mainland tiger snake, *Notechis scutatus*, one of the most poisonous of all snakes, which causes a high incidence of snakebite in Australia.

which may be indistinct in many individuals. Both species of tiger snakes take a wide range of food, including frogs, small mammals, birds and even other snakes.

Oxyuranus

The largest and most dangerous snake in Australasia is the taipan, *Oxyuranus scutellatus* (Pl. 12). Although represented by just the one species, there is an endemic race found in New Guinea. In Australia the taipan is restricted to the north of the continent, being found in Queensland and the northern part of Northern Territory. It is uniformly coloured light to dark brown with yellowish brown on the lateral surfaces; there is usually a distinctive yellow coloration around the head region. The body is slender and there is a similarity to the African mambas. The taipan is said to reach 400 cm, but adults of between 200–300 cm are more usual. It is truly an extremely aggressive snake and there are a number of records of unprovoked attacks. A wide range of habitat is occupied, from savanna and woodland to tropical forest. Food consists mainly of small mammals.

Demansia

The whip snakes, *Demansia*, are slender agile medium-sized elapids consisting of four species with at least one representative in all parts

77

of continental Australia. The largest of these is the black whip snake, *D. atra*, which grows to 100 cm and occurs only in the coastal and low-lying areas of north eastern and north Australia and Papua New Guinea. It is olive brown to black above, becoming lighter on the lateral surfaces. Lighter coloured specimens have the scales edged with black. It is found in dry habitat and is said to be of a nervous disposition.

The most widespread of the whip snakes is the yellow-faced whip snake, *D. psammophis*, which occurs throughout Australia except the north central regions, and the extreme south west, south east and Tasmania. Coloration is notably variable but usually steely grey with dark-edged scales forming a network pattern. There is a dark streak, edged with yellow or cream, which runs from the eye to the angle of the mouth. Maximum size is around 80 cm, and food consists mainly of small lizards. The remaining two species of whip snakes are *D. olivacea* from northern central Australia and *D. torquata* from north eastern Australia.

Pseudonaja

The eastern brown snake, *Pseudonaja textilis* (Fig. 20), was until recently included in the genus *Demansia*. In fact, the classification of many Australian snakes is unsatisfactory and the situation appears to be in a state of flux. The brown snakes consist of six species all contained in the genus *Pseudonaja*. The eastern brown snake occurs in the eastern, more densely populated part of Australia and is reputed to cause the highest incidence of snakebite in the country. It also occurs in eastern Papua New Guinea. This species is variable in both colour and pattern, and ranges from light to dark brown, orange and almost black. The body may or may not be marked with bands of varying intensity. The brown snake is swift and agile and grows to 160 cm. The diet consists of small mammals and reptiles.

The western brown snake, *P. nuchalis*, is the most widespread of the genus and in fact its range overlaps with the eastern race. The body colour is similar to that of *P. textilis*, but this species exhibits a bold reticulated pattern. It attains a similar length to that of the eastern race.

The ringed brown snake, *P. modesta*, is a small species which rarely exceeds 60 cm and is found in central and Western Australia.

The remaining three species have a very restricted range and little

Fig. 20 Brown snake, *Pseudonaja textilis*, a large and agile elapid which occurs in the drier regions of eastern Australia.

is known about their habits and status. *P. affinis* occurs only in extreme south western Australia, *P. guttata* in central Queensland and *P. ingrami* in the northern parts of Northern Territory.

Pseudechis

The most widespread elapid of Australia is the mulga or king brown snake, *Pseudechis australis*, which is only absent in the extreme south of Western Australia, and the southern parts of eastern Australia. This is a large species, growing to 200 cm, and the body colour is a rich reddish brown with the ventral surface cream, often pinkish or orange. This species occupies a wide range of habitat including rain forest where it is active by day. In the desert areas to the south it tends to be more nocturnal. Food consists largely of small mammals, but reptiles, including other snakes, are often taken. The genus *Pseudechis* contains three other species, two of which have a limited distribution in the eastern parts of Australia. *P. guttatus*, the spotted black snake, is found only in southern Queensland and extreme north of New South Wales. Collets snake, *P. colletti*, is restricted to central Queensland.

79

Fig. 21   Black snake, *Pseudechis porphyriacus*, a diurnal species usually found in damp situations. It produces live young.

The red-bellied black snake, *P. porphyriacus* (Fig. 21), has a much wider range in eastern Australia, being found along the entire east coast and the south eastern corner of the continent. This species is particularly handsome with an iridescent black body and with the lower scales of the lateral surfaces coloured bright red which shades to a duller red on the ventral surface. It is a large species, growing to 150 cm, and is capable of spreading a 'hood' by flattening the anterior part of the body. This species feeds mainly on frogs and small mammals.

Burrowing genera

Quite a number of Australian elapids are burrowing forms and are largely nocturnal. The most widespread and well-known is the bandy bandy, *Vermicella annulata*, which occurs in most of the regions except southern Western Australia, northern parts of Northern Territory, and the extreme south east. As the name implies, the body is banded with black and white rings which usually encircle the entire body. Maximum size is around 40 cm.

The northern bandy bandy, *V. multifasciata*, is often regarded as a sub-species of *V. annulata*, but is more slender with a somewhat smaller head. Coloration, however, is very similar. Distribution is confined to the extreme northern parts of Northern Territory. Food consists largely, if not entirely, of blind snakes (Typhlopidae).

Another burrowing genus is *Simoselaps*, which contains six species all of which are brightly coloured and have representatives in all regions of Australia. All are small snakes rarely exceeding 50 cm and very little is known of their habits.

Other burrowing genera are *Cacophis*, *Cryptophis* and *Neelaps*, all of which are largely nocturnal. In addition, many species of Australian elapids which are nocturnal, or at least partly so, spend the daylight hours under leaf litter or logs representing varying degrees of activity.

An example of this type of behaviour is found in the monotypic genus *Suta*, which is represented by the curl snake, *S. suta*, which is widespread in central and eastern Australia with the exception of coastal regions. It is a small species rarely exceeding 60 cm and occurs in a wide range of habitat from woodland to arid scrub.

A medium-sized snake which is considered to be potentially quite dangerous is the rough-scaled snake, *Tropidechis carinatus*, which again is represented by the single species and has a patchy distribution in the coastal regions of eastern Australia. Maximum size is around 80 cm and this snake is said to be very aggressive when aroused. As the name suggests, the body scales are strongly keeled, and this distinguishes it from all other Australian elapids. The body is brownish with irregular dark crossbars; the ventral surface is cream or greenish. Food is variable and consists of small mammals, frogs and reptiles.

It is true to say that there is still much to learn about the Australasian snake fauna. Distribution and habits for many species still remain a mystery, particularly the status of species in Papua New Guinea and the remote areas of the Australian continent. There is an obvious problem of examining the habits of secretive burrowing types, but even some large active terrestrial snakes remain virtually unknown with regard to their habits and behaviour. A good example is the monotypic species, *Parademansia microlepidota*, sometimes called the fierce snake. This is a very large species, growing to 250 cm, and resembles the taipan in general appearance. It is confined to a central area towards eastern Australia and it is known to be active by day, but otherwise its habits remain a mystery.

Sea snakes

A major problem involving the study of animals in remote areas is the inhospitable nature of such environments. Desert regions and thick jungle each present their own difficulties, which are usually associated with heat, lack of water, and the general strain and fatigue which result from any physical excess in such conditions.

An alien environment which contains a major group of elapids is the sea. The sea snakes are fully adapted to marine life and consist of forty-seven species contained in two sub-families. The sub-families Hydrophiinae and Laticaudinae differ from their land relatives in that they have laterally compressed oar-like tails and valvular nostrils which open above the snout. Sea snakes do not occur anywhere in the Atlantic Ocean and are essentially creatures of Asian and Australasian coastal waters with only a few species occurring well out to sea (Fig. 10). In fact, only one genus (*Pelamis*) is truly pelagic and occurs across the Pacific to the western coasts of Central and South America. It is also found as far south as New Zealand and the Cape of Good Hope. The distribution of individual species is dealt with in Chapter 2. As can be imagined we still know very little about the ecology of the sea snakes, but in recent years there has been a notable increase in the study of marine environments and no doubt many more facts about this group of venomous snakes will be revealed.

Sea snakes are indeed puzzling animals to study. One instance is that often unrelated species show a marked similarity to each other. Others, however, are quite distinctive.

Bites from sea snakes are unlikely to occur whilst the snake is in deep water; they are said to be indifferent to swimmers, although it must be appreciated that temperament must vary from species to species and even amongst individuals of the same kind. In fact, most accidents occur when these snakes are hauled up in fishing gear, or else trodden on in shallow water. On land most sea snakes are helpless and others can at best manage a clumsy crawl. One group of sea snakes, Laticaudinae, can be described as partly terrestrial. This group favours mouths of rivers, mangrove swamps and shallow reefs. However, the most important factor regarding this group is that they lay their eggs on land. The Laticaudinae also show a greater affinity to their land relatives than the Hydrophiinae, particularly the kraits. The sea snakes are often referred to as the sea kraits.

Sea snakes feed largely on fish, some take eels and prawns, and one species, *Emydocephalus annulatus*, feeds exlusively on fish eggs.

The majority of the sea snakes are contained in the sub-family Hydrophiinae and the largest number of species are found in the genus *Hydrophis*, with a total of twenty-two species distributed over the entire sea snake range. All the species of *Hydrophis* are either banded or blotched and are usually under 100 cm in length. One species, however, *H. elegans*, is said to attttain a length of 200 cm.

The genus *Astrotia* contains just one species, *A. stokesii*, 120 cm long, which is the largest of all sea snakes due to its great bulk. Coloration is usually uniform yellowish, grey or black, and some individuals may have an indistinct reticulated pattern on the posterior part of the body.

Another monotypic genus is represented by *Acalyptophis peronii*, which is moderate in size, growing to 100 cm and is cream or brownish with darker crossbands which may be obscure in some adults. This species also has a wide range, from the Gulf of Siam to the Gulf of Carpentaria.

From the Persian Gulf to Australia is distributed yet another monotypic genus, *Enhydrina*. The beaked sea snake, *E. schistosa*, is a relatively large species, growing to 120 cm, and is greenish in colour with dark narrow crossbands. As far as is known the venom of this species is the most toxic of all known snake venoms.

Among the smaller of the sea snakes are such genera as *Ephalophis* and *Hydrelaps*, which rarely exceed 50 mm and only occur in Australasia.

Hardwickes sea snake, *Lapemis hardwickii*, is the only member of the genus and ranges from the Persian Gulf to northern Australian waters. Average length is around 100 cm and the body colour is greyish above and creamish below which meet on the mid-lateral surfaces. The pattern consists of fused dark blotches on the mid-dorsal line.

The genus *Microcephalophis* contains two species, one of which, *M. cantoris*, is confined to the Arabian Sea and the Bay of Bengal. *M. gracilis* is found from the Arabian Sea to the Flores Sea.

The pelagic sea snake, or yellow-bellied sea snake, *Pelamis platurus*, has already been mentioned; it is a distinctive species with a unique colour pattern, with the upper half of the body black or dark brown and a contrasting lower half of yellow or cream. Maximum size is around 80 cm.

The sub-family Laticaudinae contains three genera consisting of eleven species, six of which are contained in the genus *Aipysurus* (Pl. 10). This genus contains moderate to large sea snakes with a wide distribution in Australasian waters with the exception of *A. eydouxi*, which is also found in the Gulf of Siam. Most of the genus are marked with

83

crossbands, but two species, *A. duboisii*, and *A. fuscus* are often uniform brownish in colour.

Emydocephalus is a monotypic genus with a distribution from the Yellow Sea to northern Australia. *E. annulatus* is highly variable in colour and pattern; the body colour may be black, brown, or grey above and below with a varying degree of banding. It is a medium-sized snake growing to 80 cm.

The genus *Laticauda* contains four species of similar appearance. All are bluish or grey with black crossbands and average 100 cm in length.

The breeding habit of the sea snakes still remains much of a mystery, but it is known that all the species contained in the Hydrophiinae give live birth and those in the Laticaudinae come on land to lay their eggs.

1   Boomslang *(Dispholidus typus)*

2   Mangrove Snake *(Boiga dendrophila)*

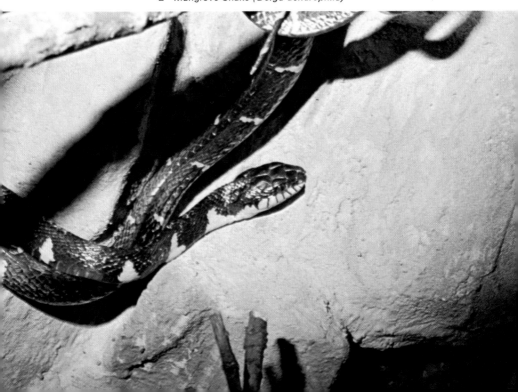

3 Coral Snake *(Calliophis maculiceps)*

4 Coral Snake *(Micrurus frontalis)*

5 Banded Krait *(Bungarus fasciatus)*

6 Jamesons Mamba *(Dendroaspis jamesoni)*

7 Green Mamba *(Dendroaspis angusticeps)*

8 Cape Cobra *(Naja nivea)*

9 Black and White Cobra *(Naja melanoleuca)*

10 King Cobra *(Ophiophagus hannah)*

11 Tiger Snake *(Notechis scutatus)*

12 Taipan *(Oxyuranus scutellatus)*

13 Death Adder *(Acanthophis antarcticus)*

14 Olive Sea Snake *(Aipysurus laevis)*

15 European Adder *(Vipera berus)*

16　Sand Viper *(Vipera ammodytes)*

17　Russells Viper *(Vipera russelli)*

18   Horned Viper *(Cerastes cerastes)*

19   Puff Adder *(Bitis arietans)*

20 Gaboon Viper *(Bitis gabonica)*

21 Rhino Viper *(Bitis nasicornis)*

22   Malayan Pit Viper *(Agkistrodon rhodostoma)*

23   Copperhead *(Agkistrodon contortrix)*

24 Cottonmouth *(Agkistrodon piscivorous)*

25 Pope's Pit Viper *(Trimeresurus popeorum)*

26 Eyelash Viper *(Bothrops schlegelii)*

27 Argentine Pit Viper *(Bothrops ammodytoides)*

28 Western Diamondback Rattlesnake *(Crotalus atrox)*

29 Red Diamondback Rattlesnake *(Crotalus ruber)*

30 Rock Rattlesnake *(Crotalus lepidus)*

31 Speckled Rattlesnake *(Crotalus mitchellii)*

32 Massasauga *(Sistrurus catenatus)*

33 Pygmy Rattlesnake *(Sistrurus miliarus)*

5
The Vipers

The remaining venomous snakes are to be found in the major family, Viperidae, which embraces some one hundred and sixty species found throughout both the New and Old Worlds with the exception of Australasia.

The Viperidae is further divided into three sub-families, the largest sub-division being represented by the Crotalinae which are better known as the pit vipers and embraces about one hundred and twenty species. The largest number of species are found in two genera, *Bothrops* and *Trimeresurus*, which are distributed through Central and South America and Asia respectively.

However, number of species is no indication of actual abundance and the sub-family Viperinae, although only numbering thirty-nine species, contain some of the most widespread of all venomous snakes. Furthermore, one of these, the European adder, *Vipera berus*, has the widest known distribution of all the world's snakes. Two other notable examples are the saw-scaled viper, *Echis carinatus*, which ranges from West Africa across to peninsular India and Sri Lanka, and the puff adder, *Bitis arietans*, which is the most abundant venomous snake to be found in most of Africa. All the members of the Viperinae are restricted to the Old World.

The third sub-family of the Viperidae contains just one species, the obscure Fea's viper, *Azemiops feae*, which is a montane species found only in upper Burma and parts of adjacent India and China.

The vipers display many similar characteristics to each other in general appearance; the head is triangular or spade-shaped and notably distinct from the body. The bodily form is usually comparatively short and robust but exhibiting a great degree of variability. This is exemplified by such extremes as the large heavy-bodied snakes to be found in the genus *Bitis*, and the relatively slender arboreal vipers which are contained in the genera *Bothrops* and *Trimeresurus*. In between these extremes fall such groups as the European vipers and the North American rattlesnakes, although there are exceptions such as the eastern diamondback rattlesnake, *Crotalus adamanteus*, which can attain a considerable body weight.

Due to their dissimilarity to other groups the vipers are the most readily identified of all the venomous snakes. Very few colubrid snakes could be mistaken for vipers, although there are two possible exceptions. The first is the hog-nosed snake, *Heterodon spp.*, of North America which has a bodily form and markings similar to that of some viper species. In fact, throughout many parts of this species' range it is referred to as 'spreading adder', 'blowing adder' and 'bastard

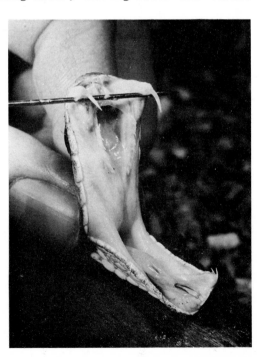

Fig. 22   Maximillians viper, *Bothrops neuwiedi*, showing large fangs of this young specimen housed at the Poole Serpentarium.

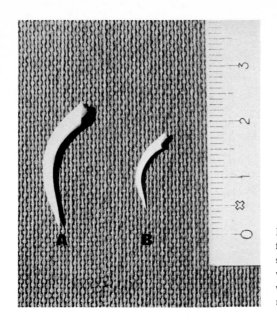

Fig. 23 Relative sizes of fangs (in cm) from vipers of similar lengths: A, gaboon viper, *Bitis gabonica*; B, western diamondback rattlesnake, *Crotalus atrox*.

rattlesnake' just to name a few examples. The second colubrid snake which causes some confusion is the African egg-eating snake, *Dasypeltis scabra*, which is often mistaken for the highly dangerous saw-scaled viper in regions where they are sympatric. In addition to similarities in appearance both the egg-eating snake and the saw-scaled viper share the habit of rubbing the strongly keeled body scales together to produce a rasping sound.

The vipers are the élite amongst venomous snakes due to the highly sophisticated venom apparatus. All vipers possess folding front fangs which lie on the roof of the mouth when the jaws are closed. The fangs can be erected independently of each other, and this can be seen quite clearly when a viper yawns or else uses the fangs to 'walk' the prey into the mouth (Figs 22, 23). The fangs are shed periodically and are replaced from a cluster of reserve fangs which lie just posterior to the functional fang on each side of the upper jaw.

The aspect which mainly sets the vipers apart from other venomous snakes is the means by which their bite is delivered. In fact, the term bite is a misnomer as the movement is best described as a strike terminating in a stabbing motion with the jaws at an angle of almost 180 degrees. The speed at which the strike is effected has to be seen to

87

be believed. Prior to the strike a viper will adopt the familiar 'S' shaped position with head and forepart of the body. This attitude varies considerably from species to species; some rattlesnakes will raise a third of the body well up from the ground, pulling the head and neck well back, while other vipers, usually smaller species, may content themselves by just adopting a loose 'S' shape before striking. This defensive attitude of vipers is usually enhanced by a slow meaningful flickering of the tongue as the snake confirms the reality of possible threat. The rattlesnakes will also maintain a steady 'buzz' of the rattle during such stress situations; and in fact many of the pit vipers vibrate the tail when coiled in a defensive position.

A viper can strike and resume the defensive attitude almost before one can register the fact the snake has indeed moved at all! The speed of the strike varies from species to species, and it is said that the rattlesnakes are particularly rapid in their striking movement. However, there is little to differentiate between the species with regard to the swiftness of the strike. The vipers must possess the most efficient means of predation that exists in our natural world – the ability to deliver a lightning lethal dose of venom and then to be able to retreat whilst the prey, mortally wounded, is hardly aware of the nature of its aggressor. The snake can then follow the scent trail of the prey at leisure.

This means of overpowering prey is a wonderful ability when one considers the potentially dangerous nature of some prey species, which may include large rodents, or small carnivores such as the mustelids. The ability of killing with the minimum of bodily contact is only exceeded by man himself, who has reached beyond his natural resources and has resorted to modern weaponry.

The sixteen genera of vipers exhibit a wide range of variety and habits, and can be found in all habitat types with the exception of the marine environment. One species, the European adder, occurs so far north as to enter the Arctic Circle. In fact, both the northerly and southerly extremes of snake distribution are occupied by two viper species.

Two genera of vipers which are the most primitive of the group are *Azemiops* and *Causus*. Fea's viper, *A. feae*, which has been mentioned earlier, is the only member of this genus and little is known about its habits. It is a small snake growing to around 80 cm with a broad flat head which is distinct from a moderately slender cylindrical body.

Causus

The African genus *Causus* contains six species commonly known as night adders. This genus is unique amongst the African Viperinae in that the scales on the top of the head are large symmetrical shields as opposed to the small imbricate scales typical of other African vipers. The night adders are also amongst the very few viper species that lay eggs as opposed to giving birth to live young. As the common name suggests, this genus is essentially nocturnal and the diet consists almost wholly of toads and frogs. The venom glands of *Causus* are unusual in that they are elongated and extend some 3 cm back into the body.

The most widespread of the genus is the rhombic night adder, *C. rhombeatus*, which occurs throughout the larger part of Africa south of the Sahara. Coloration is usually olive or brownish with darker brown or black rhomb-like markings or chevrons which may be margined with white or creamish white. There is a variable degree of black striping or spots on the lateral surfaces. This is the largest of the genus, growing to 85 cm or exceptionally more. In common with other night adders this species, when threatened, will flatten the anterior part of the body. The rhombic night adder is said to favour damp situations.

The green night adder, *C. resimus*, is essentially a creature of tropical forest occurring mainly in east and central Africa, but as far south as Angola and Mozambique. This species has a striking appearance: the body is usually velvety vivid green with dark chevrons on the dorsal surface. The head may be partially orange or yellowish. Maximum size is around 60 cm.

The snouted night adder, *C. defilippii*, is so called because the snout is pointed and upturned at the tip. It is essentially an eastern species, occurring from Tanzania in the north to northern Natal in the south. This is a small species rarely exceeding 50 cm. The coloration is light brownish or greenish with a bold V marking behind the head. Body markings consist of crescent-shaped dark markings on the dorsal surface; in many individuals markings may be indistinct. This species also favours a tropical environment.

Lichtensteins night adder, *C. lichtensteinii*, is another tropical species found in the rain forest regions of west and central Africa, and as far east as western Kenya. The body coloration is greenish or olive with dark chevrons on the dorsal surface. Maximum size is around 55 cm.

The two remaining species of *Causus* are *C. bilineatus*, which is

89

found in Angola, Zambia and Katanga, and *C. maculatus* from west and central Africa.

Atheris

Arboreal species of the viperinae are represented by just one genus, *Atheris*, which contains eight species commonly known as leaf or bush vipers. Two species, however, are terrestrial and were formerly included in the genus *Vipera* and their status is still uncertain. The remaining six species are truly adapted for arboreal life and have tails which are strongly prehensile. All the arboreal members of the genus are of small size, rarely exceeding 60 cm, with large prominent heads and relatively slender bodies.

The bush vipers are usually restricted to forest regions, including montane forest, swamplands and lake shores.

The most widespread of the genus is *A. squamiger*, which is found throughout the main rain-forest regions of west Africa, eastwards to western Kenya, and southwards to Angola. This species is usually some shade of green with variable degrees of light crossbands on the dorsal surface. The body scales are very strongly keeled and are usually edged with yellow. Food consists mainly of small mammals.

The rough-scaled bush viper, *A. hispida*, is an extraordinary-looking snake; the scales are exceedingly rough and give the species a bristly appearance and for this reason it is also called the hairy bush viper. The body colour is brownish with an irregular pattern of alternate light and dark bars.

The sedge viper, *A. nitschei*, occurs in the eastern parts of central Africa, southwards to northern Zambia, and it is said to be locally abundant in its distribution. The body coloration is bright or olive green with irregular black markings and a black V-shaped mark on the top of the head.

The remaining three arboreal members of the genus are *A. ceratophorus* of central Africa, *A. chlorechis* of west Africa and *A. katangensis* from the Congo Republic.

The current terrestrial members of the genus, *A. hindii* and *A. superciliaris*, are somewhat problematical forms and both have a very restricted range and are considered to be rare. The montane viper, *A. hindii*, is a small species with a maximum length of 60 cm and occurs only in the region of the Aberdare Mountains in Kenya. The lowland viper, *A. superciliaris*, grows to around the same size and is found only in some lowland areas of southern Tanzania. Some authorities feel that these two species have a closer affinity to some of the small members of the genus *Bitis*, but it is equally likely that they belong in a genus of their own.

Another obscure species that was once included in the genus *Atheris* is the small worm-eating viper, *Adenorhinos barbouri*, which is the only member of the genus and occurs only in parts of Tanzania. It is typically viper-shaped with large prominent eyes. As the name implies, this species is said to exist on earthworms and is not considered to be dangerous to man.

Arid and sandy desert areas of Africa, the Middle East, west Asia, and India are well stocked with members of the Viperinae. As with most desert-dwelling species these snakes are mainly nocturnal and tend to be of a small size.

The genera *Echis, Cerastes, Pseudocerastes, Eristocophis* and some of the smaller species of *Bitis* are all creatures of sandy, arid habitat. In areas of loose sand, all can adopt the sidewinding mode of locomotion with equal efficiency to the North American sidewinder, *Crotalus cerastes*.

Echis

The most widespread of these small vipers is the genus *Echis*, which contains two species known as carpet, or saw-scaled, vipers. *E. carinatus* is the most widespread, occurring from west Africa across west Asia to peninsular India and Sri Lanka (Fig. 24). The range of this species is broken in the Middle East where it is replaced by *E. coloratus*. Both are very similar in habits and appearance and each grows to a maximum length of around 80 cm, although the average size is much more likely to be around 60 cm. *E. carinatus* is considered to be probably the most dangerous snake in the world. This is due to the fact that in addition to its geographical status populations occur in high densities, often in areas of rural agriculture. In the past the puff adder, *Bitis arietans*, has probably taken the blame for many incidents of snakebite that should have been attributed to the saw-scaled viper. The dangerous nature is further enhanced by the fact that it is extremely short-tempered and belligerent and will strike without provocation.

The coloration of *E. carinatus* is variable and can be almost any shade of brown or reddish, grey, buff or olive. The pattern is also

Fig. 24   Saw-scaled viper or carpet viper, *Echis carinatus*, a small aggressive snake with a wide distribution which is probably the most dangerous snake in the world.

variable but usually consists of light dorsal blotches edged with black which may become fused to smaller blotches on the lateral surfaces. The head is spade-shaped with large eyes, and the marking on the top of the head appears in many individuals in the form of a light cross. The body scales are strongly keeled and the habit of rubbing the scales together has been mentioned earlier. There is some evidence to suggest that certain colour phases may be typical of certain areas and several sub-species exist throughout various parts of the range of the saw-scaled viper.

Horned Vipers

In north Africa and the Middle East are to be found the horned vipers contained in two genera, *Cerastes* and *Pseudocerastes*. The genus *Cerastes* consists of two species, *C. cerastes* (Pl. 8) which is usually referred to as the desert horned viper, and *C. vipera*, usually known as the Sahara horned viper. An interesting point regarding the local distribution of these two species is the fact that populations rarely if ever overlap.

The desert horned viper is yellowish, greyish or buff in colour with darker markings on the dorsal surface which may be blotched or there may be a regular series of crossbars. Most individuals have a long spike-like horn above each eye. The body is thick and short with a

92

short tail, and the head is broad and flat and very distinct from the neck. Maximum size is 75 cm, but individuals of around 60 cm are more common.

The Sahara horned viper is a smaller species, growing to a maximum of 50 cm. In appearance it is very similar to *C. cerastes*, but the markings are more faded and the horns above the eyes are absent. Both species feed on small mammals and reptiles.

The Persian horned viper, *Pseudocerastes persicus*, occurs from the Sinai peninsula eastward to the southern part of west Asia. This species Closely resembles the desert horned viper, but the horns above the eyes are made up of small scales and not the spiky projections as seen in the preceding species. The colour is greyish or buff with a series of regular dark crossbars on the dorsal surface. Bodily proportions are similar to that of *Cerastes* and this species grows to 85 cm.

Macmahons viper, *Eristicophis macmahonii*, occurs in sand-dune areas of Afghanistan and Pakistan. It is a comparatively rare species and little is known about its habits. The body colour is reddish brown with a regular series of dark spots edged with white on the lateral surfaces. The dorsal surface may be uniform or else marked with faint irregular spots. The head is broad and wedge-shaped and the body is moderately stout. This species grows to around 70 cm.

Bitis

The genus *Bitis* contains several desert forms, two of which are very small indeed, being just a little larger than the new born of their close relative the puff adder.

Peringueys viper, *Bitis peringueyi*, is a tiny species, the maximum length being just 30 cm but usually 25 cm or less. This species is typically viper-shaped with a broad flat head distinct from the neck and a stout body. The colour is brownish grey or buff with a series of three rows of small dark spots on the upper surface. This sidewinding species is confined to southern Angola and Namibia and feeds largely on lizards.

The dwarf adder, *B. schneideri*, is the smallest of the genus with an average length of 20 cm. It is very similar to the preceding species, but the head is more heart-shaped and the eye somewhat smaller. The range of this species is restricted to the coastal areas around the mouth of the Orange River in Namibia.

The horned adder, *B. caudalis*, is somewhat larger, growing to 45 cm or more. This species is more colourful; the ground colour is usually some shade of grey or brown with a series of elongate dark dorsal markings which are interspaced with light grey. The markings vary and may appear indistinct in some individuals. There is a single horn above each eye which projects slightly backwards. This species is found in Namibia and its range extends eastwards into the Kalahari. Like other small desert species of viper this species buries into soft loose sand, leaving just the eyes and tip of tail above the surface. Many of the desert-living vipers are said to use the exposed tail as a lure when buried in this fashion.

The many-horned adder, *B. cornuta*, as its name suggests, has a cluster of upright scales or 'horns' above each eye. Coloration is usually reddish brown or greyish and there are a series of spots on the upper surface which may be black or dark brown and form three or four longitudinal rows which may be interspaced with light patches. The size is similar to that of *B. caudalis*.

The mountain adder, *B. atropos*, is an attractive species found in southern Zimbabwe and the eastern parts of South Africa. The body colour is brownish with opposed semicircular black markings on the dorsal surface. There is a distinctive lateral stripe and beneath this is a series of regular pale circular spots. The head is more elongate than other members of the genus. Maximum size is around 50 cm and although this species occurs mainly in montane rocky situations it is often found at sea level in the southern parts of its range. Food consists mainly of small rodents and nestling birds.

Other, lesser-known and small members of the genus are *B. heraldica*, from Angola, *B. worthingtoni*, from Kenya, and *B. xeropaga*, from southern Africa.

The remaining three members of the genus are considerably larger and exhibit the most grotesque forms of all vipers. The most well known of these large vipers is the puff adder, *B. arietans* (Pl. 19, Fig. 25), which is widespread in Africa and also occurs in Syria and Jordan. An adult puff adder could hardly be mistaken for any other snake; the head is flat and spade-shaped and very distinct from the neck. The body is extremely stout, giving a bloated appearance. Large examples of this species are incredible creatures with a girth of perhaps 30 cm or more. Individuals have been known to reach a length of 180 cm. The largest puff adder that I have seen was a little over 150 cm, and at this size was a terrifying creature to behold.

Fig. 25   Juvenile puff adders, *Bitis arietans*. This species is live-bearing and females produce large litters. The puff adder accounts for a high snakebite incidence throughout its range.

The body colour is usually some shade of brown, sometimes greyish, with bold regular chevrons of white or cream on the dorsal surface. The pattern and colour appear to vary from region to region and some individuals are pinkish and much lighter in coloration. Typical South African puff adders are brown or reddish brown with yellow or cream chevrons. The large size attained by the puff adder has just been mentioned, but lengths of between 60–100 cm are more commonly encountered.

The puff adder prefers semi-arid habitat but is often found around farms and other areas of human habitation. The food of this species consists mainly of small mammals, including small deer such as duiker. Young puff adders are said to feed largely on toads and frogs.

The gaboon viper, *B. gabonica* (Pl. 20) is a snake of rain-forest regions and thickets. It matches the puff adder for size and in fact is recognised as the largest viper of Africa, and for sheer bulk is probably the largest viper in the world. The bodily proportions of the gaboon viper are similar to that of the puff adder, but the grotesque appearance is further enhanced by the bizarre coloration and pattern. It is difficult to describe with accuracy the actual coloration as the whole body appears to be an intricate fusion of many shades of browns, cream, purple and other shades not so readily noticeable. The head is an immaculate shade of creamy white or buff with a vivid black triangle running from the point of the eye to the lower jaw. There may or may not be a black hairline bisecting the top of the head. The body pattern consists of very regular oblong buff markings on the dorsal surface which are enclosed by elongated ovals of rich brown that are again enclosed in a chain-like row of purplish markings. On the lateral surfaces are large triangles with the points towards the dorsal surface. These triangular markings are purplish or rich brown. The head is large and triangular and very distinct from the neck. There are two horn-like appendages on the snout which are absent in some individuals. Several species of viper possess these appendages and their function is not known.

The gaboon viper occurs in west and central Africa, western parts of east Africa and southern Tanzania, and has a patchy distribution in Zambia, northern Zimbabwe and northern Natal. Food consists mainly of small mammals.

The rhinoceros viper or river jack, *B. nasicornis* (Pl. 21), is associated with west African rain forest and also occurs eastwards to Uganda, western Kenya and southern Sudan, and southwards to Angola. Although a large member of the genus, it is smaller than both the puff adder and the gaboon viper, but there are records of individuals in excess of 150 cm. The average size appears to be around 70–80 cm, and the body, although stout, is not as massive as the other large members of the genus. This snake exceeds even the gaboon viper with regard to coloration; the late Raymond Ditmars described this species as the most amazing snake of Africa. Coloration is seen at its best when the snake is freshly shed, when the beautiful hues are blending shades of carmine and olive. Along the dorsal surface are a row of large pale blue oblong markings each separated on the midline by a narrow yellow line. These blue markings are enclosed in black rhombs. In many individuals the blue is replaced by a lime green with the scales edged with black. On the lateral surfaces are large triangles which are crimson or rich brown and margined with blue or green. The top of the head

96

has a distinctive black javelin-shaped marking which points towards the snout. The snout itself possesses a variable cluster of spiky 'horns' which give this species its common name. The diet consists of small mammals and sometimes amphibians.

Vipera

The remaining genus of the Viperinae is *Vipera*, a major group with representatives throughout Europe, the Middle East and parts of Asia. Of the nine species most are small or medium sized snakes, but three are large and robust and are included amongst the world's most dangerous snakes.

The most well known of the genus is the European adder, *V. berus* (Pl. 15, Fig. 26), which occurs over much of Europe as far south as north west Spain and northern Italy and then eastwards across Russia to the Pacific coast.

Fig. 26 European adder, *Vipera berus*, the only poisonous snake of the British Isles, and also the snake with the widest distribution.

97

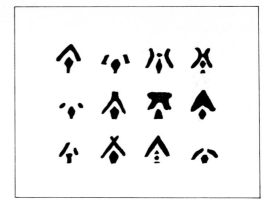

Fig. 27 Variations in the head markings of the adder, *Vipera berus*. Sketched from individuals in the field.

The European adder is unusual in that it exhibits sexual dimorphism; the males are usually some shade of white, grey, yellow or straw, and the females brown, reddish, buff or olive. Both males and females possess a dark dorsal zig-zag pattern with dark blotches on the lateral surfaces. There is usually an inverted V- or X-shaped mark on the head and Fig. 27 shows how variable this particular marking can be. In some individuals the zig-zag may be broken up to form blotches or the snake may be striped. Uniformly coloured black adders are quite common, but uniform red or brown individuals are much rarer. Female adders are somewhat larger than the males and the average size is around 65 cm, but monsters in excess of 90 cm have been recorded. The diet of the adder consists of small rodents and their young, lizards and nestling birds.

The European adder is one of the few species of venomous snakes that has enjoyed a certain amount of field study and observation. My own study of this species has indicated quite a complex life style which involves such aspects as distinctive seasonal movement and variable female breeding cycles. This small viper is also suprisingly resourceful, which is exemplified by the manner in which it can adapt to sudden changes in its habitat. More will be mentioned at a later stage regarding the habits of this species.

The aspic viper, *V. aspis*, is of a similar size to the adder and occurs in western and central Europe throughout Italy and also on the islands of Elba and Montecristo. Coloration is brownish, olive or buff, and in most parts of the range the pattern consists of regular dorsal crossbars, but in Italy and south western France this pattern may be

98

replaced by a broad wavy vertebral stripe. Identification is sometimes confused due to the fact that hybrids of *V. berus* and *V. aspis* occur occasionally.

Latastes viper, *V. latasti*, occurs throughout the Iberian peninsula with the exception of the extreme north and it is also found in Tunisia and Morocco. This species grows to 60 cm, sometimes larger, and the body colour is greyish or reddish with a zig-zag of a shade darker than the ground colour on the dorsal surface. The zig-zag is margined with black or dark brown. There is usually a small horn at the end of the snout, but this may be absent in some individuals.

The meadow viper, *V. ursinii*, is the smallest of the genus and rarely exceeds 45 cm. It is nowhere common and populations tend to be localised in Europe where it occurs in southern France and central Italy, through the Balkans to west and central Asia. In appearance it is very similar to the adder, but the zig-zag marking is narrower and may be broken up into blotches. The head is oval in shape and not very distinct from the body. The meadow viper has an exceptionally mild manner and feeds largely on lizards and grasshoppers.

The caucasus viper, *V. kasnakovi*, is often described as a sub-species of the meadow viper. It has a somewhat stouter body than the preceding species and the head is broad and quite distinct from the neck. The coloration ranges from yellowish to brick red with a dark brown or black irregular dorsal stripe and two series of dark spots on the lateral surfaces.

The long-nosed viper or sand viper, *V. ammodytes* (Pl. 16), is a handsome species which occurs in southern Austria and the extreme northern parts of Italy, eastwards through the Balkans to the extreme northern parts of Iran. Maximum size for the species is around 75 cm, but males, which grow larger than the females, can reach 90 cm. A variable amount of sexual dimorphism is displayed by this species; the males are usually light- or silver-grey with a bold black dorsal zig-zag, and the females tend to be brownish with a dark brown zig-zag. The sub-species, *V. a. meridionalis*, has a grey dorsal zig-zag in the male with black edging and a light brown zig-zag in the female with a darker brown edging. All the European vipers have several sub-species which represent a wide range and variety of colour and pattern. The horned appendage of the long-nosed viper is made up of small scales usually numbering from ten to thirteen.

Ottomans viper, *V. xanthina* (Fig. 28), is a large heavy-bodied viper

Fig. 28   Ottomans viper, *Vipera xanthina xanthina*, a robust species from eastern Europe which is of a nervous disposition and quick to strike.

Fig. 29   Palestine viper, *Vipera palaestinae*, a large and aggressive species from the Middle East where it is often found around human habitation.

which ranges from the Middle East to European Turkey; this species also occurs on several eastern Aegean islands. The males are more boldly marked than the females with a bold black zig-zag or a blotched dorsal surface on a light grey ground colour. Females tend to be more brownish. This species can grow to over 100 cm and is a potentially very dangerous snake.

The Palestine viper, *V. palaestinae* (Fig. 29), is much more colourful and more vividly marked.

The blunt-nosed viper or kufi, *V. lebetina* (Fig. 30), is a robust species occurring in parts of the Middle East, north Africa, north west Pakistan and the Cyclades. The coloration is brownish, reddish, buff or pinkish, with darker crossbars on the dorsal surface which may be indistinct in some individuals. The blunt-nosed viper can grow to 120 cm, but lengths of 70–80 cm are more usual. This is a bold and dangerous species and prefers hilly habitat and rocky areas. Food consists of small mammals, birds and lizards.

The last member of the genus is the much feared russells viper,

Fig. 30   Levantine viper or kufi, *Vipera lebetina*, one of the largest of the genus with a powerful haematoxic venom.

V. russelli (Pl. 17), which is found from the eastern parts of Pakistan across India and into South East Asia. The russells viper has a patchy local distribution, but where it does occur it tends to be very common. It is a large robust snake growing to 150 cm, but Indonesian island races are notably smaller. Coloration is variable; olive, brown, yellowish, buff, with a series of dark oval rings on the dorsal and lateral parts of the body. This species is largely nocturnal and feeds mainly on small mammals.

The russells viper figures high on the list of the world's dangerous snakes; it is short-tempered and is often trodden on, whereupon it will strike without hesitation.

Agkistrodon

The remaining group of vipers are contained in the large sub-family Crotalinae, better known as the pit vipers. Although only represented by six genera the pit vipers embrace some one hundred and twenty species. All this group possess a loreal pit situated below the eye which is a heat receptor and is a functional part of prey detection.

The most primitive of the pit vipers are contained in the genus *Agkistrodon* which has species in both the New and Old World. Three species occur in North and Central America. The cottonmouth moccasin, *A. piscivorous* (Pl. 24), is a semi-aquatic species found in swamps and streams of the southern lowlands of the USA. It is a stout- bodied snake that can reach 150 cm or more. Coloration is variable; large adults are often uniform black or dark brown, but most individuals are brown or light chestnut with dark crossbars which may encircle the body. Food consists mainly of fish and amphibians, but small mammals are also taken. The cottonmouth owes its name to the habit of displaying the white interior of the mouth when threatened.

The cantil, or Mexican moccasin, *A. bilineatus*, is rather similar in habits to its North American relative but is somewhat smaller, the average size being around 90 cm. The body colour is either uniform black or rich chocolate with a thin yellow or cream line running from the snout and along the upper and lower jaw. These pale lines are also present to a variable degree on the body.

The copperhead, *A. contortrix* (Pl. 23, Fig. 32), is a boldly marked snake which occurs mainly in the eastern half of the USA. The body is comparatively stout with broad triangular head. Maximum size is around 100 cm. The body colour is buff or orange brown with rich

Fig. 31   Mangrove pit viper, *Trimeresurus purpureomaculatus*, an abundant species of pit viper inhabiting coastal areas of South East Asia.

brown crossbands which vary in shape and regularity. Due to their habit of frequenting areas of human habitation accidents are quite common, but fatalities are almost unknown.

The other ten species of *Agkistrodon* are to be found in Asia and the Far East. The hump-nosed viper, *A. hypnale*, is found in southern India and Sri Lanka. It is a small species rarely exceeding 50 cm which earns its name from the upturned snout. Coloration is light greyish with a varying intensity of brown mottling, sometimes with a double row of dark spots on the dorsal surface. This species is a snake of dense jungle but is also found on plantations.

Another member of the genus that adapts well to life on plantations is the Malayan pit viper, *A. rhodostoma* (Pl. 22). This is a sedentary snake which due to its abundance and uncertain temper causes a large number of accidents each year. The body colour is rich chocolate brown or light pinkish brown with dark triangular blotches on the dorsal surface that may extend down the lateral parts of the body.

Fig. 32   Copperhead, *Agkistrodon contortrix*. A uniformly coloured male from Douglas County, Kansas.

The Malayan pit viper has a large triangular pointed head with a fierce staring eye that gives this species a malignant expression.

Some members of the genus have a fairly restricted range and one species, *A. nepa*, is endemic to Sri Lanka.

The sharp-nosed pit viper, *A. acutus*, is a short-tempered species and is considered to be the most dangerous snake of the Far East, where it occurs throughout southern China, northern Vietnam and Taiwan. The ground colour is greyish or light brown with dark brown triangular crossbands. There is a dark streak running from the eye along the top of the head. The snout is pointed and upturned. This dangerous snake can grow to 120 cm.

A. halys has a wide distribution ranging from eastern European Russia, eastern parts of the Middle East, Japan and eastern China. In Japan it is known as the mamushi and is represented by the sub-species *A. h. blomhoffii*. It is a small species growing to around 70 cm. It is usually yellowish or reddish with dark brown crossbands. Some two thousand incidents of snakebite per year are attributed to this species in Japan alone, but fatalities are rare.

Bothrops

The genus *Bothrops* is a large genus with forty-eight species distributed throughout Central and South America and the West Indies. This group contains small slender arboreal forms and large-bodied terrestrial forms, many of which are a hazard to man.

Due to the large number of species in this genus it will suffice to describe the more prominent members. The arboreal members of *Bothrops* are all small slender species with strongly prehensile tails and large heads.

The eyelash viper or palm viper, *B. schlegelii* (Pl. 26), occurs from southern Mexico throughout Central America and into Venezuela and Equador. The ground colour appears mainly in two phases, either green or light brown. The pattern may consist of brown or reddish crossbars or it may have an irregular pattern of red blotches. Maximum size is around 60 cm and the scales above each eye are raised into small spikes.

The yellow-lined palm viper, *B. lateralis*, occurs in Costa Rica and the eastern parts of Panama and is of a similar size to the eyelash viper. The body colour is green with a pale line on the lower part of the lateral parts of the body. This species closely resembles some of the green-coloured members of the Asiatic genus *Trimeresurus*.

The black-spotted palm viper, *B. nigroviridis*, has a somewhat wider range in Central America, and as the name suggests it is heavily speckled with black, with prominent blotches on the dorsal surface. The body colour is usually yellowish.

The Amazonian tree viper, *B. bilineatus*, is found in the northern parts of South America to central Brazil and Bolivia. It grows to a similar size to that of the preceding species and the colour and pattern are variable.

Amongst the small terrestrial members of the genus is the jumping viper, or mano de piedra, *B. nummifer*, which occurs in low-lying rain forest throughout Central America. This short thick-bodied viper grows to 60 cm and when striking the whole body moves forward several centimetres. Its Spanish name refers to the resemblance of the body to an instrument used for thrashing corn.

The larger members of the genus are important as they often clash with man throughout much of their range. The most notorious species found in both Central and South America is the barba amarilla, *B. atrox* (Fig. 33), which is often wrongly referred to as the fer-de-lance.

Fig. 33   Barba amarilla, *Bothrops atrox* (juvenile), often wrongly referred to as the fer-de-lance. It is the most dangerous snake of Central and South America where it is commonly encountered on plantations.

It is one of the largest of the genus, growing to 180 cm with individuals recorded in excess of 240 cm. The colour is greyish, brown or olive green, with large dark pale margined triangles, their points meeting on the dorsal line. Like many other members of the genus the head is triangular and pointed. This species is common on plantations and causes a high incidence of snakebite throughout its range. Food consists mainly of small mammals.

The true fer-de-lance, *B. lanceolatus*, is found only on the island of Martinique in the West Indies. This is also a large species, growing to 180 cm, with a greyish or brownish olive body colour with a series of dark hourglass-shaped blotches on the dorsal surface. Although the larger members of this genus are typically viper-shaped they are moderately slender when compared to the large African vipers. This is seen to full effect when even individuals of 120 cm or more appear quite small when coiled in the resting position.

Another island species is the St Lucia serpent, *B. caribbaeus*, which as the name implies occurs only on the island of St Lucia. Average size is around 150 cm and the body colour is greyish with indistinct darker blotches on the upper parts of the body. This species is considered to be very dangerous and like its relatives often occurs on plantations.

B. insularis is also an island species and is only found on the island of Queimada Grande off the coast of Brazil. The venom of this species is known to be highly toxic.

The jararaca, *B. jararaca*, is often confused with *B. atrox*, and there are similarities in appearance. The body is olive or brownish with brown crescent-shaped blotches margined with paler markings. This snake grows to 130 cm and occurs in grassland and open country in southern Brazil, northern Paraguay and northern Argentina.

The jararacussu, *B. jararacussu*, occurs over much of the same range as the above but is said to prefer damper situations. It is basically a black and yellow snake with a pale network of yellow triangles on a black ground colour. The lateral parts are paler and have a row of dark spots. This species grows to 160 cm.

Maximillans viper, *B. neuwiedi* (Fig. 22), is smaller, growing to 90 cm and occurs throughout southern Brazil to northern Argentina. It is a snake of open country and in Argentina it is a major cause of snakebite. The pattern is distinct; a series of alternating dark triangles on a light grey or tan body.

The urutu, *B. alternatus*, shares a similar range and is the most handsome of the genus. The body colour is brownish with dark 'telephone' type markings on the lateral surfaces which meet on the dorsal line. There is a row of pale-centred dark spots on the lateral ventral line. This species grows to 120 cm and causes a large number of bites each year.

The venomous snake with the most southerly distribution is the Argentine pit viper, *B. ammodytoides* (Pl. 27), which is a small species with an upturned snout. The body colour is usually reddish brown with dark saddle-like blotches on the upper parts of the body.

Many members of the genus have a comparatively restricted range with some exceptions such as, for example, lansbergs viper, *B. lansbergii*, which occurs throughout Central America into Colombia and northern Venezuela. Godmans viper, *B. godmanni*, is also widespread in Central America.

Lachesis

Although several species of *Bothrops* attain a large size for viperid snakes, none can compare in length with the bushmaster, *Lachesis mutus*, which is the only member of the genus. This fearsome-looking snake can reach lengths in excess of 300 cm and is found in the tropical rain forests of the southern parts of Central America and the southern half of the South American mainland. The bushmaster is also found in Trinidad. Apart from its large size this snake is distinctive in that the body scales are strongly keeled and 'knobbly' in appearance; only the tropical rattlesnake, *Crotalus durissus*, displays this exceedingly rough texture of the body scales, and in addition the prominent rattle instantly identifies this species. However, the bushmaster has a distinctive tail which resembles a narrow spiky fur cone. This unusual aspect of the tail is formed by many divided sub-caudal scales at the end, and the terminal spike. The body colour of the bushmaster is tan, often pinkish, with large dark brown or black triangular rhombic markings usually edged with, or centred with, white. There is a dark stripe which runs from the eye and extends well into the neck. The body section of the bushmaster is distinctively triangular. Although potentially very dangerous this species occurs in areas well away from human influence. However, in these days of increased erosion of the world's wilderness areas there are obviously occasions when man must encounter the bushmaster. The bushmaster is largely nocturnal and feeds on small mammals and birds. This large pit viper is unusual in that it lays eggs.

Trimeresurus

The Asiatic pit vipers represented in the genus *Trimeresurus* are very similar to the New World *Bothrops* and systematists often prefer to group the two in one genus, i.e. *Trimeresurus*. The thirty or so species contained in this genus are small to medium sized snakes, many of which are arboreal and display marked similarities in appearance. The terrestrial members of the genus are either fairly large and relatively slender-bodied with long tails, or short squat-bodied snakes, the former usually being more brightly coloured and the latter typically brownish with varying degrees of dull blotches.

The largest species is the Okinawa habu, *T. flavoviridis*, which occurs only in the Ryukyu Islands and grows to around 150 cm— sometimes up to 200 cm. This slender-bodied pit viper is said to be irritable and in fact causes a high incidence of snakebite throughout much of its range. The coloration is distinctive, usually light brown or olive with dorsal blotches of dark green or brown which are edged with yellow. The blotches are often fused to form a stripe which may or may not run the entire length of the body.

The Sakishima habu, *T. elegans*, occurs in the southern part of the Ryukyu Islands and is similar in appearance to the Okinawa habu but is much smaller.

The himehabu, *T. okinavensis*, is found throughout the same range as that of the Okinawa habu. However, this species is a short-bodied snake growing to a maximum of 80 cm. The coloration is usually dull brown with indistinct dorsal blotches.

The Chinese habu, *T. mucrosquamatus*, is very similar in habits and appearance to the other habus and is found in southern China, Taiwan and westwards to eastern Burma. This species is often found near human dwellings and on agricultural land.

The montane viper, *T. monticola*, has a wide range, and is found from Nepal, across mainland China and also through much of the Malayan peninsula. This species can be found at elevations of up to 2400 m and is a creature of mountain forest. It is a fairly stockily built snake growing to around 100 cm and is usually grey or olive in colour with brownish blotches on the dorsal surface. This species also lays eggs and is said to be sluggish in its habits.

The mangrove pit viper, *T. purpuromaculatus* (Fig. 31), can be seen as essentially terrestrial but is also commonly encountered in low bushes. As the name suggests, this snake is particularly common in mangrove swamps, and its range extends from eastern Bengal, southern Burma, through the coastal areas of the Malayan peninsula, to Sumatra and the Andaman Islands. The average length is around 80 cm, but sometimes this species grows to 120 cm. Large individuals can be quite robust, but smaller snakes are comparable to some of their arboreal relatives. This snake is alert and vicious and will strike blindly at anything that moves.

The body coloration is purplish brown or grey with greenish spots and dark saddle-like markings on the dorsal surface. As with other members of the genus the head is large and 'chunky' looking and very distinct from the neck.

The arboreal species of *Trimeresurus* are well suited to their mode of life and all have strongly prehensile tails. Several of the species are basically greenish in colour, and three of these, *T. albolabris*, *T. stejne-geri* and *T. popeorum*, are superficially almost identical to each other. The white-lipped tree viper, *T. albolabris*, has a somewhat paler green body than the other green tree vipers and the end of the tail is dark red. All the green tree vipers have a pale lateral line, which in the case of the white-lipped tree viper is only present in the males. This species ranges from north eastern India to south eastern China and averages 60 cm in length.

The Chinese green tree viper, *T. stejnegeri*, is a much brighter green and a somewhat smaller species growing to around 50 cm. The pale lateral line is edged with orange or reddish in males and the eye is usually copper-coloured; the eyes of the other two species are usually yellowish. This species occurs in central and south eastern China. The red at the end of the tail of this snake is paler than the other green tree vipers.

Pope's tree viper, *T. popeorum* (Pl. 25), is probably the largest of the species and grows to 90 cm. The pale lateral line is either absent or indistinct in adults, and a positive means of identification is that the structure of the hemipenes is notably different when compared to the preceding species. The pope's tree viper has a wide range and occurs from Assam and Burma to Cambodia and south through Malaysia and Indonesia.

The Indian green tree viper, *T. gramineus*, is also predominantly green in colour, but is unusual in that most of the dorsal scales are smooth, there is usually dark speckling over much of the body and the end of the tail is also greenish. This species is also confined to peninsular India.

Waglers pit viper, or temple viper, *T. wagleri*, is a handsome snake which is usually of a rich green body colour with bright yellow cross-bands. The head is particularly large and very distinct from the neck. Although the basic coloration has been mentioned there is a great deal of variation usually associated with the density of pale spots which may obscure the more usual pattern; and some individuals have been seen to be almost a uniform green. This snake is common in lowland jungle and is found throughout Thailand, Malaysia, Indonesia and the Philippines. This is the snake to be found in the famous temple of Penang and it is also tolerated around human dwellings although its bite is potentially dangerous.

Many of the other species of *Trimeresurus* have a restricted range, although *T. puniceus* has a wide range in South East Asia and *T. jer-donii* ranges from north eastern India to eastern China and Vietnam. However, one of these species, *T. puniceus*, is rarely seen and is considered to be scarce over much of its range.

T. trigonocephalus is endemic to Sri Lanka where it is said to be locally abundant. The coloration is green with darker markings, with a prominent dark streak running through the eye. Maximum length for this arboreal species is around 70 cm.

The horseshoe viper, *T. strigatus*, is found in southern India and is probably the smallest of the genus, growing to just 45 cm. It is usually some shade of brown with variegated dark markings and a distinct pale horseshoe mark behind the head.

Crotalus

The remaining group of pit vipers are the rattlesnakes, which are well known to most people as a result of the many misleading roles that they have played in western movies. There is no doubt that some of the larger rattlesnakes are very dangerous indeed, particularly the large diamondbacks. However, many are small to medium sized snakes which vary in temperament from inoffensive to easily provoked creatures.

The rattlesnakes are so named due to the 'rattle' which is situated at the end of the tail. The rattle is made up of loosely jointed horny segments and varies in shape from species to species. This unique appendage instantly identifies a rattlesnake, although it is only vestigal in one species, the rare Santa Catalina Island or rattleless rattlesnake, *Crotalus catalinensis*. In addition, the rattle of the pygmy rattlesnakes, *Sistrurus spp.*, is very small and not always easily observed. It is also likely that many individual rattlesnakes may lose their rattles due to natural damage.

The rattle is a sophisticated warning device and the sound of a vibrating rattle can be described as a buzzing noise rather than a rattle. The sound has also been likened to that of escaping steam.

The rattlesnakes consist of twenty-eight species found in two genera, *Crotalus* and *Sistrurus*, most of which have a number of distinct sub-species which increases the number of variants to around sixty-five races. The races of two species are shown in Table 2 and Table 3.

The largest rattlesnake of the North American west is the western diamondback rattlesnake, *C. atrox* (Pl. 28). This is a snake of semi-

Table 2

Crotalus viridis and its sub-species

C. v. viridis	Prairie rattlesnake	Central USA from southern Canada to northern Mexico
C. v. abyssus	Grand Canyon rattlesnake	Grand Canyon, Arizona
C. v. caliginis	Coronado Island rattlesnake	Coronado Island off the coast of California
C. v. cerberus	Black rattlesnake	Arizona
C. v. concolor	Midget faded rattlesnake	Colorado and Green River basins
C. v. helleri ·	Southern Pacific rattlesnake	Southern California and northern Baja, California
C. v. lutosus	Great Basin rattlesnake	Great Basin of Rocky Mountains and Sierra Nevada
C. v. nuntius	Hopi rattlesnake	Northern Arizona
C. v. oreganus	Northern Pacific rattlesnake	Pacific Slope from British Columbia to California

Table 3

Crotalus durissus and its sub-species

C. d. durissus	Central American rattlesnake	South eastern Mexico and Central America
C. d. culminatus	Neotropical rattlesnake	South western Mexico
C. d. terrificus	South American rattlesnake	South America to northern Argentina
C. d. totonacus	Totonacan rattlesnake	South eastern Mexico
C. d. tzabcan	Yucatan rattlesnake	Extreme south eastern Mexico, northern Guatemala and northern British Honduras

Note: In recent years as many as thirteen different races of this species have been described; e.g. *C. d. dryinus* of the Guianas, *C. d. cascavella* of Brazil, *C. d. collilineatus* of Brazil, Bolivia and Paraguay, *C. d. marajoensis*, from Marajo, Brazil, *C. d. ruruima* from Venezuela, *C. d. cumanensis* from Venezuela and Colombia.

It is now generally accepted that this large sub-division is somewhat artificial and the above table is more representative of the group. However, two former sub-species, *C. d. unicolor* and *C. d. vegrandis*, have now been given specific status; i.e. the Aruba Island rattlesnake, *C. unicolor*, and the Uracoan rattlesnake, *C. vegrandis*.

arid habitat throughout much of the south western parts of the USA and as far south as central Mexico. The body colour is greyish brown or pinkish with dark diamond-shaped dorsal blotches. These markings are often faded and many individuals may have a dusty-looking appearance. The tail is distinctive—boldly ringed with black and white. Average size is around 150 cm, but much larger individuals of up to 210 cm have been recorded. The western diamondback is a robust species with a large spade-shaped head which is very distinct from the neck. This species is considered by many to be the most dangerous snake of the USA. Food consists of small mammals which are hunted mainly by night.

The red diamondback, *C. ruber* (Pl. 29), is similar in appearance to *C. atrox*, but the body colour is decidedly more reddish or pinkish and the markings less distinct. It is also a smaller species, growing to a maximum of 150 cm, and is said to be more placid. This snake prefers arid and semi-desert coastal regions in southern California and Baja California, and northern Mexico.

The eastern diamondback, *C. adamanteus*, is the largest of all the rattlesnakes, growing to 240 cm, and is heavier in body than its western relative, *C. atrox*. The pattern is also more consistent; large dark brown or black diamonds on a body colour of olive, brownish or blackish. This large rattlesnake occurs in sparse woodland and lowland coastal regions of south eastern gulf states of the USA, and is found throughout Florida, including the Keys. Food consists of mammals and birds.

The timber rattlesnake, *C. horridus*, has a wide range and is the only rattlesnake of the well-populated north eastern USA. Its range extends into much of the central and southern states, excluding Florida. However, due to urban pressure this species has been exterminated in many parts of its range. *C. horridus* occurs in two distinct races, the timber rattlesnake, *C. h. horridus*, which is representative of the northern part of the species' range and is a creature of pine forest country and wooded slopes, and the canebrake rattlesnake, *C. h. atricaudatus*, which occurs in the southern lowlands and is at home in cane thickets and swamplands.

The timber rattlesnake is a large species growing to 120 cm or more and has a robust body with a large flat head. The colour is yellowish brown or dark brown with darker crossbands which may form chevrons. Completely black individuals are not uncommon.

Fig. 34 Southern Pacific rattlesnake, *Crotalus viridis helleri*, from San Diego County, California, in typical defensive posture.

The canebrake rattlesnake is more brightly marked with a pinkish buff or brown body colour with bold black crossbands and an orange or reddish dorsal stripe on the anterior part of the body. A prominent feature is a bold dark stripe running from the eye and extending well behind the neck. This is a larger snake than the timber rattlesnake and can grow to 150 cm.

The majority of rattlesnake species are concentrated in the south western parts of North America and two of these have already been mentioned. The most widely distributed is *C. viridis* (Fig. 34), which has nine distinct races distributed throughout central and western parts of the USA and as far north as British Columbia.

The individual ranges for these races are given in Table 2 and there are several records of intergrade forms. The various races represent a size range of between 60–150 cm and all are marked with dark blotches of varying intensity. The ground colour ranges from olive, grey, brown, reddish, buff and yellowish. A great variety of habitat is occupied, including sparsely covered coastal dunes, rocky outcrops and mountain woodland.

114

The Mojave rattlesnake, *C. scutulatus*, is a large robust species growing to 120 cm and distributed in the southern parts of the south western states and well into Mexico. This is a snake of desert regions and lower mountain slopes and it avoids dense vegetation. The ground colour is greyish or olive brown with distinct dorsal diamond markings with pale edges. The tail has contrasting light and dark rings.

The tropical rattlesnake, *C. durissus* (Fig. 35), is also called the cascabel or cascavel, and is the rattlesnake of mainland South America as far south as northern Argentina and as far north as southern Mexico. Two other closely related species occur within the South American region—the Aruba Island rattlesnake, *C. unicolor*, and the Uracoan rattlesnake, *C. vegrandis*, of northern Venezuela. The tropical rattlesnake has five distinct sub-species and these are shown in Table 3.

This species is boldly marked with pale-edged diamonds which are joined by similarly coloured triangles on the lateral surfaces. Extending from the top of the head are usually two wide dorsal stripes that extend to varying lengths into the neck. In South America these stripes extend for 20 cm or less and in Central American and Mexican snakes perhaps for 60 cm or more. The ground colour is usually brownish or olive or yellowish, and Mexican snakes are often more brightly coloured. The tropical rattlesnake is notably triangular in body section and the head is not so distinct from the neck as in other rattlesnakes.

Fig. 35 Tropical rattlesnake, *Crotalus durissus terrificus*, a highly dangerous rattlesnake from South America with a strong neurotoxic fraction in the venom.

The maximum size is around 160 cm. Dense jungle is avoided and this species shows a preference for open grassland. The combination of a highly toxic venom and an uncertain temper makes this species a very dangerous snake indeed and throughout much of its range it is only outmatched by the barba amarilla, *Bothrops atrox*.

The rock rattlesnake, *C. lepidus* (Pl. 30), is a handsome species and occurs in the southern parts of Arizona and New Mexico and southwards to northern Mexico. It is a medium-sized snake, growing to 70 cm, with bold widely spaced dark crossbands on a pale grey or greenish grey body. Rocky ledges in low mountain areas are a favourite haunt.

The speckled rattlesnake, *C. mitchellii* (Pl. 31), is found in similar habitat in Arizona, southern Nevada, southern California and southwards throughout Baja California. This species grows to around 100 cm and is yellowish, buff or pinkish, with a high density of dark speckling on the body scales. The more prominent markings consist of dark crossbands which may be indistinct in some individuals.

The ridged-nosed rattlesnake, *C. willardi*, is a rare species with a limited distribution from southern Arizona to central Mexico. It is a small species, growing to just 60 cm. This is a snake of mountain woodland and is seen most often in clearings with rocky outcrops. As the name suggests, there is a prominent ridge which follows the outline of the snout. The body coloration is reddish brown or grey, with pale crossbars edged with black.

The sidewinder, *C. cerastes*, is a well-known species which occurs in windblown desert areas, and its sidewinding mode of locomotion is shared by other Old World viper species. The sidewinder is a small snake which rarely exceeds 70 cm and the males are notably smaller than the females. The colour is sandy brown, or yellowish, even pinkish, with pale spots on the dorso-lateral surface which are sometimes fused to form crossbars. The supraoculars are raised and pointed, which gives the species a horned appearance similar to the north African vipers. The range of the sidewinder is confined to the desert areas of the south western USA and northern Mexico.

Sistrurus

The smallest of the rattlesnakes consist of the three species contained in the genus *Sistrurus*, better known as the pygmy rattlesnakes.

One of these, *S. ravus,* is confined to central Mexico while the remaining species have a much wider range in North America.

The massasauga, *S. catenatus* (Pl. 32), has a very wide range, from Pennsylvania in the north and south west to Texas. This species grows to around 60 cm and is grey or brownish with large dark blotches along the dorsal surface. The pygmy rattlesnakes are distinct from the other rattlers as they have nine plates on the crown and not the usual small imbricate scales typical of *Crotalus.*

The pygmy rattlesnake, *S. miliarus* (Pl. 33), has several recognised sub-species, as do many of the rattlesnakes, and these races are usually quite distinctive.

The dusky rattlesnake, *S. m. barbouri,* ranges through much of Florida, and northwards to southern Carolina and southern Mississippi. The body colour is grey with dark dorsal blotches interspaced with blotches of orange red which may or may not merge into the darker markings to form a stripe. This species is also usually heavily flecked with white.

The western pygmy rattlesnake is very similar but has two conspicuous rows of lateral spots. The range extends from southern Missouri to southern Kentucky.

Both species rarely exceed 60 cm and are usually found near streams or rivers, or else in marshes or swampland.

6
Habits and Behaviour

Snakes, and indeed all reptiles, exist within certain levels of tolerance which are governed chiefly by climate and habitat. The many species of snakes can be described as very successful creatures which exhibit a high degree of variety in their way of life and actual abundance. It is obvious that some snakes are more successful than others and this is exemplified by species which have adapted to a wide range of habitat, and which may also accept a wide range of food. Species that show a limited choice of habitat and a limited range of food are the ones that are usually more susceptible to changes in their immediate environment. These changes are often quite subtle, and usually man-made; a few felled trees or bushes, or a small grass fire, can have drastic results on small snake populations.

There is nothing to suggest that venomous snakes should be more successful in their survival than their non-venomous relatives, although it is a fact that some of the more prominent of abundant species are indeed venomous. The European adder, the saw-scaled viper and the puff adder, for example, all tend to occur in rather high densities.

Adaptability is the key to the success of any species—the ability to cope with man's encroachment and persecution and in some cases to go one step further and actually flourish under the hand of man. This may seem odd, and needless to say it is not a state of affairs consciously encouraged by man!

Our lack of knowledge with regard to the life styles of the varied snake species is only equalled by our seeming lack of concern. Even contemporary zoologists appear reluctant to inquire into the lives of these creatures, and in my own experience this attitude is not totally unbiased. The snake is a predator like any other predator and is an integral part of the natural community in which it occurs. We need to know about these creatures and, to take a completely selfish view, we need to know why in many areas of the world venomous snakes occur in high numbers around areas of human influence.

Temperature requirements

Reptiles are usually referred to as cold-blooded, a description which is synonymous with the scientific term ectothermic, which means that the regulation of body temperature is reliant on external sources of heat. Although this means that the body temperature of a reptile can basically be correlated with that of the surroundings, many reptiles can achieve a higher body temperature. This is brought about by various behavioural patterns which vary according to climate and, of course, the type of reptile.

Snakes are no less efficient in controlling their body temperatures than other reptiles, and indeed have some advantage which is made apparent by their life style; for example, they are usually less active than lizards and feed at longer intervals. Even the ungainly tortoise is in some ways more active as it makes daily excursions in search of food.

It is true to say that a snake does not move for the fun of it. If a snake is in fact seen on the move then it is either hunting, mating, migrating, seeking a basking spot or, more likely, just moving off after being disturbed.

The geographical distribution of snakes suggests that the various species possess a wide range of individual optimum temperature requirements; temperate species such as the European adder are more tolerant to low temperatures, and desert species such as the African horned vipers can withstand quite high temperatures. However, this rather over-simplifies the matter. Firstly, it has already been mentioned that reptiles can improve on the surrounding ambient temperature. The adder achieves this by extended periods of lying out which vary in duration according to time of year and vagaries of climate. Figs 36–38 show the modes of lying out, each mode usually

119

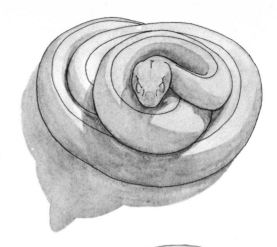

Fig. 36 The tight spiral
lying-out attitude, most often
adopted when the snake first
emerges or during inclement
weather, with its head in the
centre of the coils and the
snake usually fully alert.

Fig. 37 The loose spiral
attitude. This is the most
often adopted attitude and is
employed over a wide range
of weather conditions. The
snake is usually relaxed and if
the head is depressed it may
well be asleep.

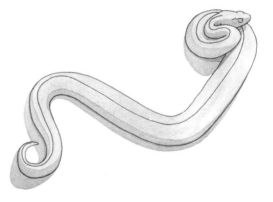

Fig. 38 The elongate
stretched attitude, adopted
during periods of weak sun or
overcast weather, exposing
maximum body surface. The
attitude is often enhanced in
many species by a horizontal
flattening of the body surface.

determined by weather conditions. Snakes, even desert species, rarely expose themselves to direct sun, and optimum temperatures of desert species are achieved by concealment usually effected by burying themselves in sand or else hiding in rocky fissures. In addition, desert species tend to be nocturnal.

It has also been mentioned that a snake's mobility is restricted to necessity, and this means that much of its life is spent immobile, just lying around, apparently doing nothing. Many visitors to zoos often comment on this aspect with remarks to the effect that they are stuffed or made of plastic.

The most obvious reason for immobility is that a snake may be basking. However, the term basking suggests that the snake is seeking to raise the body temperature in order to meet the demands of the daily routine, which may include feeding, mating or other functions which involve some degree of activity. In temperate climates the early spring activity of snakes consists almost wholly of basking with just a short amount of travel at either end of this basking period (Fig. 39).

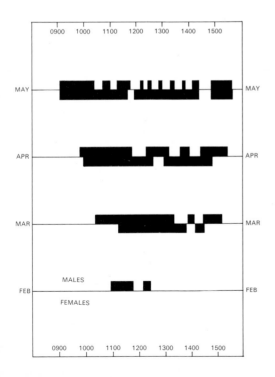

Fig. 39 Daily lying-out periods throughout the early active year recorded for the adder, *Vipera berus*, in southern England.

121

This tells us that long periods of basking are not necessarily a pre-clusion to high activity on that particular day and that other reasons are involved. In many temperate zones male snakes are the first to emerge from their period of winter torpor. During this time a new skin is developing and sperm has to mature, and this is achieved by lying out for long periods. Until the females emerge male snakes have literally nothing to do that involves any activity. For example, no feed-ing takes place during this early period, and in fact male snakes of many species do not feed until the finish of the breeding period. Dur-ing other periods of the year lying out can also be related to new skin growth, digestion of food, and embryo development.

Basically, a snake will succumb to excesses of both heat and cold, and the optimum preferred temperature range lies between 12°C and 32°C. Although this is a general assumption, and some species of snakes exhibit a limited amount of activity outside these preferred limits, the actual critical mean temperatures—the lower and upper danger limits—are around 5°C and 42°C respectively. Critical tem-peratures at either end of the scale vary from species to species, but in general snakes exhibit a higher tolerance to cooler conditions than to excessive heat where the critical range is much narrower.

Desert species, such as the sidewinder, have a preferred temperature range of between 28°C and 32°C, a narrow range which is achieved by alternate exposure and concealment of the body, or parts of the body surface. Prolonged exposure to direct sun at a temperature just a few degrees higher than the maximum preference would prove lethal for even desert species.

A reptile's obligation to regulate its own temperature to within opti-mum limits, sometimes referred to as the reptile's voluntary tempera-ture, is achieved by various means according to the many shapes and forms and varied life styles of contemporary reptiles.

Although we can, in general, describe a snake's way of life as either terrestrial, arboreal, aquatic or semi-aquatic, there is in reality a con-siderable amount of overlap which is exemplified by the fact that all snakes can climb and swim, and even large so-called sluggish species such as the puff adder and gaboon viper will climb and swim as a matter of routine.

However, there are snakes that are so consistently allied to their mode of life as to be described as one type or another. Obviously, a tree-living species will effect its preferred temperature range in a somewhat different manner than a terrestrial or semi-aquatic species. During periods of great heat, which may be daily in many parts of the world, snakes are obliged to seek cooler conditions by burrowing, entering water or, as in the case of arboreal species, adjusting themselves within a tree canopy. The green mamba is a well-known arboreal species and during the heat of the African day will lie, often in groups of three or more, in high canopy where they may be subjected to soft breezes. The green mamba is most active during early morning and evening when it will be found in low canopy or else scrub or thornbush.

Water-loving species such as the cottonmouth moccasin like to bask but can equally 'cool off' by just lying half submerged in the water, usually out of sight under a bank or log.

The intensity of thermoregulation in snakes varies with regard to the size of the species. Large species, although slower to warm up, generally retain heat more efficiently than medium-sized or small species. During cooler conditions many medium-sized and small species, such as the European adder and some of the smaller rattlesnakes, will flatten the body when basking, allowing a greater body surface to be exposed to the sun. Even so, the daily lives of smaller species of snakes involve a shuttle routine seeking alternate sun and shade.

In the past it was often thought that snakes were lovers of great heat, and in fact many people still believe that a scorching hot day is the best weather to be able to observe snakes. It is of course possible to encounter a snake during the heat of the day; good eyesight could discern the mamba in the high canopy, or else the snout of the cottonmouth protruding above the surface of the water. However, we would be observing just sedentary behaviour which could hardly be regarded as typical of the habits of that particular species.

Most people know that, due to vagaries of climate, snakes spend periods of inactivity which are usually referred to as hibernation and aestevation. Hibernation is really a word of convenience as it applies to both reptiles and mammals and it can be appreciated that the metabolism of each is somewhat different. The most obvious difference in the mode of winter torpor is that mammals are reliant upon their fat reserves to sustain them and their hibernation may not be continuous. Snakes, on the other hand, can enter hibernation with little or no fat in the body, although many may have good reserves at this time, and activity is determined by temperature alone (Fig. 40). For

123

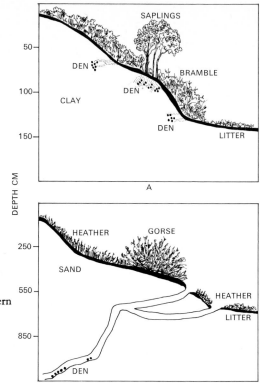

Fig. 40 Examples of hibernation dens for the adder, *Vipera berus*, in England and Wales: A, southern Dorset, hibernation occurring at shallow depth in sandy soil; B, western Wales, hibernation occurring at much greater depth in disused rabbit warren in clay.

this reason, a mild winter may prove disastrous for temperate species as they will be lured out only to be smitten by a sudden frost. Ideally, a consistently cold winter is preferable as this does not induce premature emergence.

Aestevation is the opposite concept: a snake's obligation to retire from excessive heat. However, this usually involves periods of a much shorter duration, almost daily in many cases, compared with hibernation periods of sometimes six months or longer for temperate species. Rain-forest species are also governed by distinct wet and dry seasons and for many tropical species the start of the rains heralds the birth of young.

During hot weather such species as the gaboon viper or Malayan pit viper may bury themselves in the peaty soil of the forest floor or else just lie below the surface amongst leaf litter.

Whether a snake is diurnal or nocturnal, or perhaps crepuscular, is an indication of optimum temperature preference. It does not follow that a tropical species necessarily has a higher temperature preference than a temperate species. Tropical nights can be quite cool and a nocturnal species such as the fer-de-lance probably exhibits a similar preferred temperature range to that of the European adder.

In addition, climatic conditions are somewhat more consistent in tropical zones, and temperate species are often subjected to 'untypical' weather conditions such as heat waves and drought, or else prolonged cool and wet summers, both of which can adversely affect a snake's annual cycle.

Some snakes can be described as both diurnal and nocturnal, and this must be true of many species that occur in regions where the nights can be both warm and cool, depending on the time of year. Many of the larger elapids such as the cobras and the black mamba are good examples of how a snake can 'turn' its way of life around according to the seasonal fluctuation.

Habitat

The influence of climate is the most obvious factor that controls a snake's activity, and the actual nature of climate is a general indication of a species' life style. However, the nature of the climate must be co-ordinated with the type of habitat. Habitat types are usually referred to distinctly as rain forest, savanna, desert, heathland and so forth. These are just general indications and it is obvious that many 'grey' areas exist within these basic botanical regions (Figs 41–8).

This is exemplified by the way in which the world's rain forests have been denuded or else replaced with coffee or cocoa plantations. We extract minerals and literally turn parts of the earth's surface upside down. Much of the heathland of northern Europe has been encroached upon by mineral extraction and further fragmented by housing and other development. There are many other examples, and all lead to a rethink of how we describe many forms of existing habitat. Consideration must now be given to the high number of snake populations that exist on plantations and in areas which can be termed remnant forest. Urban heathland is a term often used to describe the habitat type of adder populations in southern England. Other venomous snakes appear to have adapted to an urban existence; the North American copperhead and the African puff adder are two

Fig. 41 Remnant heathland in an area of major afforestation in southern England. Ideal habitat for the adder, *Vipera berus*.

examples. However, it would be extremely unlikely to find a snake living free and wild in a busy city centre. The outlying town areas, with perhaps typically large gardens, are the most usual haunt for these town-dwelling snakes, and, furthermore, the surrounding countryside is usually more typical of the particular species' habitat type. However, snakes do enter gardens, and even houses, for a number of reasons. It may be that the snake is seeking shade, or perhaps food; but a lesser-known fact is that the house or garden in question may occupy what originally was, and still is, the snake's migratory route.

The earth's surface is changing continuously, influenced both by man and natural forces, and the favourable habitat type for many species is often difficult to determine. Railway embankments, quarries and rubbish tips are all types of habitat where snakes are to be found, but these are all products of relatively modern times and observations have shown that snake populations are often of a high density. Why are these man-made habitats so popular with snakes? Firstly, such

Fig. 42   Habitat for the ridged nosed rattlesnake, *Crotalus willardi*, and rock rattlesnake, *Crotalus lepidus*. Santa Rita Mountains, Arizona.

Fig. 43   Habitat for western diamondback rattlesnake, *Crotalus atrox*. Eagle Pass, Texas.

Fig. 44 Summer habitat for the cottonmouth moccasin, *Agkistrodon piscivorous*. Winters Pond, Pine Hills, Union County, Ill.

Fig. 45 Hill prairie habitat; denning area for timber rattlesnake, *Crotalus horridus*, and cottonmouth moccasin, *Agkistrodon piscivorous*. Pine Hills, Union County, Ill.

128

places attract rodents, a valuable food source. Secondly, embankments and quarries possess a sunny aspect, a very favourable condition for basking and hibernation.

Plantations attract more than their extra quota of small rodents and in many cases populations of various species such as *Bothrops*, *Trimeresurus* and *Agkistrodon* sometimes occur in almost double their normal numbers.

Snakes certainly take advantage of man's disorder and are quick to invade our bits of cast-off machinery, deserted buildings and disused quarries. An empty hut in the middle of the African bush soon collapses for lack of maintenance and then it may become home for several species of venomous snakes. Exploring one such hut I discovered four puff adders, two spitting cobras and an Egyptian cobra!

In tropical America and parts of Asia there are whole cities and temples that have been swallowed up by the jungle. These are eerie places, made even more weird when one observes arboreal vipers occupying the various nooks and crannies amongst the ancient carvings and masonry. In one such place in Thailand cobras favoured the cool dark corridors and galleries long empty of man and only accessible through thick tangled vine. The sight of a king cobra sliding gracefully through these long forgotten chambers leaves one in no doubt as to who are the masters now of these ancient monuments to man's edification.

It would be almost impossible to think of a habitat that is, or is likely to remain, unchanged; perhaps the deep interior of the Amazonian jungle is safe for now, but encroachment on the world's rain forests is rapid and who can say with any certainty that a halt to this destruction will be brought about? If a comparison were made with regard to the status of species, one could say that in some respects the adders at the bottom of some rural garden in southern England have a more hopeful future than, say, the gaboon viper and rhinoceros viper in the Kakamega Forest in western Kenya.

Man will continue to invade the world's wild places, but natural events also greatly influence habitat. Fire, flood, storms, all can have disastrous effects on habitat. Fire is a common event in such places as Australia and the African plains and woodlands, and such fires seem to destroy all and everything in their path. However, it is not so; fire shapes the habitat, it is responsible for its very creation. Many animals and plants of course perish in the flames, but surprisingly, new life arises from the ashes and in a short while the land is lush and teeming

Fig. 46   Malineau Gorge, Mulu National Park, Sarawak. Habitat for the arboreal *Trimeresurus* spp.

with life. Snake populations seem to be able to maintain the status quo in such conditions, which suggests that many must have the ability to seek refuge successfully. How snakes do this is sometimes a mystery, but I have dug out large aggregations of snakes from termite hills and other refuges following a fire. The very nature of the catch—Egyptian cobras, spitting cobras, puff adders, mole snakes, sand snakes, plus various lizards—indicates that this usually incompatible group sought refuge in a hurry.

Heath and grass fires in northern Europe are usually man-made and are usually disastrous, as heather can take twenty-five years to mature and such plant life as bracken and birch are quick to encroach, permanently changing the habitat.

Flooding is an annual occurrence in many parts of the tropics and at the start of the rains semi-arid valleys may be come huge lakes. At such times such terrestrial species as the puff adder may suddenly find themselves both aquatic and arboreal as the only 'land' space available may be the top of a tree protruding above the water. An extreme

130

example was the flooding incurred by the construction of the Kariba dam; this was of course man-made and permanent, and although many snakes were rescued many others perished.

Other natural causes are sometimes more subtle. Elephants often push over whole trees, usually acacia trees, and in doing so may dislodge a mamba or a boomslang which is then demoted to terrestrial life until another suitable tree can be found. Similarly, a buffalo may use an old termite hill as a scratching post and eventually reduce it to rubble. As a consequence the Egyptian cobra or black mamba that may have taken up refuge is obliged to seek a new home.

Habitat, be it man-made or truly wild, must provide both shelter and access to the sun, and in addition must also maintain a consistent source of food. However, general descriptions of habitat types are inadequate; for example, it is quite vague to describe the European adder as a creature of moorland and heath, or the western diamondback rattlesnake as a snake of semi-desert. One has to look further, and examine in depth just what part of the habitat the snake actually occupies.

Fig. 47 Rain forest, Mulu National Park, Sarawak. Habitat for a wide range of venomous species, including *Bungarus fasciatus*, *Naja naja*, *Trimeresurus popeorum* and *T. sumatranus*.

131

Fig. 48   Rain forest, River Santiago, Equador, showing habitat for snakes enhanced by limited clearance in areas marked X. Ideal habitat for the barba amarilla, *Bothrops atrox*.

There is a lot of heathland in northern Europe, but it is a fact that adders are not evenly distributed overall. Furthermore, it is now known that the adder occupies quite different habitat types throughout various parts of the year. Dry, well-drained, south-facing slopes of heath are favoured for hibernation and spring activity, but marshy valleys are utilised during the summer months. When one reflects that this occupation of wet habitat by the adder is a fairly recent discovery, and that this species is probably one of the most well known of all snakes, it shows just how little we in fact know about how snakes live.

Populations

The world's distribution of snakes is not as haphazard an affair as one might imagine. The importance of habitat has been mentioned and it is the habitat that influences distribution with regard to limits and avenues of dispersal.

It is important to understand what is meant by the term 'population' as this infers that all snakes exist in colonies or are to some extent social creatures. In fact, the subject is quite complex and there are no general rules that can be applied. However, if we were to generalise it could be said that vipers are more likely to exist in colonies and that the elapids are solitary by comparison. While this holds true for most species of viper, some elapids exhibit gregarious behaviour—some species of sea snakes are notable examples. The Australian tiger snake occurs in colonies, and green mambas occur in at least small groups. It may be that many elapids, such as the coral snakes, some species of cobra, and the kraits, are habitual snake-eaters, including their own kind. This of course does little to encourage social behaviour. Furthermore some species of cobra are notoriously territorial.

Communal behaviour is highlighted in regions where large numbers of snakes gather in hibernation. These aggregations are notable in the European adder and many of the North American pit vipers. Courtship and mating also take place in these areas, usually followed by dispersal to summer areas, the same routes being taken each year. Communal hibernation is not always restricted to one species; rattlesnakes may group with other species of snake, such as the copperhead, or the harmless gopher snake, and even lizards and toads. In southern England I have found the adder during hibernation in company with the grass snake, smooth snake, slow worm and viviparous lizard, the latter being a normal prey species.

Seasonal migration is typical of temperate species and the amount of distance involved varies even amongst snakes of the same species. This can range from just 200 metres to a distance of 5 kilometres or more.

Sedentary behaviour is probably more typical of some of the tropical species, and even large snakes such as the Egyptian cobra and black mamba will often occupy just a surprisingly small area.

Because most snakes exist within certain levels of tolerance with regard to habitat it follows that the majority of species can be termed locally abundant. This means that rather than a blanket coverage over a general area, numbers of snakes are more likely to occur in scattered concentrations with obvious fluctuations throughout the year in seasonal movement, breeding and other social behaviour (Fig. 49).

Rattlesnakes, for example, can occur in very large numbers during the spring when they are just emerging from hibernation. However, during the summer months they are much more thinly dispersed and tend to be nocturnal or crepuscular. Large numbers are again recorded

133

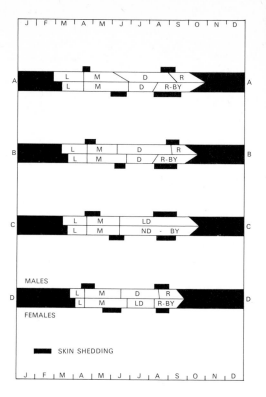

Fig. 49   Four separate
populations of the adder,
Vipera berus, showing marked
similarities in the annual
cycle. The black areas
represent periods of winter
torpor.
L—lying out; M—mating;
D—dispersal to summer
areas; ND—no dispersal;
LD—limited dispersal;
R—return to denning area;
BY—birth of young.

in the autumn when the snakes return to the hibernation den and once
more adopt more diurnal patterns of behaviour as in the early spring.

Many of the viper species occur in distinct populations which are
autonomous, that is to say that they maintain their numbers within
a distinct area. It is in fact possible to assess numbers of snakes within
a population, but it is a prolonged process which involves identifying
individual snakes. It is important when assessing snake populations
to start at the beginning, that is the start of the species annual cycle.
This is most readily obvious in temperate species when large numbers
will be concentrated at the hibernation dens. At this time there may
appear to be an infinite number of snakes and marking each individual
can be a hectic affair. However, over a period of time a pattern evolves
and one finds that certain snakes may occupy the same basking spot
year after year. Ultimately, by the method of mark and recapture, one
finds that fewer new snakes are being found and that shortly afterwards
a finite number can be allotted to that particular population; as can

134

other data such as sex ratio, ratio of immature, etc. The practicalities of studying snakes in the wild are dealt with in Chapter 10.

Due to the limitations of studying snake populations—the restrictions of time, accessibility, etc.—it is hardly surprising that we know so little about most species. Various observations on different aspects of behaviour are of course useful, but they do not tell the whole story, and it is only those species that have been the subject of sustained field study that actually give us an insight into how snakes occupy their particular niche in the highly complex natural world.

I suppose there may be a dozen such species that have undergone any serious research and the majority of these are probably North American. The European adder, however, has been studied by a number of workers, including myself, and many facts about this fascinating snake have now been revealed.

It is often tempting when beginning fieldwork on a new species to speculate and to compare with past work on other species. Although there is no room for guesswork, and field study of any species should run its full course, it is usually helpful to compare one species with another, and in fact many species have been found to lead very similar lives.

The work of Henry Fitch on the copperhead, and that of Ray Burkett on the cottonmouth moccasin, is well known in herpetological circles, and the annual cycle of these North American snakes bears many similarities to that of the European adder. Such aspects as seasonal movement, communal behaviour, female biennial breeding cycle, for example, must indeed be inherent in many species of venomous snakes.

To illustrate just how snakes live it will be necessary to state examples from some of those species that have been studied in depth.

Firstly, let us look at some of the species that have already been mentioned: the copperhead, the cottonmoth moccasin and the well-known European adder. The adder has a very wide range, and although we appear to know quite a lot about its habits, this may not be relevant for parts of its range, particularly in the east. However, the facts are that this widespread species occurs in distinct populations which are self-governing, and are not dependent on recruitment from outside; that is, they maintain their numbers by their own breeding effort. Furthermore, a lengthy period is spent in hibernation, which results in an active season in areas where females breed on alternate years. This is due to a low feeding factor during actual breeding years which means that the fat body, i.e. breeding condition, cannot be maintained for two consecutive years.

How then does this brief summary of the adder's life style compare with, say, that of the copperhead and cottonmouth moccasin? Firstly, basic seasonal patterns such as hibernation and communal behaviour are very similar in the three species. The copperhead exhibits seasonal movement, as does the cottonmouth, and the females of both species show a bias towards a biennial breeding cycle.

So, we have both New and Old World species that exhibit marked similarities in their way of life, and perhaps it would not be too presumptuous to suggest that all the European viper species, and many rattlesnake species of North America, may lead very similar lives.

We need not confine this comparison to Europe and North America, for many species of viper in Africa and Asia occur in local concentrations which fluctuate in numbers throughout the year. The russells viper is a typical example; a common snake in some areas, but seemingly absent in others. This is probably due to a limiting factor in the habitat which imposes a somewhat local preference, as this dangerous snake can be found in both scrub and forest with a migration between each, or else be restricted to just one habitat type.

The saw-scaled viper is considered by many to be the most dangerous snake in the world and its wide range is second only to that of the European adder. This small snake occurs in arid regions but is also abundant in areas of rural agriculture. Fieldwork on this species is a priority, especially for those areas where it is a major hazard to man. In addition to its wide distribution, this snake occurs in remarkably high densities with a peak of numbers between May and August, according to locality. The actual abundance of this species is exemplified by the fact that, just in the space of a few hours, whilst engaged on preliminary work on this species in northern Kenya, I recorded twenty-two specimens. The late C. J. P. Ionides caught thirty-nine specimens in one day also in northern Kenya. Even more astonishing was that in 1935 one hundred and eighty-six of this species were caught in one day at Parachinar in Pakistan. If that were not enough, there is a record that, during 1890, 115,921 saw-scaled vipers were killed in the Ratnagiri district of India over a period of just eight days!

The large African vipers of the genus *Bitis* are quite distinctive in appearance, but much less is known about their actual habits. The

136

puff adder is perhaps the most well known of these large snakes and my own work on the species has shown that populations are often difficult to define and there is almost definitely some overlap. This is probably due to this snake's wide choice of habitat. Although avoiding rain forest, it can be encountered almost anywhere where conditions are suitable. Savanna or semi-arid habitat is often put forward as the favoured habitat for the puff adder. This, while being generally true, is misleading as I have often found this species in urban gardens amongst lush vegetation, and even in dense montane scrub.

The puff adder certainly shows a great deal of variance in its populations, but some are easily pinpointed. A developed area may contain some remnant habitat that supports a small sedentary group, or a prominent kopje within savanna may have its permanent colony of puff adders.

The other two large African vipers, the gaboon viper and the rhinoceros viper, are usually referred to as forest species. However, as mentioned earlier much of the forest is now disappearing and these two species may occupy additional habitat in the form of remnant forest or plantation.

Both these species are considered to be local in their distribution, but populations can be quite high. The gaboon viper is a sedentary creature and at certain times of the year males are much more in evidence than females. This has probable connections with the breeding cycle, but my own programme of fieldwork was too shortlived to confirm this.

The gaboon viper can be quite abundant in areas where it does occur, and in southern Tanzania C. J. P. Ionides took over two thousand specimens and stated that this did not appear to reduce noticeably the numbers of local populations.

The vipers that we know less about are the arboreal species contained in the genera *Atheris*, *Trimeresurus* and *Bothrops*. Some observations indicate that this group may be fairly sedentary with regard to population, but much more work is needed to confirm this.

Elapid populations must be given quite different consideration and the various species show great variety in their individual ways of life. Firstly, some of the socially inclined elapids have already been mentioned. The green mamba will often occur in groups of varying numbers; I have recorded up to six mambas in the same tree. During the breeding season behaviour and movements become erratic and the

137

males will show considerable excitement, descend to the ground and show great activity in low bush and thickets. This may involve a mamba travelling a distance of just 50 metres or perhaps several hundred metres. Outside the breeding season groups of mambas do not appear to show a bias towards one sex or the other, and may consist of mixed groupings or just males or females.

The jamesons mamba spends much more time on the ground, and populations and numbers are difficult to determine.

The black mamba is an interesting creature and is a snake that is most likely to establish a permanent home base. This may be in some rock outcrop, disused termiteria, ant bear hole or decaying human dwelling place. At such refuges it is usual to observe a pair of black mambas, and they appear to pair outside the breeding season. Occasionally a single mamba may be in evidence or a group of four or five. Black mambas are nervous and irritable snakes and their co-existence with one another seems to be one of excitable tolerance. Although this species shows preference for a permanent refuge regular excursions to hunt are made and this may involve travelling a considerable distance. Identification of mambas has to be by sight alone—once captured and marked they are prone to vacate their homes and hence disrupt the very nature of the study. In general, vipers are much more tolerant of such abuse.

Some of the African cobras are amongst the most anti-social of all the elapids. The forest cobra, spitting cobra and Egyptian cobra all tend to be solitary creatures and, in addition, all are prone to make a meal of other snakes. I observed a spitting cobra that had established a home amongst tree roots actually attack and eat a smaller member of its own species that had ideas about moving in.

The Egyptian cobra is probably the most anti-social of all and appears to occupy the same refuge for considerable lengths of time. A large female in Kenya that I marked during 1961 was still in residence during 1963. Obviously, these so-called anti-social snakes must get together to breed. However, this can often be a savage affair which involves much biting and chewing accompanied by loud hissing and hood spreading. Both the Egyptian and spitting cobras are common and both prefer drier situations, and single refuges can be scattered about various pieces of savanna or scrub. In addition, the spitting cobra is quite likely to enter huts and urban gardens if sufficient cover is available.

The Asiatic cobra is sometimes found in large aggregations, but it is much more likely to occur in small groups or else singly. The difficulty in determining the habits and population status of many such species is that populations may have become drastically altered during adaptation to life in the plantation or paddy field or other man-made habitats.

King cobras are sometimes said to pair for life. It is true that they are often seen in pairs, but they are just as often encountered singly, although it is appreciated that another king cobra may well be lurking nearby.

Mention so far has been made of how the various species exist as individual populations. However, throughout most areas of world snake distribution more than one species is to be found in any one particular area. Even in southern England there are areas where the three British snake species, the adder, smooth snake and grass snake, occur within the same habitat.

Composite snake populations are by no means rare and each species usually occupies an individual niche. Snake species that have similar habitat or food preferences, however, rarely occur side by side and there is usually a subtle demarcation line with regard to their local distribution. For example, the large eastern diamondback rattlesnake and the pygmy rattlesnake occur within the same habitat, and although they both prey on mammals there is obviously no competition as each accepts prey only of the relevant size range. This, plus the fact that the pygmy rattlesnake will also take amphibian prey, means that the two species can co-exist happily together.

It can be appreciated then that the term 'population' covers a wide range of type and composition which, in many instances, is constantly changing. The status and composition of snake populations in many cases must be very different from what they were just two decades ago.

Many snake species lead very secret lives; the coral snakes, sea snakes, snakes of deep forest, are all difficult subjects for the field herpetologist, and it is still very true that many more prominent species yet await serious study.

Breeding

Courtship and mating amongst snakes is not just a case of male meeting female but a rather more complex affair which is dependent on certain rituals and defined patterns of behaviour within snake populations.

139

Firstly, male snakes are usually the more activated section of a population during the breeding season; in temperate climates such species as the European adder and North American rattlesnakes actively seek out females and at this time there is often great rivalry between the eager males. This rivalry often manifests itself in a ritual display, which is often referred to as a dance. This combat ritual usually takes place when one male is already in possession of a female and is in fact warning off another male. In the case of the European adder it was noted that the male in possession at the time was always the victor of such encounters.

At this time male snakes are alert and vicious and are usually displayed at their best having recently moulted. Female snakes in such circumstances play a placid role until approached by a male. Then, both snakes exhibit what is probably the most beautiful of all aspects of snake behaviour. The courtship of snakes is an amazing spectacle and varies in its intensity from species to species. During the time of courtship it is as if both male and female become synchronised to each other's movements. The two snakes move as one; as the female moves then the male follows, both snakes exhibiting a fluency which has to be seen to be appreciated.

On the ground, such species as the European adder and the copperhead are examples of this fluent togetherness; in the trees, two green mambas flowing and entwining amongst the green foliage of high canopy is indeed a wonderful sight.

Other snakes are not so gentle or subtle in their courtship routine; and many species of cobra will bite and chew their way to consummation.

The mating period occurs at a specific time during the year. There have been many records of so-called off-seasonal mating behaviour, but this is often confused with territorial behaviour which exhibits many similar characteristics. Temperate species usually mate shortly after emergence from hibernation; tropical species are influenced by either distinct wet and dry seasons or else the end of the rains in parts of Africa.

Little is known about the female breeding cycle in many species, but field work has shown that many temperate forms exhibit an individual biennial female breeding cycle. Some temperate species can be induced to breed each year in captivity, but records have shown that this often results in erratic feeding and other symptoms that suggest a divergence from normal behaviour.

The breeding cycle for female snakes in the tropics may be quite a different story, but records have shown that the actual duration of the active annual cycle usually determines a female snake's breeding potential. For example, the adult females of a population of puff adders in southern Kenya produced young each year, and although there were inconsistencies in active behaviour, the active season was of sufficient duration to allow each female to feed constantly. Female snakes in temperate climates feed little during a breeding season and exhibit a high feeding factor during the following year which is a non-breeding year for that individual. Female puff adders in southern Africa tend to breed on alternate years due to the marked vagaries of climate.

It can then be concluded that the criteria for consistent breeding potential is the maintenance of the actual bodily condition in females. In temperate climates, due to the relatively short season, females are obliged to breed on alternate years.

The biennial female breeding cycle also means that during any one year only a certain section of the female population is available for mating. Many snake populations exhibit a male:female ratio of 1:1 and this means that in a total population of say sixty adults only fifteen females would be available for mating. Male snakes, although highly active during the breeding season, maintain a good bodily condition from year to year, so in our hypothetical population of sixty adults this would mean thirty males in competition for fifteen females. However, this does not necessarily mean that only half the male population would be successful in finding a mate because each breeding female usually receives more than one male.

However, this does portray how essential male rivalry is during the course of natural events leading to a successful breeding population.

Distinct seasonal movement is perhaps more marked with regard to temperate species. At the conclusion of the mating period there is usually a dispersal to summer areas; this dispersal can be quite sudden. Snakes that were thick on the ground one day may quite suddenly seem to vanish or become hard to find. In fact, the bulk of the population would have started their way along well-worn routes which are sometimes quite direct and migration is completed in a day or so, or else there may be detours on the way with individuals stopping to feed. The non-breeding section of a population, i.e. immature snakes and non-breeding females, may well have migrated some weeks before the conclusion of the mating period. However, population behaviour varies considerably in this respect and it is difficult to generalise

Tropical species are often more sedentary in their behaviour and large terrestrial elapids such as cobras, black mamba and some Australian forms may mate and live out their lives in just a small section of habitat, providing this can give enough food and shelter for sufficiently viable breeding individuals.

The majority of snake species are oviparous (egg-laying), whilst others are viviparous (live-bearing). With regard to the venomous species it can be generally stated that the elapids and colubrids are typically egg-layers and that the vipers are live-bearers. There are, however, exceptions on both sides; the ringhals cobra of southern Africa and some species of sea snakes are examples of elapids that in fact are viviparous. Egg-laying vipers also exist, and the bushmaster of Central and South America, and the Malayan pit viper are notable examples. Vipers that exhibit both oviparity and viviparity are known to occur; the levantine viper, *Vipera lebetina*, normally a live-bearing species, is known to lay eggs in parts of its southern range.

New-born snakes are fully independent from birth and in the case of many of the vipers are mini replicas of the parent snakes. The young of colubrid and elapid snakes are often more brightly coloured, sometimes barred or blotched, whilst the parents may be of a uniform hue.

Snakes do not show any maternal attachment to their young and the same can be said of most species of reptile. However, the maternal actions of the Nile crocodile, *Crocodilus niloticus*, has recently been well documented on film, probably the most unlikely animal to have been attributed with any such instinct.

In the case of egg-laying snakes, the eggs are usually deposited in sand, leaf litter or other form of suitable substrate, and then left to incubate unattended, often to be dug up and eaten by some prowling predator.

The king cobra is a notable exception. This, the largest venomous snake in the world, constructs a nest of leaves, grass and twigs, which contains two chambers, an upper and a lower. The lower chamber contains the eggs, whilst the upper chamber houses the guarding female. It is at this time that it is said the king cobra is most likely to attack. However, people have passed very close to such nests oblivious of the snake's presence.

Growth and longevity

New-born snakes grow rapidly and are usually fully adult by their fourth year. However, it is not always a simple matter to determine sexual maturity in snakes. To determine the actual age when sexual maturity occurs with accuracy would mean mass post-mortem examination of individual snakes of varying sizes representing many species. This is of course a herculean task, but it has been accomplished with a few species (Fig. 50).

In southern England it was determined that any adder of 40 cm or over could safely be termed as adult. This, however, was determined by the examination of almost two hundred snakes of various age groups, the presence of sperm or ovaries being the determining factor.

With regard to most species we can only assume what is considered to be the average adult size for that particular species. Many observations of sexual maturity have largely been made with captive species. Some of these observations have provided a few surprises. At the Poole

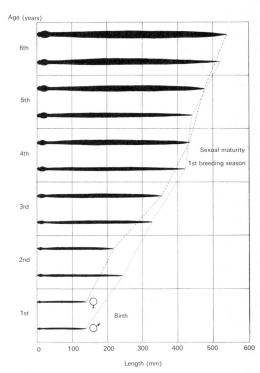

Fig. 50   The growth of the adder, *Vipera berus*, taken from field records for southern England.

Serpentarium in Dorset, England, a male puff adder just 50 cm in length successfully mated with a female some 100 cm in length. Considering that this species can grow to lengths in excess of 150 cm, then this would mean that the sexually mature members of a puff adder population would represent a very wide range of individual sizes. In addition, this particular female puff adder consequently gave birth to twenty-four young; three more in fact than after a previous mating with a 90 cm male. This is an interesting aspect; and it seems likely that the size and number of a litter are determined by the status of the mother. Henry Fitch in his paper on the copperhead states that in fact the size of new-born copperheads is determined by the health of the mother, and that many copperheads born in captivity for example are often stunted.

It is possible to induce rapid growth of snakes in captivity, and the small mature male mentioned above was in fact just a little over two years old.

The growth of snakes is less rapid when sexual maturity is reached, and once what can be termed as the average size for the species has been attained, growth is reduced drastically. When does a snake stop growing? The answer is that no one really knows. It is my own personal belief that snakes never in fact cease to grow, although in most cases growth over a certain length may be almost indiscernible each year. Although size can be related to age, in many instances there is a notable difference in attainable sizes of snakes from region to region amongst members of the same species. This sometimes suggests that growth may be more rapid in one area, perhaps because more favourable conditions exist. Although it is easy to make assumptions, I have noted that many individuals of the Malayan pit viper appeared to attain a larger size on plantations than those occurring in more 'natural' conditions. A more consistent food supply is the obvious conclusion, but again, this can only be properly assessed by long-term study.

The term 'average length' is in reality misleading. Current literature, field guides, etc., may tell you that a spitting cobra may grow to 200 cm, or a gaboon viper reach a size of 150 cm. In reality, one usually encounters individuals of half this size.

The black mamba is a large species and can grow to 360 cm, and I have in fact observed and even on occasion caught black mambas of 300 cm or more in length. However, there is a much greater abundance of this species in the size ranges from 180 to 210 cm. In fact, although several species are said to contain the largest individuals of their kind, it is much more usual to come across much smaller specimens. It is a fact that a bushmaster of 300 cm or a king cobra of 500 cm would be exceptions rather than common occurrences. Even so, a bushmaster 200 cm in length or a king cobra 400 cm in length are imposing creatures and well worthy of their status.

So, there would appear to be disagreement as to whether or not size is an accurate guide to age. With so many influences at work pertaining to habitat, climate, food, etc., it must be assumed that individuals of the same species may well exhibit differences in growth rate from region to region.

It was mentioned earlier that I believe that snakes continue to grow throughout their lives. This is sometimes difficult to ascertain in the wild, but is a relatively simple matter with regard to captive snakes. A forest cobra at the Poole Serpentarium has been in captivity for twenty-five years. This snake was originally caught in southern Kenya and at that time measured 120 cm. During its period in captivity this snake has fed well but has shown a tendency to fast for two months of the year. On measuring this cobra during the early part of 1980 it was found to be just under 210 cm, an increase of 90 cm over a period of twenty-five years!

The achievement of old age in snakes is determined by several factors. Firstly, a snake must be free of predators, or at least be successful in evading them, and these predatory elements do of course include man. Man in his role as super predator is a destroyer of habitat, and many snakes have been denied the achievement of old age simply because their environment has literally been torn up from under them.

Remote and isolated areas are the most likely places to find large old individuals. At the mention of such areas one tends to think of such places as the Amazon, or Papua New Guinea. However, I know of an area on the Isle of Wight in southern England where many individuals of an adder population are 70–80 cm in length. These are definitely old individuals, and it is well to remember that, apart from man, there are no habitual snake predators in Britain. In addition, the field guides tell us that the 'average' length of the adder is 50 cm, and that the maximum size is 60 cm.

Food and feeding

Snakes feed much less often than most other creatures, but this does not mean that they in fact consume less. Their capability of feeding on large prey items means that the actual food intake is comparable to that of most other carnivorous vertebrates.

Many species of venomous snake accept a wide range of prey and this range is extended by young individuals of some species which prey on completely different or less 'popular' food items. Young puff adders often feed on small frogs and toads whilst the adults definitely have a preference for warm-blooded prey.

Other species appear to be specialised feeders and only accept a narrow range of food. Some snakes are particularly adapted for specialised feeding; the non-venomous egg-eating snake, *Dasypeltis scabra*, of Africa is a well-known example. Some of the sea snakes feed solely on eels, or even just fish eggs. Many of the arboreal rear-fanged colubrids may be primarily lizard-feeders and it is these species that often prove difficult in captivity as they may refuse to be induced by alternative food. Other venomous snakes are well known as snake-eaters; the king cobra is perhaps the best known of all such snakes.

However, many species of venomous snakes can be described as opportunists with regard to feeding habits and will accept a wide range of food both cold and warm blooded. Most species of the genus *Naja* will prey on small mammals, birds, amphibians, lizards and other snakes. Other prey items generally acceptable to many species are eggs,

Fig. 51   Young puff adder, *Bitis arietans*, swallowing a small mouse. Young puff adders in the wild also consume a large amount of amphibian prey.

nestlings and fish. One species, the cottonmouth moccasin, is said to feed occasionally on carrion in the form of dead fish.

The front-fanged venomous snakes are probably the most efficient predators on earth. The ability to kill prey rapidly and without risk of injury is something few other creatures share. Even the so-called super predators such as the big cats often receive mortal wounds in their efforts to secure food; many a lion bears the scars from encounters with wildebeest or zebra.

Potential prey animals such as cane rats, or rock hyraxes, are powerful animals in their own right and if not subdued could inflict serious injuries to such species as the puff adder. In truth, such animals rarely see or are aware of their adversary. A puff adder will lie in wait beside a well-worn rodent path and suddenly strike as the prey passes. The puff adder will have inflicted a mortal wound and does not need to dash after the prey. There follows a leisurely follow-up to where the prey lies, warm but usually quite dead (Fig. 51).

The elapids are also efficient, albeit a little clumsy in comparison. Elapids will actively chase prey with great excitable darting and rushing; the prey is then seized and held in the jaws while the venom does its swift work. Mambas will often just 'pluck' a bird out of the air, as will boomslangs. Snakes will often 'raid' a nest of young birds or rodents and on such occasions there is no need for envenomation.

The frequency of feeding is of course dependent on the type of food; a night adder that feeds on toads will feed more often than a puff adder that feeds on large rodents. Even so, I once witnessed a night adder feed on three toads in quick succession.

There are also indications that many species exhibit a peak feeding period during a particular season; the erratic feeding of breeding females is one example, but this is certainly not applicable to all species.

Enemies and defence

Man is of course the greatest enemy of all snakes, mainly due to urban expansion and afforestation and other means of habitat destruction.

However, there are many other enemies of snakes including creatures that habitually prey on snakes. The mongoose is perhaps the most famous of all snake-hunters, but its prowess has been much exaggerated. Mammals that prey on snakes include the meerkat, honey badger, hedgehog, jungle cat and quite a number of other predatory

147

Fig. 52 Bateleur eagle,
Terathopius ecudatus. This
handsome bird of Africa, in
common with other raptors,
will often include snakes in its
diet.

mammals. However, only a relatively few of these can be described
as habitual snake-killers.

By far the most consistent snake predators are the raptors, the birds
of prey (Fig. 52). The most famous of these is the African secretary
bird, which resembles more a hybrid between a stork and an eagle
than a true raptor (Fig. 53). This bird is super-efficient at seeking out
such large species as cobra and puff adder. The wings are spread and
used as a decoy for the snake's fruitless strikes, then at the appropriate
moment the bird moves in and tramples the snake with the long stork-
like legs which are protected by their hard scales.

Other birds which prey on snakes include the hornbill (Fig. 54),
and several species of shrike, or butcher bird as they are also called.

Very young snakes are vulnerable to predation. New-born adders,
for example, have been taken by thrushes and even shrews. In fact,
the mortality of young snakes is very high and is thought to be as much
as 80 per cent in some species during the first three years of life.

The humble domestic cat often becomes an efficient predator of
snakes; a cat in Dorset in southern England was reputed to have caught

Fig. 53   Secretary bird,
Sagittarius serpentarius, a
highly efficient snake predator
of the African plains.

and killed some sixty adders until one particularly large adder put an end to this feline's ophidian adventures.

Most people are of the opinion that a venomous snake's first line of defence is to bite. In fact, most venomous species will only strike as a last resort.

It should be remembered that the poison fang is primarily a means of securing prey and not for inflicting mortal wounds on every *Homo sapiens* that happens to wander by. The first line of defence for most snakes is immobility. Many snakes are difficult to detect on both the ground and in the trees. The large African vipers such as the gaboon viper and puff adder are sometimes virtually invisible on the ground where they lie. Unfortunately, this is sometimes their undoing as they often get trodden upon as a consequence and many people have been bitten in such circumstances, particularly by the puff adder.

In most cases, although the snake is probably aware of a threatening

Fig. 54   Great hornbill,
Buceros bicornis, an
omnivorous bird that will
prey on both snakes and
lizards in addition to its more
well-known diet of fruit.

149

presence, it will remain immobile; if then it feels threatened it will move off. If prevented from doing this or restrained in any way then it is likely that the snake will resort to biting. Some snakes may just use threatening behaviour such as the hood spreading of the cobra, the rattle of the rattlesnake, the scale rubbing of the saw-scaled viper and even the tail waving of the coral snakes.

Spitting cobras will eject their venom at any threatening object, be it man or bird, with little or no provocation. Other snakes, such as the ringhals cobra, will sham death, rolling over on its back with its mouth gaping and tongue lolling out.

Many species of venomous snakes when adult have few natural enemies, and those that exist only have an even chance of outmatching a large venomous snake. Even the notorious mongoose comes off worse on many occasions.

Temperament

Much has been said in past literature on the temperament of certain species: the aggressiveness of the mambas, the placid natures of the gaboon viper and the kraits, for example.

It is in fact impossible to generalise about the temperament of any species. This has been brought home to me by experience of many species both in the wild and in captivity.

The nature of the black mamba has been exaggerated. This species is without doubt a very dangerous snake indeed, but stories of unprovoked attacks and whole villages being wiped out by this snake are incredible. Firstly, the black mamba is a nervous creature, and is quickly provoked if cornered or interfered with. However, as with most snakes this species will make off in the opposite direction if allowed to do so. It must be true that snake-catchers who habitually seek out and restrain such species must observe the worst side of their nature. I have even had mambas held in a grabstick that still have refused to bite, just struggling desperately in their efforts to get away.

The green mamba is a placid species and due to its arboreal habits rarely encounters man—other than tree-climbing snake-catchers.

The gaboon viper is said to be a placid creature and I must admit that this species, although the largest viper of Africa, is easy to handle and very slow to become even slightly annoyed. However, I received a shipment containing several of this species and all went well until the last bag was tipped gently on to the floor. On this occasion a female gaboon viper of around 90 cm eased her bulk on to the floor from the bag in a leisurely fashion. Suddenly, this normally placid species, without warning, lunged at me and sunk her fangs into the toe of my boot. Luckily the leather was of good quality and the fangs did not penetrate. On another occasion which I and many others recall, at a meeting of a herpetological society in England a guest speaker tipped a gaboon viper on to the stage from which he was delivering his talk. This snake, which was about 80 cm in length, had hardly touched the stage when it made off in the manner of a much more agile species, much to everyone's consternation.

Another venomous species with a reputation for being docile is the banded krait. To anybody who thinks this I suggest they try and catch or handle one at dusk or night time. I can assure you that this species, which is indeed seemingly quite placid during the day, is an active and dangerous snake during the hours of darkness.

The reputation of many species of snakes is largely a matter of hearsay and I am only willing to judge from those people who have had actual experience with the species in question.

I have been lucky enough to observe and catch snakes in both the Old and New Worlds. The criteria for assessing a snake's temperament are quite simple; firstly, judging a snake's reaction to just being observed but aware of the observer, and secondly, the snake's reaction to being physically restrained. Using these criteria I have selected species with which I am familiar. These are as follows: the European adder, the levantine viper, the sand viper, the russells viper, the saw-scaled viper, the puff adder, the gaboon viper, the Asiatic cobra, the king cobra, the Egyptian cobra, the spitting cobra, the black mamba.

Of these species observed in the wild state all but two remained passive when observed but aware of my presence. The two exceptions were the saw-scaled viper, and the russells viper. Both of these species were ready to strike from the word go, and in fact on several occasions saw-scaled vipers have even advanced towards me, rubbing their scales furiously. When restrained all the species with the exception of the gaboon viper put up savage resistance.

The lesson to be learned from this is the golden rule: leave well alone, unless of course you are an experienced snake-handler.

More will be said later on the temperament of various species, but

I personally rate the saw-scaled viper as the most irascible snake in the world.

However, I have it on good authority from colleagues in the USA and South Africa, that both the barba amarilla and the Cape cobra need little provocation to initiate a meaningful attack.

7
Venom and Snakebite

Snakes, it would seem, have exceeded themselves by becoming top of the unpopularity polls in the ranks of the world's fauna. A snake's very appearance and bodily form is enough to send shivers of horror down the spines of many people, and the fact that some snakes can deliver a lethal bite to boot has safely assured these creatures a lowly place in the mind of prejudiced man.

It is a difficult, almost impossible, task to argue a case in support of venomous snakes, despite their place in the complex ecological chain and the fact that snake venoms are actually helping to save life. These arguments and others, which are all quite valid and reasonable, are of little consequence to the prejudiced mind—a snake is a snake, end of argument.

People in the so-called civilised Western world are often more prejudiced in their outlook towards snakes, and this is due to total ignorance. In Europe, for example, the adder poses little threat to most people, and is a creature that may be encountered on a picnic or a country walk. The sight of a snake for the first time in the wild can have a startling effect on some people, but most of us do tend to overreact at the sight of an adder, reactions which vary from shock to pure hysterics. It is strange that in the regions of the world where the real 'top snakes' occur—cobras, mambas, etc.—the local inhabitants have a much more philosophical view. This is not to say that they do not respect or fear snakes, but just that they have learned to live with them.

Why in fact are some snakes venomous? The term venomous indicates that a creature can secrete a poisonous substance by means of a bite or sting. Such creatures include spiders, scorpions, some species of fish, bees, hornets, wasps, and even some species of mammals, in addition to snakes and two species of lizards. This ability to deliver a venomous bite has two functions: protection and the acquisition of food.

Snake venoms are amongst the most complex of all biological toxins and are composed of numerous enzymatic substances. In fact, upwards of twenty different enzymes have been identified in snake venoms, although no one species possesses all of these. Most species possess between seven and ten different enzymes.

These various enzymes have different functions in their action when secreted and there is no one 'magic' substance in snake venom that accounts for its toxicity. Therefore, any type of venom is reliant on a multiple reaction to be effective. Modern science is now able to separate these enzymes and it is this fact that has made snake venom such a valuable substance in the field of modern drugs.

One mystery does in fact exist with regard to the amount of venom that each venomous snake possesses in relation to sizes and types of prey. A puff adder, for example, has enough venom in its glands to kill many rodents, and the king cobra has been known to kill an elephant. It is as if each snake had man in mind as an enemy as it evolved a capacity for storing large exaggerated amounts of venom.

The action of venom on living organisms is a highly complex affair and would be difficult to relate in simple terms. In general, there are firstly haemotoxin types which break down tissue, and are said to be typical of the viper family. Secondly, there are neurotoxin types which affect the central nervous system, and these are said to be typical of the elapids.

However, this is rather over-simplifying matters as there exists a great deal of overlap between all the groups of venomous snakes. They, in fact, have many individuals which possess both haemotoxic and neurotoxic factions in the venom. For example, the tropical rattlesnake of Central and South America has a positive neurotoxic faction in the venom, and the spitting cobra of western and eastern Africa has tissue-destructive factions in the venom. Table 4 lists some of the enzymes found in snake venom.

Snake venom, when expelled from the venom glands, is a viscous

Table 4

Some enzymes found in reptile venoms

	Biological action	*Source examples*
PROTEINASES	Aids digestion and breaks down proteins. Largely causes clotting in snakebite cases, also local gangrene	Most pit vipers, puff adder
L-AMINO ACID OXIDASE	Gives yellow colour to venom and aids digestion. Also activates other venom enzymes	Blunt-nosed viper, cotton-mouth
HYALURONIDASE	Dissolves tissue and enhances rapid absorption of venom	Most snake venoms, aspic viper, eastern diamond-back rattlesnake
CHOLINESTERASE	Probably a nerve depressant but true function uncertain	All elapid venoms, banded krait, forest cobra, brown snake
RIBONUCLEASE	Function in venom uncertain	Most snake venoms, Asiatic cobra, russells viper
PHOSPHOLIPASE A	Promotes histamine production in tissue. Also probably largely responsible for shock factor in snakebite	Black mamba, taipan, cotton-mouth
PHOSPHOMONESTERASE	Function in venom uncertain	Most elapid venoms, and some vipers. Egyptian cobra, waglers viper

fluid which can be yellowish, amber or pale straw in colour. There is some variation, even amongst snakes of the same species; for example, most juvenile snakes exhibit an almost colourless venom. Colourless venom is also typical of many sea snakes and some species of krait. The percentage of solids in venom varies and this is of course apparent by the actual viscosity of a particular venom.

Probably the most popular question with regard to venomous snakes is, 'Which is the most poisonous?' What the question usually means is, 'Which snake is the most deadly to man?' These are of course two entirely different questions, and it should be remembered that many snakes with highly toxic venom hardly rate in snakebite statistics.

If we take the first question concerning which snakes possess the most toxic venom, then a means must be established whereby venom

155

can be tested with some measure of accuracy. In the past various laboratory animals were used to test the values of snake venom, but nowadays the white mouse has become the standard medium for work involving animal toxins. Using snake venom on a set group of mice a result is obtained which represents half the lethal dose, which is known as the LD_{50}. This method on mice has shown that the beaked sea snake tops the list and is found to be twice as toxic as the Asiatic cobra. The Australian tiger snake and brown snake are also high on the list.

Some snakes exhibit marked differences in both toxicity and composition of the venom for members of the same species. The subspecies of the Asiatic cobra in the Philippines, for example, has a much more toxic venom than the other races, and in addition, antivenin produced in India is ineffective in treating the bite.

Venom extraction

The process of extracting the venom from snakes is often referred to as 'snake milking' and involves some skill and a little nerve, and quite a bit of knowledge about venomous snakes.

The actual art of handling snakes in such situations is dealt with in another chapter. Suffice to say that the snake is gently but firmly restrained and the fangs hooked over a beaker or other receptacle, and then encouraged to expel its venom (Fig. 55). This is often achieved by the snake itself, which understandably being annoyed will deliver its venom with angry chewing motions. However, the venom glands usually have to be squeezed gently to encourage the flow.

The demand for types of venom by the pharmaceutical industry usually only embraces a narrow range of species at any one time. This means, for example, that if the particular demand is for eastern diamondback venom then venom extraction laboratories will usually pool the venom from a number of snakes into one receptacle. This is very efficient, but one obvious disadvantage is that one snake may have a mouth infection which could spoil the entire batch. It is of paramount importance to inspect the mouth of each snake prior to extraction and to use an antiseptic swab on both receptacle and snake after extraction.

The uses of snake venoms fall mainly into two categories: firstly, its use in the research and development, and actual manufacture of modern drugs; and secondly, as the necessary ingredient for the production of antivenin for the treatment of snakebite. Much of the latter

156

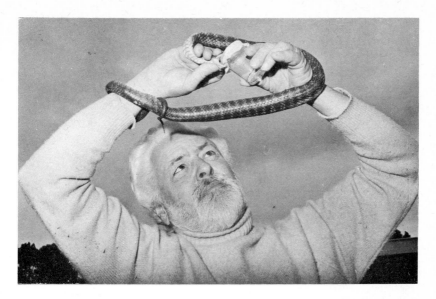

Fig. 55   Eric Worrell, the director of the Australian Reptile Park, milking a tiger snake for venom research.

demand is fulfilled on a local basis; that is to say, antivenin produced in Australia, South Africa and Asia is mainly dependent on venom supplies from within these countries.

However, major drug houses in Europe do produce antivenin which covers species on a worldwide basis. In the past, and even today, these European drug houses have been reliant on procuring venom from source, i.e. the country of origin. These sources were often found to be unreliable, and it was partly for this reason that the Poole Serpentarium Laboratories became established in southern England during 1979. At the time of writing the Serpentarium houses fifty different species of venomous snakes which represent a variety of types from Europe, Asia, Africa and North and South America (Fig. 56).

The economic success of a venom extraction enterprise is dependent on pure market research. Although demand for the many types of venoms varies usually only a dozen or so species are actually being used for extraction at any one time. Snakes can be expensive to purchase and import charges and freight can be costly, so it is essential to concentrate on those species that are in current demand.

If drug houses are looking for particular enzyme sources for research

Table 5

Some venom yields for venomous snakes

(From data taken from the Poole Serpentarium Laboratories)

Species	Yield (milligrams)	Lethal dose for man (milligrams)
Banded krait Bungarus fasciatus	20–80	Not known, bites very rare
Black mamba Dendroaspis polyepis	50–100	10
Asiatic cobra Naja naja	100–300	20
Egyptian cobra Naja haje	150–350	25
Spitting cobra Naja nigricollis	150–350	50
Puff adder Bitis arietans	150–250	100
Gaboon viper Bitis gabonica	350–600	60
Saw-scale viper Echis carinatus	15–40	5
Blunt-nosed viper Vipera lebetina	60–150	70
Cottonmouth Agistrodon piscivorous	80–180	100
Malayan pit viper Agkistrodon rhodostoma	40–60	40
Barba amarilla Bothrops atrox	80–200	50
Eyelash viper Bothrops schlegelii	10–20	15
Pope's pit viper Trimeresurus popeorum	10–20	Not lethal
Waglers pit viper Trimeresurus wagleri	60–100	No information
Mojave rattlesnake Crotalus scutulatus	40–100	15
Western diamondback rattlesnake Crotalus atrox	200–300	100
Eastern diamondback rattlesnake Crotalus adamanteus	300–500	150

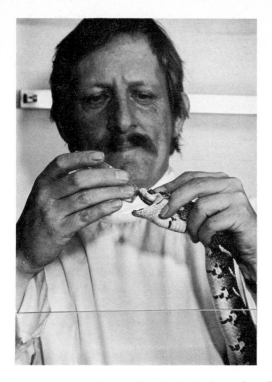

Fig. 56   The author taking a sample of venom from a puff adder, *Bitis arietans*, at the Poole Serpentarium.

or drug manufacture then it is obvious that the relevant species should be chosen with regard to the quantity of the yield. Gaboon vipers, eastern diamondback rattlesnakes, Asiatic cobras and banded kraits are all examples of high-yielding snakes, and these, and other high-yielding snakes, should be chosen wherever possible.

Although antivenin exists for most species of venomous snake there is still much scope for producing specific antivenins; many species are still only covered by polyvalent antivenins which may embrace venomous snakes from an entire region or country. Specific antivenins require specific venoms and it would be an awesome task to house and extract the venom from the many species involved. Luckily, the market does not usually work like that, and drug manufacturers can limit their efforts to perhaps one or two species at any one time. This is perhaps just as well as some species of reptiles are not always readily available. However, it is true to say that several species will be in demand for some time to come and, with good husbandry, breeding techniques should be enhanced which will ensure the maintenance of captive stocks. The reason why the Poole Serpentarium holds so many different species of venomous snakes is that many of these are on show to the public in the reptile house and, in addition, many are used in public displays of venom extraction. This of course means that there are extra funds from the actual gate money which a normal laboratory would be denied.

The processing of venom at the Poole Serpentarium Laboratories is quite simple. The venom is placed in a desiccator over silica gel and dried in a high vacuum. It is then placed in a cool dark place for several days and the process is repeated. The venom is then scraped into granule or 'needle' form, packed and stored in a refrigerator until shipped.

The methods of processing venom are varied. Some institutions freeze-dry (lyophilise) venom and others place the venom into a centrifuge. Others extract venom into a receptacle packed with ice, as venom loses its potency at room temperature and above. At Poole I extract venom in a cool room which also has an obvious quietening effect on the snake.

Some institutions concentrate on one particular species that may be in demand, particularly for drug manufacture. Twyford Pharmaceutical Services of West Germany extract the venom from sixty Malayan pit vipers daily. This venom is used principally for the manufacture of 'Arvin', a drug now used to treat such ailments as coronary occlusion. This venom has a high anti-coagulant factor.

Snakebite

Man is without doubt the greatest enemy of snakes, but even so the sophisticated venom apparatus, which has some obvious importance as a defensive weapon, evolved long before man appeared on this earth. It is, then, somewhat of an enigma to learn that man is so highly susceptible to many snake venoms.

Snakebite is an emotive subject which is shrouded in myth, folklore and other exaggerated misconceptions. It is without doubt a traumatic event; even the dedicated herpetologist would find it difficult to suffer a serious bite with calm dignity. However, the chances are that if you are bitten you will not die, however unpleasant the symptoms.

Snakebite is not an exceptionally unusual event, even in Europe, but most of us tend to assume that most cases are fatal. Actual mortalities as a result of snakebite are much rarer and are more typical of

Third World countries, and to some extent countries such as Australia, where the venomous snake population is high. In most parts of the western world the majority of the population rarely if ever encounter snakes. Only agricultural workers, forestry staff and others engaged in pursuits which take them to 'snake' areas present themselves to any element of danger.

However, the present trend is for city people to flock to the countryside at weekends and holidays, and many are obviously ignorant of 'country ways' and even the existence of venomous snakes. It is a fact that people in Europe and North America that get bitten are those that attempt to pick up a venomous snake or else encroach upon the countryside with inadequate footwear.

Snakebite is much more of a hazard in countries such as Africa, Asia and Central and South America, where many people have to cope with snakes literally in their own backyard. Many cases of snakebite in the Third World are suffered when people are at their place of work, either on plantations or working the fields with hand implements.

Actual snakebite statistics are usually unreliable, especially when attempting to attribute cases to specific species. A bite from a non-venomous snake can be painful and can result in shock symptoms—the so-called victim being convinced that he or she has suffered a serious venomous bite.

It is often advised that the offending snake should be killed so identification can be accurately concluded. However, whilst it can be appreciated that this would greatly enhance the speed and method of treatment, there have been cases where further bites have been received in an attempt to kill the snake. Furthermore, there would be little point in killing an adder in England, or any other area where only one species of venomous snake is indigenous.

Many people who are bitten do not even see the offending snake; a woman gathering firewood may suddenly feel a stabbing pain in her finger, and although she probably knows that she has been bitten by a snake her immediate reaction is to seek help. By the time others come to seek out the snake the probability is that it has crawled away. Similarly, people often tread on snakes during the hours of darkness. The fact is that if a person is seriously bitten by a venomous snake it will soon become obvious and characteristic symptoms will appear which will be a guide to diagnosis of type of envenomation.

However, it would be wrong to describe a case of typical snakebite as there are so many variables. The most important fact is that we now know that many snakes can actually control their venom output when biting. This means that there is in fact such a thing as a non-venomous bite from a potentially lethal species. This aspect is more typical of some of the viper family; the delayed action of some of the elapid venoms is well known, and the last thing this book wishes to do is to encourage complacency.

Many cases of snakebite never find their way into an official record, and in much of the Third World may be of only local concern. Therefore the figures for the annual mortality worldwide are usually thought to be too low. In 1954 the World Health Organisation (Swaroop and Grab) estimated the annual mortality of 30,000 to 40,000, with a total incidence of around 300,000. The gathering of such data is a haphazard affair when much information is reliant on untrained personnel in remote areas.

It is my own belief that most statistics can be safely discarded, especially when one considers that the still quoted death rate each year in India, 20,000, is based on information gleaned in 1869! Nowadays with modern treatments one can safely halve that number.

Probably the highest incidence of snakebite is exemplified in the Ryukyu Islands where there is about one case per five hundred people.

It is obvious that venomous snakes do present a very real hazard in areas of the Third World and actual incidents can usually be correlated with density and proximity of both human and snake populations.

Bites by members of the viper family are very painful (Figs 57–8). The immediate sensation is an intense burning pain at the site of

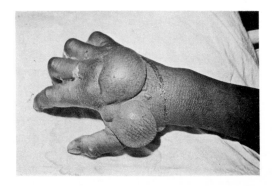

Fig. 57　The effects of puff adder bite showing local swelling and blistering.

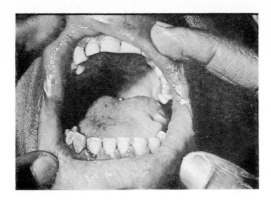

Fig. 58 Saw-scaled viper bite, showing the typical symptoms of bleeding from the gums.

the bite followed by numbness of the affected part which may eventually become gangrenous. The absorption of the venom is accompanied by local swelling which spreads along the stricken limb. There may be severe pain in the kidneys with much vomiting. However, symptoms vary and all is dependent on the amount of venom injected. Antivenin should only be used when envenomation has been confirmed, remembering that it is possible that little or no venom may have been absorbed.

The symptoms of elapid bite are not so apparent as that of viper

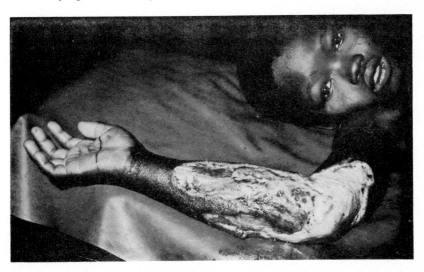

Fig. 59   Effects of a bite from the spitting cobra, *Naja nigricollis*, showing local gangrene, a symptom not usually associated with elapid envenomation.

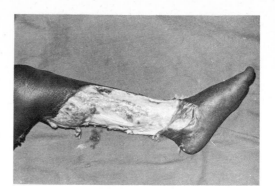

Fig. 60   Gangrene caused by
the bite of the spitting cobra,
showing the sloughing of
gangrenous tissue.

envenomation. Firstly, there is little pain at the actual site of the bite
and true symptoms do not begin until at least fifteen minutes afterwards. The first serious indication that the bite is a serious one is the
drooping of the eyelids, difficulty in swallowing and slurred speech.
This is accompanied by giddiness, and a pronounced gasping. In some
cases of elapid bites the symptoms do not become apparent until up
to six hours after the bite (Figs 59, 60).

During the years that I have been involved with venomous snakes
I have been bitten three times by 'exotic' species, and twelve times
by the European adder. The most serious bite occurred in Kenya
where I was bitten on the right hand by a large puff adder; this cost
me six weeks in hospital and a nice scar. I have also been bitten in
the calf by a western diamondback rattlesnake and just under the eye
by a pope's pit viper.

All these bites occurred in the field and were, in my own estimate,
a result of carelesness. However, the odds are quite good, as I have
captured and marked over 5000 European adders, numerous African,
Asian and American front-fanged snakes, which include black mamba,
puff adder, saw-scaled viper, gaboon viper, king cobra, tropical rattlesnakes and eastern diamondback rattlesnakes.

In addition to exploits in the field I have extracted the venom from
40,000 front-fanged snakes. With this in mind it must be true that
the people who invoke the highest incidence of snakebite must be those
who work with venomous snakes for a living.

8

Snakes and Man

The present-day relationship between snakes and man has its roots deep in past history dating back to prehistoric times. Early man could appreciate the lethal danger of the large carnivores for example, but such a terrifying death from such a relatively small creature as a venomous snake must have appeared quite mysterious and sinister.

It is little wonder that so much myth and superstition has accumulated over several millennia, and this is reflected in the cults and religious festivals that have their origins in serpent lore. These contemporary 'snake activities' are alive and well; some are exemplified by tribal rituals such as can be seen in parts of Asia, or else such events as the famous Hopi snake dance where live rattlesnakes are used. However, the latter has more or less adopted the status of just a tourist attraction, and many of the venomous snakes have been substituted for such harmless species as the non venomous gopher snake.

During the passage of history snakes have been associated with such aspects as supreme power, wisdom and fertility (both human and agricultural), and in addition many species of snake have been bestowed with certain curative powers.

Venomous snakes have also figured as a means of warfare; Hannibal masterminded the scheme to have jars of live snakes thrown into the Pergamenian ships, a tactic that brought about victory. In the seventeenth century there were accounts of Amerindians infiltrating basket loads of venomous snakes to Martinique in the West Indies where they were at war with the native population. Whether or not this resulted in the present populations of venomous snakes on the island is uncertain. *Bothrops atrox*, the mainland species, differs somewhat from the fer-de-lance, *B. lanceolatus*, which is endemic to Martinique.

Close relationships between man and snakes is probably best illustrated by the art of snake charming which is practised in many parts of the world in some form or other. However, the peak of this profession is witnessed in India and South East Asia where the 'charmers' show great skill and knowledge with regard to the handling and the actual habits of their captives. Doubtful elements exist in some areas whereby snakes have been mutilated in an attempt to 'defang' them, or else in some instances the lips of the snakes have been wired together to prevent them from biting.

The actual 'kit' of the snake-charmer is familiar to most people—the gourd flute and baskets are stock in trade of most oriental snake-charmers. All the objects of the snake-charmer's trade are usually transported around in gaily coloured bags. The actual performance is variable, it may be quite basic, or else rather elaborate, including other fakir arts such as fire-eating and sword-swallowing. In cities it is very important that the performer chooses his site well, and a performance usually takes place outside a large hotel or perhaps a railway station.

The classical part of the performance involves the seated flute-player with the swaying cobra before him, giving the illusion that the snake is in all appearance responding to the music. Snakes are, of course, deaf to airborne sounds and the snake is only responding to subtle movements of the snake-charmer himself. These consist of slow head movements, and a subtle movement of the feet co-ordinated with a change in pitch or tempo can result in the illusion that the snake is really responding to the music. This is because an erect cobra is perceptive to any movement and its focal interest can change direction accordingly.

Other snakes used in these performances include species such as large rat snakes, sand boas, saw-scaled vipers and russells vipers.

The practice of snake-charming is by no means restricted to men—women often participate in performances with equal skill. In certain regions of Burma girls use king cobras in a performance which reaches its peak when the girl bends over and kisses the erect cobra on top of the head. These girls capture their own snakes and are said to treat them with great care and affection. In addition, each snake is eventually returned to its place of origin.

The art of snake-charming is of course not without risk, and quite a number of ophidian entrepreneurs do get bitten, often with serious consequences.

Other snake entertainments include staged fights between cobra and mongoose or other equally bizarre spectacles. In many parts of North America rattlesnake sideshows are a familiar sight; some of these can be quite educational as they exhibit species found in a particular region. Others, however, are just sensational pulls for the tourist and many rattlesnakes may be mutilated by crude defanging methods.

The attitude of people in the Western world towards snakes can be summed up quite simply: the majority either hate or fear snakes; many, however, tolerate them; and a tiny minority are actually fond of them. To most people the distinction between a venomous and non-venomous snake is irrelevant as it is the very appearance of a snake that usually turns people cold. A fear of snakes is very real in many cases and people who suffer from 'ophidiaphobia' should be given the respect that they deserve as no amount of education or familiarisation will have any useful effect. Many of my friends who lecture regularly with live snakes often relate that there is usually one person who is likely to become hysterical if approached too closely with snake in hand. Many people, however, can be 'converted' by skilful and informative persuasion. It is certainly wrong to force a snake on to someone who has definitely no desire to touch or hold the creature. Such an action can have lasting effects on people; even the innocent practice of the little boy chasing the girls with a live snake can result in serious consequences which may not be wholly apparent at the time.

People who tolerate snakes are typical of some country folk or naturalists who, although they probably fear snakes, realise that these much maligned creatures are a necessary part of the way of things in the complex world of nature.

The worst kind of 'snake haters' are those people who actively persecute snakes by killing each one they see, be it harmless or otherwise. However, it must be true to say that most people in the so-called civilised world will never see a snake in the wild.

Mention must also be made here of the famous rattlesnake roundups which take place in parts of the south western states of North America.

These occasions are a mixture of skill, stupidity and persecution. All sections of the community are invited to participate, including children, hence the stupidity, and some even have a booby prize for those that are bitten.

The height of stupidity, however, has been exemplified recently when on several occasions individuals have 'sat in' for long periods in a confined space with such species as puff adders, cobras, black mambas and boomslangs. The actual point of this exercise is certainly beyond me, but the occasion did little to promote the science of herpetology. My own skills with regard to handling and dealing with venomous snakes has been a result of respect and there is no way that I would ever allow a black mamba to perch on my head!

Many people do have a rapport with snakes and their skills are to be admired. Some people are of the opinion that you have to be mad, or at least a little insane, to even contemplate handling a venomous snake. There are in fact quite a number of us who handle venomous snakes as part of our daily routine whether it be in the field of the laboratory. Susan Goebels, who works for Twyford Pharmaceutical Services, extracts the venom from up to sixty Malayan pit vipers each day of her working week.

Venomous snakes are not handled for the fun of it, and in reptile collections the handling of venomous snakes is kept to a minimum. There is of course the element of danger and most of us who handle venomous snakes on a regular basis have received the odd bite or two. In fact, many snake-handlers boast about the number of times they have been bitten, hardly a recommendation of their own skills.

During the years that I have been involved with venomous snakes I have met many 'snake men' who have been characters in their own right. Probably the most famous of these was the late C. J. P. Ionides, or 'Bwana Nyoka', whose life story is so aptly dealt with in *Snake Man* by Alan Wykes. Ionides spent much of the latter part of his life in southern Tanzania where he caught literally thousands of gaboon vipers, and numerous other kinds of venomous snakes such as puff adders, black and green mambas, and spitting cobras. In fact, I still have all his letters during the time that we corresponded, which are full of information with regard to the habits and details of his daily catches. Ionides, in addition to his snake-catching activities, contributed much to our knowledge with regard to the herpetofauna of Africa.

Many of the well-known names in herpetology are no longer with us, but these people have left an indelible mark on the subject as a result of a lifetime's work and dedication.

The late Raymond Ditmars was one of the first to produce a popular treatise on the subject with his book *Reptiles of the World*, which was followed by another publication, *Snakes of the World*. Both these books received popular acclaim, and even today, although much of the information is out of date, they remain a valuable source of information, as well as making extremely enjoyable reading.

Perhaps the most classic treatise ever produced is the monumental work on rattlesnakes by the late Laurence Klauber. This two-volume work covers every aspect concerning the rattlesnakes and takes pride of place in the library of any herpetologist.

In fact, when one thinks of prominent names in herpetology North America figures highly, with such people as Gloyd, Holbrook, Noble and others. The work of most herpetologists has been concentrated in their own countries of residence, and as a result when we think of the snake fauna of a particular region it is usually allied with a well-known name in herpetological circles. The snake fauna of Africa has undergone much study and when we think of South Africa the name of V. F. FitzSimons will undoubtedly come to mind. In addition to producing many publications regarding the reptile fauna of the region, V. F. FitzSimons also founded the Durban Snake Park, which is a major source for venom in the production of antivenin for all species of African venomous snake.

Several people have made their mark on the snake fauna of eastern Africa. The publication *A Guide to the Snakes of Uganda* by C. R. S. Pitman is a major work of which the title is misleading, as it would prove invaluable to any African herpetologist.

Other leading herpetological figures include Eric Worrell, who is the Director of the Australian Reptile Park at Gosford, NSW. The principal function of the park is the collection and processing of venom obtained from Australian venomous snakes. Another leading Australian herpetologist is Harold Cogger, whose book *Reptiles and Amphibians of Australia* is now a major work of reference to all students of herpetology.

Competent handlers of venomous snakes in Britain are something of a rare breed and most of them I list as personal friends. James Ashe, one-time curator of the Nairobi Snake Park, is widely experienced in

handling and milking many kinds of venomous snakes. Jim has recently returned to Africa, where no doubt he will find even more scope
for his skills. Roger Ainsley is a quiet unassuming fellow who is in
charge of the reptile house at Chester Zoo. In addition to being skilled
in the handling of venomous snakes he also has the knack of inducing
many of his charges to breed. At the Zoological Society of London
the venomous snakes come under the care of David Ball and Brian
Savage, both highly skilled in the art of handling venomous snakes.

One of the most colourful characters to emerge from the realm of
snakemen is George ('Snaky') Williams (Figs 61–2). George is barely
five feet tall and sports a goatee beard. He handles a five-metre king
cobra with the confidence of a small boy handling a harmless garter
snake. George has also simulated the Burmese snake-charming act by

Fig. 61 George 'Snaky'
Williams, versus king cobra,
Ophiophagus hannah.

Fig. 62   The moment of no return; George Williams prepares to 'kiss' the king.

actually kissing a king cobra on the top of the head. He now lives a more peaceful life in Bournemouth and has pronounced himself as retired, but he is a regular visitor to the Poole Serpentarium which is almost on his doorstep.

In North America Bill Haast of the Miami Serpentarium has probably extracted the venom from more snakes than any other man. Also in Florida is Ross Allen of St Augustine, who has handled thousands of eastern diamondback rattlesnakes.

There are many more that I could mention, people who have the nerve and the skill to render a potentially dangerous snake temporarily impotent, and in addition there are many scientists and naturalists who work with venomous snakes in the field, marking and measuring the subjects of their particular study. Even so, these dedicated people are in the minority, and the majority of mankind will continue to fear and loathe snakes.

However, it is also a fact that the reptile house is usually the most popular exhibit within a zoological garden. People would seem to enjoy being frightened, to be able to witness the subject of their own prejudice safely through thick plate glass.

171

People often ask, of what use are snakes? Such a question is born from the simple 'if we don't like them why do we need them?' type of attitude. If the world's fauna were a matter of personal choice by mankind in general the result would be utter chaos. Imagine a world without most of the insects, scavenging animals, sharks and the other animals that repel most people.

No one animal can live in isolation, and that includes man. We are part of a delicate chain whether we like it or not. If all the snakes disappeared from the earth tomorrow, we would be overrun with rats, mice and voles in a very short while; even the more attractive birds of prey and small predatory mammals would not be able to cope with the sudden surplus. This in turn would mean that man's crops would be devastated and massive food shortages would follow.

Snakebite is, of course, a very real hazard, but on balance snake and man are about even. The odds will become more in the snake's favour as far as public opinion is concerned with regard to the development of new drugs as a result of research into venoms.

However, eventually snakes will be the losers as the wild places are fast disappearing as man encroaches more and more into the rain forests and other vital refuges. Survival lies in a species' ability to adapt to these changes and there is no doubt that many species will be successful toward this end. This will mean that the relationship between snakes and man will become an even closer association, but I suspect that man will be the more unwilling partner.

9
Poisonous Snakes in Captivity

Venomous snakes are kept in captivity for a number of reasons that fall into three main groups.

Firstly, quite a number of institutions, laboratories, universities and museums, hold venomous snakes for research and medical purposes. Some of these institutions have already been mentioned, and include large pharmaceutical companies where specific species are held for the acquisition of venom which provides the basic material for the development of new drugs and the basis for manufacture of existing drugs.

The production of antivenin has resulted in a number of institutions holding large numbers of venomous snakes, often strategically placed in areas where snakebite is common. In Central and South America where the incidence of snakebite is quite high, antivenin institutions exist in Mexico, Honduras, Colombia, Venezuela, Brazil and Argentina. All these institutions cover the potentially dangerous species such as *Bothrops*, *Crotalus*, *Lachesis* and *Micrurus*.

Many institutions produce a polyvalent antivenin which may cover a number of species found in a particular region, but its effectiveness in some cases is doubtful. Specific antivenin is, of course, the ideal answer, but this must be co-ordinated with particular species/incidence information. This is often difficult to determine with any accuracy due to such factors as scant and unreliable data from remote areas. In such cases a polyvalent antivenin must be used. South America is a classic example of this problem; the barba amarilla (*Bothrops atrox*) is a major cause of snakebite due to its abundance, but it also shares a range with other potentially dangerous snakes which bear many similar characterisitics.

In regions of the world where the species of venomous snakes are restricted to one or two types the incidence of snakebite is more readily identified. In Israel, for example, the Palestine viper accounts for almost all cases of snakebite, due mainly to its abundance around human habitation. Consequently, the Wellcome Research Laboratories at Tikva have produced a specific antivenin for this species. Furthermore, a specific antivenin has also been produced for Israel's other potentially dangerous species, the saw-scaled viper.

Other major sources of antivenin include the Haffkine Institute of Bombay, the University of Tokyo, Behringwerke AG of Germany and the Commonwealth Serum Laboratories in Melbourne.

The second group of snakes to be found in captivity are those to be seen in the many public reptile houses and snake parks distributed throughout the world and includes some previously mentioned institutions that have opened their doors to the public.

In the warmer parts of the world, snake exhibitions are often dis-

Fig. 63 Port Elizabeth Snake Park, where the snakes and other reptiles are on view to the public in large outdoor enclosures.

Fig. 64   Members of the public receive an insight into venomous snakes and venoms at the Poole Serpentarium.

played in the open air in outdoor pits or similar enclosures. Some of the more well known are the Durban and Port Elizabeth Snake Parks of South Africa (Fig. 63), the Instituto Butantan in São Paulo, Brazil, and the Madras Snake Park Trust in India.

Most of the major zoological collections boast a reptile display of one sort or other and this is usually in the form of a specially designed building for the purpose of housing mainly exotic species. The world's zoological gardens usually exhibit a wide range of reptiles including turtles, crocodiles and lizards, in addition to both non-venomous and venomous species of snakes. Some of the public exhibits are more specialised; the Miami Serpentarium in Florida and the Poole Serpentarium in southern England (Fig. 64), for example, exhibit mainly venomous snakes.

The third and final group of venomous snakes in captivity covers those kept by private individuals. Emotive discussions on this issue are usually provoked by neighbours with little or no sympathy for snakes.

In many countries the keeping of venomous snakes, and indeed other potentially dangerous animals, is governed by law, and various types of legislation exist which impose certain strict conditions, and often hefty fees, on would-be keepers of venomous snakes. However unsatisfactory these laws may appear, they are to be applauded. Firstly, we must accept that there are genuine applicants who are knowledgeable and skilled in the ways of venomous snakes, and in fact these people would have little trouble in obtaining the necessary licence providing each authority responsible interprets the law in a consistent manner. This in fact has not been the case in Britain when in recent years the 'Dangerous Wild Animals Act' was implemented. The main problem has been highlighted by the variation in annual fees imposed on individual herpetologists, and these have ranged from £10 to £150.

Legislation concerning this aspect does indeed cause many moans and groans amongst snake-keepers, but it must be said that this type of restriction will discourage the doubtful elements which were commonplace prior to any legal intervention.

Many people today keep pythons, boas and other harmless snakes within the confines of their homes just as others may keep tropical fish. However, I cannot appreciate why anyone should want to keep a rattlesnake or puff adder in a domestic situation. The only satisfactory method of keeping venomous snakes at home is by using an outbuilding, a mini reptile house if you like, where proper safety and security measures can be guaranteed.

Acquisition of venomous snakes

The average person must often wonder how zoological gardens come by their stocks of exotic reptiles; it is certainly a question that I am often asked by members of the general public.

It may well surprise many people to learn that dealers exist in many parts of the Western world who trade exclusively in exotic reptiles. These are usually offered to retail custom, wholesale to pet shops and to the zoo fraternity. The traffic of exotic reptiles begins, of course, in the country of origin where the activities of the various traders vary from good to downright disgusting. South East Asia is a prime example of how varied traders can be, and this quality is reflected in the condition of the animals at their destination and the quality and nature of crating and packing. Shipments from some of the more doubtful dealers in South East Asia are often accompanied by a very strong smell, a powerful indication that a percentage of the contents have not survived the journey. This is a situation that, literally, 'gets up the nose' of customs officials.

These activities can be discouraged by just dealing only with reliable elements in the reptile trade; that is, those who have supplied two or more shipments in a good healthy condition.

Many reptile houses are conscientious in their husbandry of the reptiles in their care, and many individual species tend to be long-lived in such situations. Zoos do not often ship their requirements direct as they cannot usually warrant the quantity to make this exercise profitable. Therefore most zoos are reliant on the dealer that exists locally and who imports shipments of snakes on a regular basis. These dealers are numerous in the USA and Britain, and most of them either distribute a regular stock list or else advertise in the relevant publications.

Snakes are not cheap to buy. A gaboon viper or a black mamba, for example, may cost £40 (80 dollars) or more, and a king cobra may fetch a price of £100 (200 dollars) at the time of writing. Many of us who maintain snake collections in a temperate climate must envy the snake parks of Africa, Asia and South America with so much material readily on the doorstep, as it were. Even so, the snake parks of the warmer parts of the world may have too little time to procure their own specimens and many are dependent on local snake-catchers, who of course have to be paid.

There is, however, another method of acquiring snakes for reptile collections. With patience, and expert husbandry, many species can be induced to breed in captivity. This ultimately results in a surplus which may be offered to other institutions for exchange. In fact, one of the most pleasurable aspects of a reptile curator's job is the liaison between various reptile-orientated institutions worldwide. Many of the snake parks and reptile houses communicate with each other, which enables each and every one to be aware of each other's problems and needs. For example, at the Poole Serpentarium the ottomans vipers (*Vipera xanthina*) produce at least two broods each year. Recently, the Serpentarium received a contract to supply venom from the eastern diamondback rattlesnake—a species not in stock. It took just one letter to arrange the exchange of a number of young ottomans vipers for a number of eastern diamondback rattlesnakes.

This is just one example, and no reptile house or snake park can

Table 6

Venomous snakes bred at the Poole Serpentarium 1978–1980

		Incubation
COLUBRIDAE		
Mangrove snake	*Boiga dendrophila*	80 days
ELAPIDAE		
Egyptian cobra	*Naja haje*	75 days
Monocled cobra	*Naja naja kaouthia*	64 days
Black mamba	*Dendroaspis polyepis*	96 days
VIPERIDAE		
Viperinae		
European adder	*Vipera berus*	Live birth
Sand viper	*Vipera ammodytes ammodytes*	Live birth
Sand viper	*Vipera ammodytes meridionalis*	Live birth
Blunt-nosed viper	*Vipera lebetina*	Live birth
Asp viper	*Vipera aspis*	Live birth
Ottomans viper	*Vipera xanthina xanthina*	Live birth
Palestine viper	*Vipera palaestinae*	Live birth
Saw-Scaled viper	*Echis carinatus*	Live birth
Puff adder	*Bitis arietans*	Live birth
Gaboon viper	*Bitis gabonica*	Live birth
Crotalinae		
Malayan pit viper	*Agkistrodon rhodostoma*	30 days
Cottonmouth	*Agkistrodon piscivorous*	Live birth
Mangrove pit viper	*Trimeresurus purpureomaculatus*	Live birth
Pope's pit viper	*Trimeresurus popeorum*	Live birth
Green pit viper	*Trimeresurus albolabris*	Live birth
Grand Canyon rattlesnake	*Crotalus viridis abyssus*	Live birth
Mojave rattlesnake	*Crotalus scutulatus*	Live birth
Western diamondback rattlesnake	*Crotalus atrox*	Live birth
Pygmy rattlesnake	*Sistrurus miliarus barbouri*	Live birth

afford to exist in isolation. Apart from the valuable asset of procuring stock, much information can be gleaned on a worldwide basis.

Housing

The many species of venomous snakes exhibit a wide range of individual requirements with regard to housing in captive conditions. Light,

178

heat and space are just the very basic requirements, and the whole concept of containing snakes in captivity is a rather more complex affair.

Snakes that are on display to the public must be housed with an additional factor in mind—the aesthetic quality which will appeal to visitors and show a particular species to best advantage. It is not always possible to meet the requirements of both snake and public. For example, a coral snake placed in a vivarium with deep substrate will result in an empty cage as far as visitors are concerned as the animal will spend much of its time underground. The answer in such a case is to strike a balance whereby the coral snake feels secure but is still visible to the public. The easiest way out for some reptile houses would be not to keep coral snakes. However, many other interesting species of venomous snakes are inclined to burrow, and these include the kraits and other fossorial elapids. One method of maintaining burrowing types in full view of the public is to lay a piece of Perspex horizontally on the floor of the vivarium with enough space beneath to admit the body of the snake and leaving gaps at either end. This gives the snake security as it can feel the pressure on its back, and as far as it is concerned the snake is safely 'underground'.

It is a fact that one of the main problems that face reptile curators is to equate the needs of the reptile with the needs of the public. One of the major factors that have caused 'fits of horror' from the general public is the aspect of cage size in relation to the animal interned. In many instances this criticism is quite valid, but there are certain cases where first impressions could be misleading. The first mistake that members of the general public make is to assume that reptiles and other animals are our psychological equals and that they react emotionally to confined conditions in a similar manner to the human prisoner. Snakes, for example, given the right conditions do not suffer from any stress factor except to appear agitated perhaps when introduced into the vivarium. The settling-in process varies from species to species but usually lasts for a very short period.

Most snake men are familiar with a 'fresh' cobra that rears and strikes at the glass for perhaps several hours when first introduced into a vivarium. However, this aggressive behaviour is not a reaction to the nature of its new quarters, but to the figure standing on the other side of the glass! If a blanket is placed over the glass even the most aggressive snake will become subdued, once it is assured that the object of aggression has gone.

Many species of viper are notably sedentary by nature and it would suffice to house them in a small container. The Malayan pit viper, for example, could exist quite happily in an area just twice the size of a shoe box. However, if this species were on show to the public in a vivarium of that size then there would follow a flood of complaints. Consequently, many snakes are housed in larger vivaria than necessary in public exhibits. This of course does them no harm, but smaller, adequate, vivaria have certain advantages when it comes to cleaning and disease control.

However, some snakes, such as the larger elapids, do appreciate a large vivarium as these snakes are generally more active, and perhaps more perceptive to their surroundings.

Reptile houses in Europe, America and other areas of temperate climate share many basic similarities: a series of cubicle-like vivaria with glass frontage situated inside a building and relying to a large extent on artificial sources of light and heat. Individual designs vary, but heat sources usually consist of circulated hot air, hot water pipes or electrical tubular heaters. This source of heat is usually placed underneath the floor or at the back of the reptile house and in many cases this means that there is no individual temperature control of separate cages. In addition, evenly spaced underfloor heating results in a high even temperature over the entire floor space and gives little scope for a snake to regulate its actual body temperature. In some species this inability to 'thermoregulate' could prove fatal as the preferred temperature range may be quite narrow.

Ultraviolet heat lamps can also be used as a heat source and these can be placed strategically so a snake can 'shuttle' to and from areas of temperature preference. Heat lamps should not be the only source of light; modern vivarium lighting is best effected by the use of 'true lite', or 'vita lite', fluorescent tubes which are now readily available on the market and are the nearest thing to natural daylight.

Ventilation is an aspect which is often neglected; a single air vent situated high in the vivarium is in fact inadequate, and indeed, more than one air vent is required if a proper exchange of air is to be accomplished.

At the Poole Serpentarium each separate vivarium is fitted with at least four air vents, the larger vivaria having more. The heating system at the Poole Serpentarium consists of tubular heaters which are situated at the front of each vivarium 25 cm below the level of the vivarium floor. Just below the heater is a grille 30 cm × 25 cm which draws air from the public area; this grille is fitted with a 'hit and miss' shutter so the air flow can be controlled. At the front of the floor of each vivarium is a mesh grille some 25 cm in depth which runs the entire width of the vivarium. This allows both warm and fresh air to rise from the heater and outside vent. The other two air vents are situated in the rear door and at the top of the rear wall. In addition, a large extractor fan in the service passage can be incorporated to boost the exchange of air. This fan can also be reversed so as to cool the area during very warm periods.

Each vivarium at the Poole Serpentarium has individual thermostatic control, and due to the thermal nature of the actual vivarium construction, this means that one vivarium could exhibit a temperature as high as 30°C, while its immediate neighbour could be maintained at a temperature of around 20°C.

The heat source for each vivarium is also supplemented with heat lamps, and these are of a fairly low wattage, so as not to cancel out the thermostatic control on the heaters proper.

Some reptile houses are fortunate enough to have natural daylight via a glass roof. This of course has additional heating benefits during the warmer parts of the year.

The actual furnishing of vivaria in public reptile houses is an art in itself, and to many reptile keepers it is an enjoyable occupation. Many of the snake-keeping fraternity are never so happy as when they are up to their elbows in stone and cement or choosing the right branch or log to suit a particular snake. It is an effort to simulate a snake's habitat co-ordinated with all the practicalities of captive husbandry (Fig. 65).

The advent of 'true lite' has also given the reptile-keeper the opportunity to introduce living plants into the vivarium. The species of plants chosen is largely a matter of taste, but certain consideration must be given to the nature of the inmate. Obviously, one would not include cacti in a vivarium containing rain-forest species, but more important is the fact that the plants are subjected to the activities of snakes in a restricted space. Plants should also be chosen therefore with regard to their strength; one plant may, for example, be happy to co-operate with the arboreal wanderings of a small viper but not the bulk of a large and equally arboreal mangrove snake.

The obvious difference between venomous snake cages and most

181

Fig. 65   Black-tailed rattlesnake, *Crotalus molussus*, a handsome and docile species in captivity.

other reptile cages is that the inmates are potentially lethal, and this imposes certain additional considerations.

Firstly, in the case of large and agile species such as the mambas and other large elapids, it is advisable to incorporate a trapping system or 'shift box' into the cage. This can be built into the rear wall of a vivarium and operated by means of a sliding shutter. One disadvantage of the built-in trapping box is that it is often difficult to coax the snakes back out into the vivarium. This can sometimes be overcome by the 'light reversal' system, whereby a light in the trapping box is turned on and the lights in the vivarium turned off in the hope that the snake will seek security in the darkest place.

The ideal type of trapping box is the one that can be detached, and this is invaluable when taking large and agile species off exhibit for one reason or another. Many species of venomous snake, however, can be just lifted from the vivarium and placed in a box or sealed bin and this applies in particular to the large species of *Bitis*, and some of the rattlesnakes.

Another important factor with regard to safety is that the furnishing of the vivarium should, in general, be kept to a minimum. This of course facilitates cleaning, but more importantly, the inmates will be seen easily and will not be tangled up in some forest of greenery. A colleague of mine was rightly proud of a pair of green mambas he had just obtained and the vivarium was lavishly furnished with 'interesting' branches and luxuriant green plants. The vivarium was also fitted with an elaborate trapping system, but even with the mambas safely boxed he found he could not clean the inside of the glass window without damaging half of the carefully installed branches.

Snakes that are kept in laboratory conditions are more simply dealt with, and in the public reptile house similar methods can be employed in back up, or 'behind the scenes', areas. It has been mentioned earlier that many species of snakes can be adequately housed in quite small containers. The plastic laboratory mouse and rat cages are ideal for this purpose, and these come in a variety of sizes which have proved to be adequate for most viper species and a number of elapids, such as the kraits. These containers have the additional advantage of being able to utilise space very efficiently, and they can be racked against a wall, almost to ceiling height if necessary. For obvious reasons the conventional grille-type lid on these mouse and rat cages is to a large extent unsuitable for most species. However, it is a relatively simple job to replace the grille by rigid Perspex with a mesh insert. This can be clipped securely to the container at either end.

Absorbent paper can be used to line the bottom of each container and this makes cleaning very easy. As there are no aesthetic requirements, furnishing can be limited to branches for aboreal species. In this case it is necessary to use plastic rat cages with a depth of at least 30 cm. Branches can then be fixed from corner to corner at mid-level to form an X which still allows the removal and replacement of paper liner. This arrangement is most suitable for the arboreal members of the genera *Trimeresurus* and *Bothrops*. Large arboreal species such as the mambas and golds tree cobra require a much larger vivarium in the laboratory, as do most of the larger terrestrial elapids and large vipers. For these species a vivarium 90 cm × 90 cm × 60 cm is ideal. These vivaria can be placed side by side and each should have a glass frontage for observation. Robust plywood is an ideal material for the construction of such vivaria and, due to the agile nature of the inmates, access should be via a lid at the top. This type of vivarium is very necessary if large species are to be catered for, and each vivarium is suitable for two Egyptian cobras, four common cobras or perhaps two black mambas. The large vipers can be kept in larger numbers: four diamondback rattlesnakes, or even up to six adult puff adders, can be contained in this manner.

Larger cages may be required for exceptional species such as the king cobra. However, six of the wooden vivaria should be sufficient to contain the nucleus of species for a venom extraction programme involving the larger types of venomous snakes.

The fossorial habits of some types of venomous snakes have already been mentioned with regard to the public display of such creatures. In the laboratory or back-up area, however, this requirement can be dealt with quite simply. A method I use, and which is most successful with such species as the banded Krait, and several species of both Asiatic and American coral snakes, is to include a mass of screwed-up paper on the bottom of the container. This gives the snakes the security they require. Exposure to strong light certainly appears to have disturbing effects on such species as the kraits, and another successful method is to keep these species in darkened containers.

In addition to the adapted mouse and rat cage, the plastic ice-cream containers are very useful for juvenile snakes, particularly young vipers. All that is required is a mesh ventilation panel, which can be bonded to the lid, and a series of small holes, one in the bottom for drainage, in the event of spillage from the water dish, and several other holes at either end for ventilation.

All snakes need regular access to water, and this should be provided in a shallow dish and checked daily as many snakes tend to defecate into their water containers. Most public reptile houses include a pool in each vivarium. Many snakes, although not regarded as even semi-aquatic, like to swim or soak in a pool, and these include such species as the puff adder, black mamba and just about all the species of cobra. The cleaning of pools is a daily event in any conscientious reptile house, and these pools should be designed with an eye to easy draining and filling.

The means of providing temperature and light have been mentioned, but it should be remembered that no one species exists at a constant temperature. Allowances must be made for fluctuations in both heat and light, conditions which vary between day and night and from season to season. At the Poole Serpentarium each vivarium has a 'dimming' facility which enables a varied photoperiod to be achieved.

Records

The keeping of accurate records is an important aspect of any zoological collection, and the resulting data stored at the reptile house or laboratory are of importance as valuable reference material.

It is no good trying to think back several days, or a week, and attempt to remember what a certain snake was doing, or when it fed or moulted, etc. Events must be logged as they occur if accurate records are to be maintained. The best method is to establish a daily log where all the happenings of that particular day can be entered. In addition, it is always useful to carry a small notebook for observations made away from the office.

At the Poole Serpentarium each individual snake has its own record card. On this card are noted details of acquisition, date, where purchased, price paid, or else captive birth, approximate age, i.e. adult or juvenile, sex, size, scars, wounds and any other relevant information. In addition, each snake is allocated a code number. Some snakes have an extra card with details of venom extraction, and all individuals have a separate card with details of medical history which terminates with a post-mortem report. This method has resulted in quick reference system whereby any aspect, such as growth, feeding, breeding and ailments, can be consulted quickly.

Any system will result in quite a considerable amount of office work. I usually bring cards up to date once a week using detailed information from the daily log. In addition, events of interest to other herpetologists can be written up and presented in a journal or newsletter, and this will promote the spread of knowledge of a much neglected subject.

Feeding

The feeding of live animals to snakes in captivity is, or should be, largely a thing of the past. The maintenance of large stocks of live rats and mice is both expensive and time-consuming, and the position is often reached where the time involved in cleaning and feeding these rodents almost equals that of actually maintaining the snake stock.

Most snakes, with patience, can be induced to accept dead food. This can be offered from the end of long forceps and activated to simulate life. There are, however, a small number of species that flatly refuse anything other than live food. There is, then, a case for holding a limited quantity of live food, firstly for those snakes that refuse all other forms of food, and secondly, to establish a breeding stock for producing food items representing a wide size range. For example, pink mice are invaluable for baby snakes, as are half-grown mice for some of the smaller species. These can be killed off and held in deep freeze with the other foodstock and will result in a consistent and reliable food supply.

The most difficult snakes to maintain with regard to feeding are the snake-eaters and other specialised feeders. The king cobra, and all the species of krait are typical examples of snake-eaters, and the night adders are noted for their exclusive preference for frogs and toads.

Force feeding is one method of dealing with such snakes, and where large numbers of such species are held for the purpose of venom extraction it is standard practice to insert a stomach tube well down into the snake after it has been milked, and syringe or pump a semi-liquid food down into the snake. Force feeding is standard practice at the Miami Serpentarium, for example, where large numbers of kraits are held. Snakes can also be force fed with mice, using a sterile rod, and pushing the food well down into the stomach. In such instances it is easier to use undersize food. For example, it is easier to push three mice down the throat of a snake than it is to struggle with a large rat.

Another method, which has worked well in the past, is the 'odour related' method. Snakes sense their food largely by scent and it is possible to induce many snakes to accept artificial 'snakes' and 'toads'. My own method of accomplishing this is to skin a rat or mouse and rub it well into a toad, or else anoint it with the anal contents of a live snake. Using this method I have fed king cobras, banded krait and two species of night adders, the latter of course accepting the 'toad mouse'.

This concept has now been developed one step further. Some zoos, notably the Gladys Porter Zoo in Texas, pioneered a completely new kind of food in the form of a sausage. These sausages can be made in a variety of sizes, and with correct odour manipulation a wide variety of snakes can be induced to accept them. The actual sausage is composed of a highly nutritious carnivore diet and has the obvious advantage that it can be deep frozen and stored for later use. The reptile house at the London Zoo have also had success using this method, and staff are currently developing new ways in which to make this new food form more attractive for a wider variety of species.

The periods at which a snake should be fed are usually quite straightforward. Snakes consume relatively large prey and do not have to feed as often as other carnivores. Some reptile-keepers feed their snakes religiously once a week, except for moulting periods. This is quite acceptable, but I prefer to feed snakes at more irregular intervals. The reason being that in the wild state a mouse does not present itself to a snake for dispatch on a certain day of each week, nor does a snake seek food at such precise intervals. Snakes in the wild are opportunists, and one week they may gorge themselves on several rats or whatever, and then they may not feed for a month. There are also seasonal fluctuations in a snake's feeding habits, which in addition to periods of inactivity may be allied to mating behaviour. Pregnant snakes will also refuse food for a period which can last as long as two months.

Snakes that are held for venom-extraction purposes are usually fed at the time of extraction, as this involves, in the case of snakes that have to be force fed, only handling once. Individual snakes in these conditions are extracted on a ten to fourteen day rota and it is usual to offer food to all such stock at the time of extraction. These include species that would accept food in the normal manner. This does not mean that all the snakes would be force fed; it is usually enough to place a dead mouse in the mouth of the snake before placing it back in the container. The snake, angry at being handled, usually consumes the mouse with no further trouble. Feeding taking place after venom extraction also means of course that all the venom is conserved and not wasted into even dead food items.

Breeding

It should be the aim of every serious keeper of venomous snakes to engage in an active breeding programme; random collections of various species are not really acceptable to most zoos and most exhibits now consist of compatible groups of males and females.

There are of course some species of snakes that will always prove difficult to keep in captivity, let alone inducing them to breed. However, our knowledge and methods are improving all the time, so perhaps one day we will see such events as captive-bred waglers pit vipers and other well-known delicate species.

Some species breed quite readily; the western diamondback rattlesnake and the puff adder are two examples which appear to require little encouragement, given the right conditions. Successful breeding is not just a simple case of putting male and female together and then hoping for the best. Mating in snakes is the climax of a sequence of events, and as far as is possible these events must be simulated in captive conditions.

For many species of snake the mating period in natural conditions follows the period of winter torpor. For this reason, if breeding is the object, these snakes should undergo a period of inactivity. This need not correspond with the full time in the wild; I have found that a month's simulated hibernation is usually adequate for most species. These snakes can be kept torpid in a container at a low temperature which relates approximately to climatic conditions in the snake's wild state. When reintroduced into the vivarium the temperature and photoperiod must again relate to the snake's natural preference.

As in the wild state male snakes may be sluggish and inactive for a time and be content just to bask. The females can be introduced a week or so later. Most male snakes in my experience will moult during this period and then they can be said to be wearing their breeding livery. Male rivalry may follow, which should result in a successful pairing, but it is important that the vanquished male be removed, or else offered to another female in a separate vivarium. Copulation may occupy several hours or more and during this time the snakes should not be disturbed. This captive mating period is usually more contracted than seen in the wild state, and it is usual that no food is accepted during this period.

These methods are typical when considering the vipers of temperate regions although male rivalry and lower temperatures are requirements for some of the tropical species such as the gaboon viper and the saw-scaled viper. It is sometimes possible to use a little trickery in captive breeding methods. I once had a pair of adult sand vipers, and the male was induced to mate by the stimulus provided by the introduction of a male European adder, whereupon rivalry was seen to take place!

The courtship of the vipers involves subtle persuasion with the male following the female with jerky movements of head and body. In all aspects involving this mating period there is usually no pronounced aggression and the fighting of the males is restricted to the ritual 'dance' where one snake attempts to force its rival to the ground with much neck thrusting and twining. There are some exceptions, however; the ottomans vipers have to be watched carefully at the Poole

Serpentarium at such time as the males have been known to wound each other.

The courtship of the elapids is somewhat more direct. Male rivalry occurs on occasions, but the male is more likely to take immediate possession of a female without any form of subtle courtship. Male Eygptian cobras, for example, will chew savagely on a female, causing considerable wounds, before actually pairing.

If mating is successful then the next step is the frustrating wait for the eggs or birth of young. It is often advisable to remove breeding females in the latter stages of pregnancy as this eases the removal of eggs or of baby snakes which can easily become lost amongst the vivarium furnishings.

Most reptile eggs are incubated artificially, and wherever possible they should be placed in incubators in the position in which they were laid. The eggs may be in a 'mass' or else separate and should be treated with great care. The actual incubation medium can be composed of various substances. Some reptile-keepers prefer sand or sawdust, but I use cellulose wadding or absorbent tissue, or else granular roof insulation material that is currently on the market and is ideal for the purpose of incubating snake eggs. The actual container can be a plastic box, or a sweet jar laid on its side with allowance for a free circulation of air. The incubation medium should also be moistened from time to time.

In many ways the problems of captive breeding really begin at the birth of the baby snakes. Obtaining food for these tiny creatures can be nerve-racking. New-born Malayan pit vipers, for example, are about 8 cm in length, as are the young of most of the medium to small vipers. Some baby snakes can be made to take chopped-up mice or pieces of lean meat, but it must be admitted that there is often a high death rate amongst new-born captive-bred snakes. It is difficult to force feed these small creatures without causing them actual physical damage, and it must be remembered that even tiny vipers are fully equipped with quite adequate venom apparatus.

Baby snakes are unlikely to accept food for a week or so after birth as they have sufficient reserves to be able to cope with this short period. Many young snakes tend to be cannibalistic, usually by accident during feeding periods, and it is best to house them separately. Examples of baby snakes that show this tendency are such species as the Egyptian cobra, common cobra, puff adder and mangrove snake.

Handling

Handling is the aspect that deters many a would-be keeper of venomous snakes, and it is true that this skill does require a certain amount of confidence. However, it is equally true to say that overconfidence is the mortal sin of anyone that has to deal with these creatures on a day-to-day basis. The keeper of venomous snakes must never lose sight of the fact that he alone is responsible for the consequences of his actions.

It is virtually impossible to keep venomous snakes without coming into contact with them from time to time. No matter how elaborate the trapping system, there is always the sick snake for treatment, or perhaps a fight to break up. Of course there are situations such as venom extraction where physical contact with venomous snakes is a matter of routine.

While there is always the possibility of an accident there are certain rules which should be adhered to that will keep the odds in the favour of the keeper. None of these rules are to be found in a textbook, and in fact most aspects of venomous snake handling are a result of personal experience.

These rules are concerned with both safety and security and are as follows:

1 Beware of becoming overconfident.
2 If feeling unwell in any way do not handle venomous snakes.
3 Alchohol and venomous snakes do not mix!
4 Do not involve any 'unskilled' person in activities involving venomous snakes.
5 Always expect the unexpected, i.e. untypical behaviour. There is no such thing as a typical individual for any species.
6 All venomous snake containers should be individually locked and bolted.
7 Display clear written instructions in prominent places in case of snakebite.

All these precautions may appear obvious, but if all the cases of snakebite involving venomous snakes in captivity were examined then the actual cause could be allied to one or other of the above rules.

There is no school for snake-keepers and the moment will arrive when one has to restrain and handle one's first venomous snake. Some

Fig. 66   Lifting a puff adder using an L stick at mid-body.

books will tell you that it is good practice to handle non-venomous snakes by picking them up by the neck. But it is difficult to simulate the physical moment of 'necking' a puff adder, and the psychological factor, knowing that the snake you are about to pick up can deal out death very effectively, is very real indeed (Fig. 66).

The temperament of snakes is of course variable, and one is familiar with descriptions of such species as the gaboon viper and banded krait as being docile and manageable. However, I am always suspect of such generalisations, and I have, for example, seen a gaboon viper performing a convincing impersonation of a mamba. Hence, always expect the unexpected. With regard to the temperament of snakes in captivity against those found in the wild, a well-known snake man once said, 'A snake in the hand is worth ten in the bush.' This is largely true and even the most docile snake often strongly resents being man-handled and will show this by sometimes violent convulsions of the body.

The situations in which venomous snakes have to be handled vary from the daily maintenance of those in the reptile house, to the mass handling of snakes housed in the venom extraction laboratory. The daily routine in the reptile house usually involves making available a cage for safe cleaning. If a shift box is incorporated then the snake may have to be coaxed into it. In other cages vipers may have to be lifted into a bin or similar container. One should never be tempted to clean the vivarium with the occupants still inside, though I know many of us have done it in the past, but even a puff adder can move the length of the vivarium with considerable speed.

There are several aids which can assist the safe handling of venomous snakes. The most familiar is the snake stick with a simple L attachment at the end, which is useful for lifting heavy-bodied snakes. In fact, with experience quite a number of snakes can be handled with this simple device, bearing in mind that the stick should be of an adequate length. Even cobras can be handled in this manner. I usually hook a cobra some 30 cm behind the head, which encourages the snake to gain some leverage by turning his neck around the L piece. I then take the tail in my other hand and pull gently while the cobra continues to assert the pressure of its neck on the stick. All movements when handling venomous snakes should be slow and deliberate, except when one drops a snake, when one can excusably be nimble and quick.

Other mechanical aids include grabsticks which are operated by a lever mechanism, some of which have a locking device. These grabsticks are ideal for mambas and other agile species and they can be obtained in various lengths. It is useful to have a wide range of types and sizes of snake sticks, although most snake men have their 'special', their favourite stick. Many ordinary houshold items can be adapted to make snake sticks. For the handling of baby snakes I use stainless-steel kebab skewers with one end bent at right angles. Similarly a wire coat hanger can be adapted for the same purpose (Fig. 67).

Another method used in handling is the application of anaesthetic; halothane is the medium most commonly used. However, the recovery time for snakes is about seventy hours, although there are no harmful side effects as far as is known.

Various types of nooses are often recommended in the handling of venomous snakes, but such devices often become entangled with the snake and they are also slow to release compared with the modern grabstick.

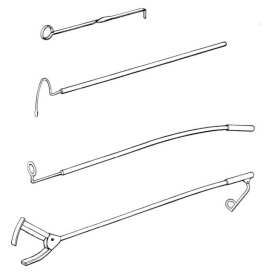

Fig. 67 Handling aids used for restraining venomous snakes. From top to bottom: converted kebab skewer used for handling baby snakes, L stick used for many kinds of venomous snakes, a larger custom-made version of the L stick used for the heavy vipers, grabstick used for some of the elapids and other agile species.

Most snake men have slightly differing methods when it comes to actually picking up a venomous snake with the hands. This involves holding a venomous snake by the head in such a manner as to render it harmless, that is to say, incapable of delivering a bite. Many people believe that to pin a snake down and take it behind the head is safest method of handling. In fact, this method is only safe if you know what you are doing. For example, there are quite different holds for vipers and cobras, and the size and strength of the snake are very important factors in deciding how a particular situation is to be approached.

My own methods have evolved over many years and I believe they are well tried and founded. With regard to vipers, the snake is first lifted gently on to a foam rubber pad 40 cm square. Using the L-shaped or T-shaped stick, the snake is then pinned gently but firmly across the top of the head, *not* the neck. To establish that sufficient pressure on the head has been attained, the tail of the snake is given a hard squeeze. This causes the snake to try and withdraw the head from under the stick. If it is unable to do so then, maintaining an equal pressure on the stick, a forefinger is placed on top of the snake's head and pressure applied downwards into the foam rubber. The stick is then discarded and the thumb and second finger are applied to the rear of the snake's quadrate bone, often referred to as the snake's

193

Fig. 68 Lifting a gaboon viper after it has been 'necked', George Williams takes the weight at mid-body with the other hand.

'shoulders' in the trade. The snake is then lifted clear of the foam pad and the weight of the body supported with the free hand. If the snake is of sufficient size then the body can be tucked under the arm, which discourages any convulsive movement on its part (Fig. 68).

The handling of elapids differs in the actual hold—a two rather than three finger hold. The thumb and forefinger are applied to the 'cheeks' of the snake, actually on the side of the rear of the quadrate bone. Another elapid hold is to place the thumb on the neck with the fore-finger across the throat, but personally I have never had full confidence in this particular hold.

Snakes of course do not always stay motionless while all this lifting, poking and prodding is going on. Most snakes in fact react violently, and it is as well to stand well back from the bench before the snake is pinned as it is quite feasible to receive a bite in the chest or abdomen. Many species exhibit individual traits when it comes to resisting hand-ling. Arboreal vipers will twist their neck and body when pinned and,

194

if allowed to do so, have the nasty habit of covering the head with a series of tight coils when being held in the hand. The saw-scaled viper has the disconcerting habit of depressing the head and, in fact, small snakes such as these are very precarious to handle. The kraits are well known for the habit of hiding the head under the body, a very frustrating habit when one is trying to pin it down.

One of the most trying snakes I have ever handled is the tropical rattlesnake, or cascabel. This snake has the habit of trying to withdraw the head from one's hand and then suddenly shooting the head forward. In fact, when a snake is in the hand one must be prepared for the sudden contortion which may occur at any time. Venomous snakes usually open their mouths quite willingly, although some of the elapids have to be coaxed by the insertion of a metal probe. Once the mouth has been opened it can then be inspected for infection and loose fangs (Fig. 69). This is an important factor that has already been mentioned with regard to venom extraction.

Once the snake has been introduced to the venom-receiving receptacle it usually gives the venom off quite willingly (Fig. 70). However,

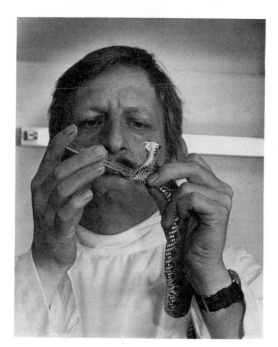

Fig. 69 The author demonstrating the hold for a viper, keeping a firm grip to the rear of the quadrate bone ('shoulders'). The snake is the mangrove pit viper, *Trimeresurus purpureomaculatus*, a highly nervous and aggressive species.

195

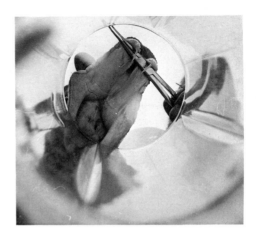

Fig. 70 Unusual view of the fangs of a gaboon viper, *Bitis gabonica*. The photograph was taken through the bottom of a beaker using a remotely controlled camera.

it is usual to aid this process by short gentle squeezes of the venom glands, using the free hand, taking care to keep clear of the front of the snake's mouth. Once the snake has been dealt with, the tricky situation arises, which is sometimes referred to as 'getting out', or in other words, releasing the snake. This can of course be aided by putting a dead mouse into the mouth of the snake. However, the procedure which I consider to be safest, when dealing with what is a very angry snake, is to take the snake to its container, place half of the body on the bottom, and then, choosing the moment carefully, gently but quickly throw the head downwards and snap the lid on.

Some venomous snakes are too much for just one man to handle; king cobras, other large cobras and mambas, large puff adders and gaboon vipers, large rattlesnakes, all require assistance. This of course adds another element of danger as one is dependent on other than one's own competence. There have been a number of accidents where an assistant has let go of the tail end of a snake at the wrong moment. I know of people who refuse to be assisted, and they would rather tackle large and dangerous species alone.

The transportation of snakes is a common event, and venomous snakes should be placed in strong cloth bags and then enclosed in a secure box which can be padlocked. The box should also be marked with a description of its contents. It is also important to remember that many snakes can bite through bags, so always handle such bags from the top only.

All institutions that hold venomous snakes should have access to

196

the necessary antivenin, and in addition local hospitals and medical centres should be aware of the fact that potential snakebite victims are in their area of responsibility.

Ailments

Snakes suffer from both internal and external parasites, the most common being mites, ticks and worms. New shipments of snakes should be examined thoroughly for parasites or any other sign of disorder. They should certainly not be placed with established snakes until a period has elapsed whereby full health and vigour can be properly ascertained.

There are not many veterinary surgeons who are willing, let alone capable, of getting to close quarters with venomous snakes. Consequently, it is the reptile-keeper who has to administer treatment to a sick snake.

However, drugs should not be administered without proper advice about type and dosage.

Mites can be overcome by using 'Vapona' in small strips in a container inaccessible to the snake and left for forty-eight hours. There are also drugs that can be diluted in water and sprayed via a vaporiser. Colds and chills can be treated with various penicillin-based drugs, but here again it is important to seek advice about dosage. Worms can be treated with regular worm mixtures or special preparations made by your vet. It is also advisable to analyse faecal samples from individual snakes at regular intervals.

Prevention is better than cure. Avoid overcrowding and be alert for signs of untypical behaviour or distress. Dead snakes should also be made available for post-mortem examination.

10
In the Field

Seeing a snake for the first time in the wild can be both a thrilling and alarming experience. The sudden appearance of an erect cobra or a coiled and angry rattlesnake causes slight symptoms of shock, even amongst ardent herpetologists.

The cobras, mambas and other large elapids, and some of the larger rattlesnakes, are examples of the types of snakes that sometimes let their presence be known. This is usually achieved by some form of defensive or warning display; i.e. hood spreading, rattling of the tail and loud hissing. However, it is of course the intention of field herpetologists to locate snakes, and it must be said that most species of snakes have to be searched for. Apart from having very efficient cryptic coloration, many snakes are secretive by nature and a number are burrowing forms.

The life styles and habits of wild snake populations still remain much of a mystery, but there are certain guidelines that can be observed that will assist in locating and assessing snake populations.

Firstly, the recorded distribution of individual species can be misleading when considering the blanket coverage offered by most conventional distribution maps. Most snake species are locally distributed and exist within certain levels of tolerance. Therefore, a species' existence in any one area can only be judged if such other factors as habitat preference, aspect of habitat, food source and urban tolerance are taken into consideration. The last-mentioned is of some importance, for it is a fact that many snakes occur in urban situations, often in what may appear to be wholly unsuitable conditions.

The question of snake habitat is often described in very general terms, and this is due to our lack of knowledge of the tolerance and adaptability exhibited by snakes in the wild state. It is the job of the fieldworkers, be they scientists or snake-catchers, to establish through their work with the various species a pattern of events which indicate status and local distribution.

Field study

The study of snakes in the wild can generally be regarded as falling into two main types—general survey, which involves assessing the snake fauna of a general region, and may also include other aspects of natural history; and specific study, which involves a study of a particular species, or a group of species where they occur together. The study of individual species may be confined to a narrow scope, for example feeding or mating behaviour, or just population density.

It is usually sufficient to conduct a general survey by sightings alone, particularly where a large area is to be covered, and time is limited. The first step in any serious fieldwork is to research the subject matter fully. All past information on the relevant species should be examined and a definite programme of work should be developed before even setting foot in 'snake country'. The recent history of an area should also be examined—changes in land use, habitat catastrophes such as fires and flooding, all will have had some effect on snake populations.

Talking to local people can also save time when trying to locate snake populations. Medical records will also give details of the incidence of snakebite. It is usually easier to approach fieldwork in a temperate climate as there are distinct seasonal variations which directly effect the annual active cycle of snake populations. In the tropics there are distinct wet and dry seasons to be considered. In any event it is important to begin fieldwork wherever possible at the start of a snake's annual cycle. This may be more difficult to determine in rain-forest or desert species, and in most cases where snakes occur in the warmer parts of the world it is useful to start research during the mating season when aggregations of snakes are more likely to occur.

It is not the aim of a general survey to identify each individual snake, it is usually sufficient to confirm a species' presence and possible range in a given area.

Even when the subject has been researched, many fieldworkers often find it baffling when confronted with what appears to be mile upon mile of identical habitat. My own experience has been that snakes very rarely occur evenly over a habitat but exist in distinct pockets.

Although a large expanse of heathland, savanna or semi-desert may appear to be similar throughout its area, a closer examination will reveal subtle differences in the terrain—a small gully, a group of bushes, a partly hidden crater or a dried-up stream. These features may not be the only ones of their kind, but may just possess that subtle difference, the right aspect to the sun, a fraction more plant growth, or some other factor that is essential to a species that can only exist within certain levels of tolerance. This is why it is necessary to research a subject before attempting any fieldwork.

Often, and it may appear quite obvious, people fail to establish whether the snake in question is diurnal or nocturnal, or perhaps crepuscular, and maybe even a combination of all three.

Many would-be fieldworkers also make the mistake of searching for snakes in great heat, even in the middle of the day, when any self-respecting snake will be coiled under the vegetation or situated in some other cooler place. Although some species do exhibit a greater tolerance to heat than other snakes they generally do not expose themselves during the hotter parts of the day. In desert and savanna areas it would certainly be a mistake for a fieldworker to be exposed to periods of great heat as he or she would soon be overcome with physical exhaustion, a condition not to be recommended when dealing with venomous snakes.

Experience has taught me to look 'into' potential snake habitat rather than at it; to put myself in the snake's position as it were. A flat stone, or a raft of dead grass, may look good to bask on, or perhaps to hide under. These subtle 'mini-habitats' must be examined thoroughly, but just visually—it is often a mistake to disturb the habitat early in any programme of fieldwork.

Specific studies of individual species can usually only be considered as long-term projects which may cover several years. This time factor is even more pronounced when considering the amateur fieldworker who can perhaps only participate in a programme of work at weekends. Even so, much of the valuable information that we now have regarding the life styles of snakes is a result of many hours of unpaid dedicated fieldwork by amateur naturalists.

Some species of venomous snakes have undergone a considerable amount of research; the work on the European adder by Ian Prestt and that on the copperhead by Henry Fitch are just two examples. Furthermore, it is highly likely that many species exhibit similarities in their way of life to those species that have undergone some degree of investigation. Therefore, it is helpful to list certain ecological criteria which could be relevant to the life style for a wide range of species. All the aspects listed below in their entirety can be considered as a full programme of fieldwork for any species, but it is appreciated that it may be necessary to be selective and maybe to concentrate on one or two related aspects.

The aspect of food is a major source for fieldwork alone, and in addition to working with snakes in the field will involve the analyses of large quantities of faecal samples.

Criteria for studying snake populations

1 Does the species exhibit a period of inactivity (i.e. hibernation or aestivation)?

2 Does the species occupy more than one type of habitat, and if so what degree of seasonal movement is involved?

3 Does the species exhibit communal behaviour?

4 What is the adult sex ratio?

5 What are the breeding potentials of (a) male, (b) female?

6 At what age and size does the species become sexually mature?

7 In what proportion do immature snakes appear in the population structure?

8 What is the mortality of (a) immature, (b) adult?

9 What are the significant predators?

10 Is the population autonomous?

11 What are the preferred food items?

12 What are the population numbers and density in accordance with range and scope of habitat?

In countries such as England and the USA, areas where snakes are abundant become well known within herpetological circles. It is important therefore that proper liaison should take place and fieldwork be co-ordinated so as to avoid duplication of work on a particular site. There is nothing more annoying than to arrive at a site for a good day's fieldwork only to find that someone has already covered the ground before you. Erosion is another problem that occurs when sites become overworked, and it is a fact that in the USA on sunny weekends snake men are thicker on the ground than the actual snakes!

Assuming that a site has been chosen and the presence of the relevant species has been confirmed, then the next step is to consider how individual snakes can be identified. This will involve making a permanent mark on the snake in some form or other. If the study is short-term then coloured paints can be used to mark the upper part of the neck. This paint will crack when the snake has fed, or else disappear when the snake moults.

Permanent marking can be achieved by clipping a number of scales on the ventral surface. The scales should be clipped in accordance with a preconceived code which will enable individual snakes to be identified (Fig. 71). The clipped scales will regrow after a time but usually in a different colour, and if the scales have been clipped neatly then these marks will still stand out plainly. The mark and recapture method of studying snakes has been well proven by a number of workers, and where large numbers of snakes are involved it is the only reliable method. Other methods, which are more time-consuming, include photographing part of a snake's pattern either on the dorsal or ventral surface. Detailed sketches also achieve the same purpose. How-

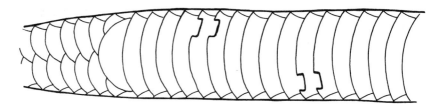

Fig. 71   Method of making a permanent identification of individual snakes by clipping the ventral scales. The scales are clipped with fine scissors. Those on the left are the master clips, and those on the right can be clipped in pairs up to the fortieth ventral scale until the master sequence is changed. The code for this individual would be 5.6/11.12.

ever, it should be remembered that a great many snakes may be involved, and I have found that, with experience, the average time that it takes to clip a snake is around two minutes from capture to release and a similar length of time is added if the snake is to be weighed and measured.

Snakes should be dealt with at the place of capture and released as soon as possible. It is no good gathering a number of snakes from various parts of the site and then trying to remember where they all came from. Record cards should also be established for individual snakes and these should be of a convenient size for carrying in the field.

In most parts of the USA and Europe we are lucky, for many sites can be reached by motor vehicle. The study of snakes in the tropics and desert regions is more trying and one must make allowances for the rigours of trekking through thick bush or rain forest even before any actual fieldwork can begin.

Equipment required for field study should always be kept to a minimum. A notebook and pen or pencil is of course a must, as are fine scissors and various spring balances to facilitate the marking and weighing of snakes. Small to medium sized snakes can be contained in strong polythene bags during the marking and measuring processes, but beware of the fact that a snake can bite through such a bag. The other advantage of clear polythene bags is that a snake can be examined in relative safety. Plastic tubes can also be used for marking and measuring purposes. It is, however, necessary to carry a range of various-sized tubes to accommodate snakes of different age groups.

The actual catching equipment should also be kept to a minimum; even just two snake sticks can become heavy by the end of the day. Unless one has the luxury of porterage then a wide range of snake sticks is a burden. One or perhaps two sticks should be chosen with the species to be studied in mind. A medium-sized L stick is probably the only requisite for small vipers; large elapids and arboreal species will, however, require a grab stick.

If study sites are situated in remote areas then it is important that the relevant antivenin be carried, and this should cover the venomous snakes of the region and not just the one species to be studied.

Many people would be content just to observe snakes, and this of course eliminates the sometimes risky business of actually handling them. In fact, one common mistake that many fieldworkers make is the failure to observe what the snake was doing just prior to capture. It is so tempting to 'pounce' immediately on spotting a snake, but a few seconds' observation can reveal much information. Firstly, the snake may be in company with other snakes, so the area all around the snake must be searched. It may even be lying on top of another.

Snakes are perceptive to ground vibration and sudden movement, and so all movements should be slow and deliberate; the 'snake walk' is something that comes with experience. Snakes are also perceptive to alien objects on the skyline, and a light coloured shirt can often aid the fieldworker in this respect. Arboreal snakes are usually content to let the world pass under them as it were and do not become unduly alarmed unless one invades the actual tree where they are situated.

Many species of snakes can be observed through binoculars of suitable focal length, and I find that the 8×40 specification is ideal for both terrestrial and arboreal species.

It is quite possible to get close to snakes without their becoming aware of one's presence. However, certain precautions should be observed when getting on close terms with potentially dangerous species. Once a position has been selected the observer should keep movement to a minimum and should not smoke or partake of refreshment.

Suprisingly enough, some of the more notably aggressive elapids make good subjects for close observation. I have observed a pair of king cobras in and around the nest from a distance of just three metres. Similarly, I have watched other cobras, and mambas, at close range.

If one maintains a rigid discipline one can become just part of the habitat as far as the snake is concerned. I have had thrilling moments when seated with my back against a tree when observing European adders in southern England. On one occasion a male in search of a mate passed over my leg several times, his mind full bent on procuring a mate, and completely oblivious to my presence. An outstanding example occurred on the same site, when in a similar position I was photographing male rivalry. The female, the cause of the action, had disappeared, and unbeknown to me had crawled on to my lap and coiled herself neatly inside my camera case.

Perhaps the most thrilling occasion of all occurred in a mango tree in eastern Kenya. I was sharing this tree with three green mambas which were quite unaware of my presence. I was seated across a branch close to the trunk, and the mambas were situated at the end of a branch just below that on which I was sitting. I had noticed that the mambas were agitated with each other, and it was the beginning of the breeding season. I was in the act of slowly raising my camera for a shot when, suddenly, and with alarming speed, one of the mambas detached itself from the group and raced on to the branch where I was perched and came to rest just six inches from what can be described as my 'middle region'. Frozen to the branch, and with camera still half raised, I watched unbelievingly as the bright green snake coiled and looped its body over the branch right between my legs. A minute or two passed, but it could have been an hour, then the snake jerked its head downwards back towards the other mambas. With a great sigh I watched as the mamba uncoiled and slid fluidly back towards its companions.

The green mamba, luckily, is an inoffensive snake, but it was certainly a lesson in expecting the unexpected.

The black mamba has a somewhat nastier reputation, and the rule here is never to put yourself in the path of a mamba. However, using common sense, even the notorious black mamba can be approached to within four or five metres. It is possible to get even closer, but safety must prevail.

Safety, of course, must always be given maximum consideration. It only takes one mistake, or a slight error of judgement, for a field study to end in tragic circumstances.

If one wishes to observe such species as large cobras or mambas then situations must be chosen where one has room to move. It would be a mistake to observe a black mamba within the confines of a thicket—more open ground must be chosen.

Photography is an obvious aid to observation and also provides a permanent record of the occasion. However, it is also obvious that photography will involve more movement on the part of the observer and as such the observation distance must be adjusted accordingly.

Fieldwork often involves a team of several people, and in such cases each person should have a specific task. Small to medium snakes only require one handler; a snake can be held by one person while others measure or photograph it. Larger snakes will probably require the assistance of another person, but it is imperative that the more experienced takes the head end. It is at such times that one seeks great faith in a colleague!

The difference between a fieldworker and a snake-catcher is that the serious fieldworker cannot study snakes in isolation; the habitat has to be considered. Hence a knowledge of botany and soil analysis is useful. Predators and food items have to be identified, and the effect and vagaries of climate have to be co-ordinated. The list goes on, and it becomes apparent that the world of the snake is no simple matter.

Snake-catching

The art of catching snakes is extremely variable: from the first efforts of a small boy as he plucks his first garter snake from a hibernation bank in North America, to the heroic struggles of Stanley Brock as he engages a large anaconda in some muddy tributary of the Amazon.

Snake-catching is regarded as almost a national sport in some areas; the rattlesnake roundups that occur in parts of the USA have already been mentioned. It is my strong belief that people should generally be discouraged from intentional encounters with venomous snakes. Children are perhaps the most ardent snake-catchers of all and it is a problem to persuade children that what they are doing could well be dangerous. However, skilled snake men do tend to learn their art from an early age; I caught my first adder at the age of eight years!

Snakes are caught for a number of reasons—to stock zoos and snake parks, for study purposes, and even for food in some parts of the world.

Many conservationists would say that it is wrong to take any creature from the wild; however, it is a fact that many snake populations have benefited and flourished through the unwitting efforts of mankind. Ionides collected and removed thousands of gaboon vipers from thickets and remnant forest areas without any noticeable depletion of the species. It should also be remembered that many snakes are killed each year throughout all parts of the world.

Some species of venomous snakes are a hazard to man; the saw-scaled viper occurs in high densities over much of its range and selective collection of this species would have obvious desirable effects. No responsible snake-catcher would wish to collect it *en masse*; it is usually enough to take just a few specimens from each area.

It is, however, practical to avoid important periods, such as when mating is at a peak, and perhaps also to avoid taking pregnant females. Wildlife conservation is a moral issue and each person engaged in taking snakes from the wild should approach the subject in a responsible manner.

The equipment needed by the snake-catcher may be somewhat more sophisticated than that of the average fieldworker. For example, it may be in the catcher's interest to carry a wider selection of snake sticks which are capable of dealing with most situations where the catching is taking place.

The freshly caught snakes should be placed in deep strong cloth bags, tied securely and labelled with the nature of their contents. If possible the bags should then be placed in a box, to avoid being trodden on, or even sat on! Snakes should never be placed in direct sun or in the confines of a car.

All the above information suggests that snake-catchers should work from a base. This is probably essential, considering that many snakes may be caught over difficult terrain. Many snake-catchers are content to sit back at base sipping beer while the local inhabitants locate the snakes. This is an idyllic method which is often more fruitful!

It is often difficult to get a freshly caught snake into a bag, and a useful device is a wire ring which can be clipped to the neck of the bag to keep it open and quickly detached once the snake is safely inside. This however, is more useful for the large vipers, as many of the elapids are too agile to permit the time required to close the bag. It is often necessary to neck elapids if they are to be restrained safely; this can be done by donning a snake bag like a glove, necking the snake through the bag, and then turning the bag inside out over the snake. The shape of the snake's head should be visible even through the bag and so the neck hold can be transferred to the other hand if necessary. One word of warning: beware of the bite through the bag and never carry snakes next to the body—always keep them at arm's length. Other useful tips are: always keep your eye on the head, and if a snake becomes tangled in vegetation, let it go!

Handling snakes in the wild is generally a more hazardous procedure than handling those in captivity as conditions are often unpredictable, and at least in captivity one has a certain amount of control.

Although there are general similarities in catching snakes of various species, different snakes often require different techniques. The obvious example is the different method used in dealing with terrestrial and arboreal forms. However, snakes vary in behaviour and temperament to such a large degree it is worthwhile here to consider a sample of species within my own scope of reference with regard to their safe capture.

Common cobra

Naja naja

Habits—Terrestrial.

Habitat—Varied, common around paddy fields, urban situations.

Temperament—Inoffensive, highly aggressive when restrained.

Method—May move off. This species easier to deal with when displaying erect with hood spread. Note positions, i.e. hood spread, body vertical—just threat; hood spread, body leaning well back, accompanied perhaps with 'whooshing' hiss—beware! pre-strike. Safe distance, two metres. Move in with grabstick to just rear of hood, force snake down and away from you. Keeping pressure on grabstick, take tail in other hand around vent region and draw body along length of grabstick. This will prevent cobra thrashing around and damaging itself. Lay grabstick and cobra on the ground and with hand in bag work up the snake's body to head. Take head through bag. Draw bag over snake and tuck body in gently. Transfer head to other hand and withdraw from bag. Twist bag quickly to disorientate. Tie bag. Snake secure.

Egyptian cobra

Naja haje

Habits—Terrestrial.

Habitat—Savanna and usually dry situations, sometimes near water.

Temperament—Quiet but inquisitive, highly aggressive when restrained.

Method—Usually displays with hood erect, strikes with little provocation. Grabstick to 30 cm behind hood in 150 cm specimen. May chew on stick. Restrain body along stick and pin head. Take head through bag but beware of constant jaw movement. When body in bag transfer hands and twist and tie. Snake secure.

King cobra

Ophiophagus hannah

Habits—Terrestrial.

Habitat—Varied, forest and areas of rural agriculture.

Temperament—Normally quiet, highly dangerous when aroused.

Method—May 'rush' forward when encountered, avoid confined spaces with this species! Grabstick directly to neck and force to ground. Assistance to restrain long muscular body. Take head through bag with two hands if large specimen. Assistant draws bag over body and ties. Release head. Snake secure.

Black mamba

Dendroaspis polylepis

Habits—Terrestrial arboreal.

Habitat—Savanna, rocky outcrops, thickets, remnant forest.

Temperament—Highly aggressive.

Method—Proceed only in open area. Grabstick to 20 cm behind head. Mamba will probably tie body in complicated coil around grabstick. Lay grabstick and snake on ground, keeping a watch for the head. Pin head and take through bag with strong thumb and forefinger grip. Preferable assistance to body. Twist and tie. Snake secure.

Green mamba

Dendroaspis angusticeps

Habits—Arboreal and highly agile.

Habitat—Forest, remnant forest, and thickets.

Temperament—Inoffensive, highly dangerous when restrained.

Method—Potentially highly dangerous situation as it usually entails climbing same tree, often to high canopy as mamba usually moves upwards when alerted. Beware

209

the presence of more than one mamba! Assistance
required! Grabstick applied to 20 cm behind head and
locked! Avoid pulling snake through rough branches,
skin very delicate. Snake locked in stick should be
passed by relay to ground, keeping head well away from
arms and legs, etc. Mamba will probably have become
well wrapped around the stick by this time. With great
care head should be pinned and taken through the bag.
Assistance to body. Twist and tie. Snake secure.

Spitting cobra

Naja nigricollis

Habits—Terrestrial.

Habitat—Savanna and areas of rural human habitation.

Temperament—Nervous and aggressive.

Method—Goggles must be worn! Grabstick to 10 cm behind head.
Pin quickly as snake tends to contort violently when
restrained. Take head through bag, pull over body, twist
and tie. Wipe venom from all parts of body and tools.
Snake secure.

Puff adder

Bitis arietans

Habits—Terrestrial.

Habitat—Savanna, and areas of rural human habitation.

Temperament—Sluggish but quick to strike with amazing speed.

Method—Small specimens up to 70 cm can be just lifted with
stout L stick and dropped into a wire-ringed bag. Large
individuals are usually too heavy to allow this method
and so they should be properly necked and the weight
taken with the other hand or by an assistant. Puff
adders may jerk the body violently so do not be caught
unawares. The puff adder can then be dropped into the
bag, taking care to 'throw' the head away from you.
Twist and tie. Snake secure.

Gaboon viper

Bitis gabonica

Habits—Terrestrial.

Habitat—Rain forest and remnant forest and thickets.

Temperament—Usually placid but capable of lightning strike.

Method—As with puff adder.

Saw-scaled viper

Echis carinatus

Habits—Terrestrial, often found under stones or logs.

Habitat—Semi-desert and dry arid regions.

Temperament—Alert and vicious.

Method—Saw-scaled vipers can be coaxed into wire-ringed bag. Beware of lightning 'jumping' strike. Long forceps can also be employed to lift this species into the bag. Several may be placed in one bag, but keep bag away from body.

European adder

Vipera berus

Habits—Terrestrial.

Habitat—Heathland, moors, quarries, railway embankments.

Temperament—Inoffensive, but quick to strike when aroused.

Method—Wait until adder moves off then place foot gently on the neck region, take the snake by the tail, play it like a yo-yo, and drop into wire-ringed bag. Twist and tie. Snake secure.

Russells viper

Vipera russelli

Habits—Terrestrial.

Habitat—Varied, both forest and open areas occupied.

Temperament—Very aggressive, will resist capture violently.

Method—One viper where a grabstick is advisable. Capture should be executed as quickly as possible, dropping the snake into a wire-ringed bag. Twist and tie. Snake secure. Great care must be taken with this species.

Western diamondback rattlesnake

Crotalus atrox

Habits—Terrestrial.

Habitat—Semi-desert and dry arid areas, also some cultivated areas.

Temperament—Alert and vicious.

Method—Beware long striking range of this species. Large examples may require grabstick. Wait until snake moves off then pin the neck region with stout L stick. Take the tail with the other hand, keeping the head at bay. Then lift the snake out to arm's length and drop into wire-ringed bag. Twist and tie. Snake secure.

Barba amarilla

Bothrops atrox

Habits—Terrestrial.

Habitat—Forest, and cultivated areas.

Temperament—Alert and vicious.

Method—As for large rattlesnakes.

Malayan pit viper

Agkistrodon rhodostoma

Habits—Terrestrial.

Habitat—Forest, plantations and other cultivated areas.

Temperament—Quick to strike.

Method—May often occur in groups, some individuals may be hidden in leaf litter, etc. Stout L stick can be used to lift, but beware of lightning jerky movements of the body. The snake should be quickly dropped into a wire-ringed bag. Twist and tie. Snake secure.

Arboreal vipers

Atheris spp., *Trimeresurus* spp., *Bothrops* spp.

Habits—Arboreal.

Habitat—Low bush to high canopy in rain forest and remnant forest.

Temperament—Variable, but many prone to strike.

Method—Arboreal vipers can usually be detached from their perches by using two L sticks, one to coax the snake on to the other L stick. When this has been accomplished the snake can then be gently shaken into a wire-ringed bag.

Various snake-catchers have their own special methods. Some will take cobras with just the aid of an L stick, or perhaps just grab it by the tail. I must admit that I have caught cobras without the aid of a stick.

However, safety is the byword, and if a snake is getting the better of one by becoming entangled in vegetation, or winning in some other way, then it is necessary that on such occasions the snake should be afforded its freedom.

If common sense prevails then both snake and man will live to fight another day.

Appendix I

Principal Antivenin Sources

Country or region	Product	Species
EUROPE		
Institut Pasteur, 36 Rue du Docteur Roux, Paris, 15, FRANCE	Serum Antivenimeux	*Bungarus flaviceps, Naja naja, Naja haje, Naja nigricollis* (monovalent) *Dendroaspis viridis, Agkistrodon rhodostoma, Bothrops lanceolatus* (monovalent) *Vipera berus, V. aspis, V. ammodytes, V. lebetina, V. xanthia, Echis carinatus* (monovalent) *Bitis arietans, Bitis gabonica, Cerastes, Cerastes vipera*
Behringwerke Aktiengesellschaft, Postfach 1140, Marburg 1, WEST GERMANY	Serum Nordafrika	*Cerastes cerastes, Cerastes vipera, Vipera lebetina, Echis carinatus, Naja nigricollis, Naja haje, Bitis arietans, Bitis gabonica*
	Serum Zentralafrika	*Bitis arietans, Bitis gabonica, Bitis nasicornis, Hemachatus haemachatus*
	Serum Naher und Mittlerer Orient	*Cerastes cerastes, Echis carinatus, Vipera lebetina, Vipera ammodytes, Naja haje*
	Serum Europa	*Vipera ammodytes, Vipera lebetina*
	Serum Mittle und Sudamerika	*Crotalus durissus, Bothrops atrox, Bothrops jajaraca*
	Serum Kobra	*Hemachatus haemachatus, Naja nivea, Naja haje, Naja nigricollis*
INDIA		
Haffkine Institute, Parel, Bombay 12, Maharashtra	Polyvalent Anti-Snake Venom Serum	*Naja naja, Bungarus caeruleus, Echis carinatus, Vipera russelli*

214

Country or region	Product	Species
INDONESIA		
Perusahaan Negara Bio Farma (Pasteur's Inst.), 9 Djalan	ABM Antivenin	*Bungarus fasciatus, Naja n. sputatrix, Agkistrodon* sp.
PHILIPPINES		
Bureau of Research Laboratories, PO Box 911, Manila	Cobra Antivenin	*Naja n. philippinensis*
UNITED STATES OF AMERICA		
Wyeth Laboratories, Marietta, Philadelphia	North and South American Crotalid Antivenin	Covers most species of New World pit vipers
	Coral Snake Antivenin	*Micrurus* spp. (Not *M. mipartitus*, or *M. euryxanthus*)
CENTRAL AMERICA		
Instituto Nacional de Higiene, Czda,	Suero Anticrotalico	*Crotalus durissus, Crotalus basiliscus*
Escobedo 20, MEXICO	Suero Antiviperino	*Crotalus durissus* spp., *Crotalus basiliscus, Bothrops atrox*
	Suero Antibotropico	*Bothrops atrox*
SOUTH AMERICA		
Instituto Butantan, Caixa Postal 65, São Paulo, BRAZIL	Soro Anti-Crotalico	*Crotalus* sp.
	Soro Anti-Laquetico	*Lachesis mutus.*
	Soro Anti-Elapidico	*Micrurus* spp.
	Soro Anti-Botropico	*Bothrops* spp.
	Soro Anti-Ophidico	*Bothrops* spp. and *Crotalus* spp.
THAILAND		
Queen Saovabha Memorial Institute, Rama IV Street, Bangkok	Antivenine Serum	
	Cobra	*Naja n. kaouthia*
	King Cobra	*Ophiophagus hannah*
	Green Pit Viper	*Trimeresurus popeorum*
	Russells Viper	*Vipera russelli*
	Pit Viper	*Agkistrodon rhodostoma*

215

Country or region	Product	Species
TAIWAN		
Taiwan Serum Laboratory 151 Tong-shin Street,	Naja Monovalent	*Naja n. atra*
Nang Kang, Taipei	Bungarus Monovalent	*Bungarus multicinctus*
	Neurotoxic Polyvalent	*Naja n. atra* and *Bungarus multicinctus*
	Agkistrodon Monovalent	*Agkistrodon acutus*
	Hemorrhagic Polyvalent	*Trimeresurus mucrosquamatus, Trimeresurus stejnegeri*
JAPAN		
Institute for Medical Science,	Mamushi Venom Antivenin	*Agkistrodon halys blomhoffii*
University of Tokyo	Habu Venom Antivenin	*Trimeresurus flavoviridis*
ISRAEL		
Rogoff Wellcome Research Laboratories,	*Vipera palaestinae* Antiserum	*Vipera palaestinae*
Beilinson Hospital, PO Box 85, Petah, Tikva	*Echis coloratus* Antiserum	*Echis coloratus*
SOUTH AFRICA		
South African Institute for Medical Research, Hospital Hill, PO Box 1038, Johannesburg	Boomslang Antivenin	*Dispholidus typus*
	Polyvalent Antivenin	*Bitis arientans, Bitis gabonica, Naja nivea, Hemachatus haemachatus*
	Polyvalent Antivenin	*Hemachatus haemachatus, Naja nivea, Bitis arientans, Bitis gabonica, Echis carinatus*
	Polyvalent Antivenin	*Dendroaspis angusticeps, Dendroaspis jamesoni, Dendroaspis polylepis*

Country or region	Product	Species
AUSTRALIA		
Commonwealth Serum Laboratories, Poplar Road, Parkville, Melbourne, Victoria	Papua New Guinea Polyvalent Antivenin	*Oxyuranus scutellatus, Acanthophis antarticus, Notechis scutatus, Pseudechis papuanus*
	Tiger Snake Antivenin	*Notechis scutatus*
	Taipan Antivenin	*Oxyuranus scutellatus*
	Brown Snake Antivenin	*Pseudonaja textilis*
	Death Adder Antivenin	*Acanthophis antarticus*
	Papuan Black Snake Antivenin	*Pseudechis papuanus*
	Sea Snake Antivenin	*Enhydrina schistosa*
	Cobra Antivenin	*Naja n. sputatrix*

Appendix II

Emergency Procedure for dealing with Snakebite, compiled by Dr H. A. Reid, Liverpool School of Topical Medicine, in 1978

1 *Advice on management*
   is available from Dr H. A. Reid, Liverpool School of Tropical Medicine, telephone 051–708 9393; out of office hours 051–228 9607; if no reply, 051–733 4020 (Sefton General Hospital), ask for Ward 17, then for Tropical Consultant on Duty.

   And Dr D. A. Warrell, Radcliffe Infirmary, Oxford, telephone 0865 49891; out of office hours 0235 88344.

2 *Detain for at least 12 hours' observation, preferably in intensive care unit*
   Give tetanus toxoid injection to reassure patient.
   General charting
   Hourly blood pressure, pulse and respiration rate. Vomiting, diarrhoea.
   Daily WBC (? neutrophils increased), serum bicarbonate, creatine phosphokinase or SGOT, ECG (ECG more often if hypotension persists).
   Urine protein and output, blood urea.
   Local necrosis if relevant (extent of blisters and skin darkening, putrid smell).
   Viper bites: abnormal bleeding (injection sites, gums, skin, cerebral, etc.); daily blood clotting or non-clotting; haemoglobin; swelling (limb circumferences).
   No local swelling 2 or more hours after viper bite **excludes envenoming.**
   Elapid bites: ptosis; difficulty speaking or swallowing; breathing change.

3 *Indications for giving antivenom*
   Only a minority need antivenom, as little venom is usually injected. Clinical trials show specific antivenom is successful in severe poisoning although not given until several hours after bite. There-

fore **wait for clear clinical evidence of poisoning before giving antivenom** (but signs must be positively sought).

Antivenom is indicated when:

(*a*) **Systemic signs present = main indication** (all cases—hypotension, ECG changes, neutrophilia, acidosis; in some types of viper bite but not in adder bite—abnormal bleeding, non-clotting blood; in elapid bites—ptosis, glossopharyngeal palsy).

(*b*) Local swelling present, bite by adder (adult patients only) or by known necrotising snake, e.g. cobra, or African puff adder (all ages), and patient seen within 3 hours of the bite.

4 *Administration of antivenom*

Type of antivenom: stock for foreign venomous snakebite held at Pharmacy, Walton Hospital, Liverpool, telephone 051–525 3611; out of office hours, ask for Senior Nurse on Duty; also at National Poisons Centre, telephone 01–407 7600. Zagreb antivenom should be stocked in all regions.

Dose: adder 2 ampoules; foreign vipers usually 5 ampoules; elapid 10 ampoules. Repeat in 1–2 hours if no clinical improvement. Dose for children same as for adults.

Serum sensitivity tests: can be misleading so **not** recommended; but **'allergic' history** contra-indicates antivenom (unless envenoming threatens life).

Route: **intravenous infusion** starting slowly (15 drops/minute). If reaction occurs, stop drip, inject 0·5 ml of 1:1000 adrenaline subcutaneously. Re-start drip and slowly increase speed to complete administration in 30–50 minutes.

5 *General measures*

Give placebo injection for reassurance (unless antivenom indicated); release tourniquet if applied; leave bite site alone as interference often causes infection; steroids **only** for delayed serum reactions; cryotherapy aggravates necrosis, heparin aggravates bleeding so both contra-indicated; antibiotics needed **only** if local necrosis ensues (prompt excision, maybe skin graft then needed).

Nurse patients with dysphagia (eliapid bite) in prone position to minimise the risk of inhaling vomit or secretions; respiratory failure—intubation, artificial respiration; renal failure, conservative treatment (avoid tetracycline), dialysis.

219

Glossary

ADAPTIVE RADIATION	Development of allied groups of animals along dissimilar evolutionary paths
AGLYPHOUS	Lacking venom fangs
ALLOPATRIC	Species not occurring together within the same range or area
ANNUAL CYCLE	Used to describe the sequence of events as they occur each year with reference to wild snake populations
ANTIVENIN	Antivenene; antiserum with the ability to neutralise the effects of venom
ARBOREAL	Tree-living; applies equally to species living largely in bush or scrub.
AUTONOMOUS	Self-governing, used to describe snake populations that maintain their numbers without external recruitment or influence
BIENNIAL BREEDING CYCLE	The obligatory breeding cycle of female snakes largely in temperate climates where individuals breed in alternate years
BRILLE	The transparent scale that covers the eye in snakes
CARBONIFEROUS	Geological period some 280–350 million years ago
COMBAT RITUAL	Male rivalry in snakes during the breeding season
CREPUSCULAR	Active at dusk (twilight)
CRETACEOUS	Geological period some 65–135 million years ago
CRYPTIC	Coloration of animal that blends with background; i.e. camouflage
DIURNAL	Active during the hours of daylight
DORSAL	Pertaining to the upper surfaces; e.g. the dorsal pattern of snakes
DUVERNOY'S GLAND	Venom-producing gland of rear-fanged colubrid snakes. So called after D. M. Duvernoy, the French anatomist
ECOLOGY	The study of animals and plants in relation to their environment
ECTOTHERMIC	Cold-blooded, poikilothermic; animal reliant on external sources of heat

ENDEMIC	Animal or plant that is restricted to one area.
ENZYME	Protein catalyst that initiates a reaction without any permanent change in its structure
EXUVATION	Moult, slough, ecdysis; skin-shedding
FOSSORIAL	Burrowing; used to describe species that largely occur beneath the soil or ground vegetation
GANGRENE	Local death of tissue
GASTROTEGES	The ventral plates of snakes
HAEMOTOXIC	Used to describe the action of certain venom fractions which impair the functions of the blood
HEMIPENES	The paired sexual organs of male snakes
HERPETOLOGY	The study of reptiles and amphibians
HOOD	Used to describe the flattened part of the neck region in an erect cobra
IMBRICATE	Body scales in snakes that overlap, in similar fashion to the tiles of a roof; cf. JUXTAPOSED
INTERGRADE	Hybridisation between closely related species or sub-species in the wild; e.g. *Vipera berus/Vipera aspis*
JUXTAPOSED	Body scales of snakes that do not overlap; cf. IMBRICATE
KOPJE	Afrikaans pron. 'Koppee', used to describe rocky outcrop on African savanna
LABIAL	Pertaining to the scales that border the mouth of snakes
LATERAL	Pertaining to markings, colour, scales, etc., situated on the sides or flanks of snakes
LATERAL UNDULATION	Used to describe the most common mode of terrestrial snake locomotion
LD50	The amount of venom necessary to kill fifty per cent of animals in a test group
LOREAL PIT	The heat-receptive organ of the pit vipers situated in the region of the loreal scale on each side of the head
MIGRATION	See SEASONAL MOVEMENT
MIOCENE	Geological period some 6–25 million years ago
MONOTYPIC	Genus possessing just one species
MONOVALENT	Term applied to antivenins produced to be effective against envenomation of a specified species

221

MOULT	See EXUVATION
NEUROTOXIC	Venom fraction destructive to the nervous system
NEW WORLD	The Americas
NOCTURNAL	Active by night
OLD WORLD	Europe, Asia, Africa
OLIGOCENE	Geological period some 25–35 million years ago
OPHIOPHAGUS	Used to describe any animal that habitually feeds on snakes
OPISTOGLYPHOUS	Possessing venom-conducting teeth towards the rear of the upper jaw; i.e. the rear-fanged colubrids
OVIPAROUS	Reptiles that lay eggs
PARALLEL EVOLUTION	Development of similar species by two distinct groups
PAROTID GLAND	See DUVERNOY'S GLAND
PELAGIC	Ocean-inhabiting
POLYVALENT	Used to describe antivenins that have antitoxins which are effective against a number of different species of venomous snakes
POPULATION DENSITY	The numbers of snakes that occur within a given area
PROTEROGLYPHOUS	Possessing venom-conducting fangs towards the front of the mouth which are largely immovable, i.e. the elapids
ROSTRAL	Scale at tip of snout
SAVANNA	Large expanse of grassy plain
SEASONAL MOVEMENT	Migration; movement of snakes from one habitat to another, associated with certain periods of the year
SEDENTARY	Used to describe species of snakes that exhibit only a limited amount of movement
SEXUAL DIMORPHISM	The marked differences between male and female snakes with regard to colour, shape or size
SEX RATIO	Relative number of male and female snakes as they occur in wild populations
SHIFT BOX	Device used for trapping and catching up venomous snakes in captivity
SIDEWINDING	A mode of locomotion used by the desert-dwelling species of vipers

SOLENOGLYPHOUS	Possessing venom-conducting fangs which are hinged and situated well forward in the mouth; i.e. the vipers
SYMPATRIC	Species that exist together within a given area or region
TAXONOMY	The science that deals with the classification of organisms
TERRESTRIAL	Living largely at ground level
THERMOREGULATION	Used to describe a snake's ability to maintain its optimum temperature
TOXICOLOGY	The science and study of the effects of biological toxins on living organisms
VENT	The posterior opening situated at the beginning of the tail in snakes
VENTRALS	See GASTROTEGES
VIVIPAROUS	Bearing live young
VIVARIUM	Container or cage where captive snakes or other reptiles are housed.
VOLUNTARY TEMPERATURE	The obligatory regulation of body temperature in reptiles
WINTER TORPOR	Period of obligatory inactivity exhibited by reptiles during the cold months of the year
ZOOGEOGRAPHY	The study of the geographical distribution of animals

Selected Bibliography

APPLEBY, L. G. (1971) *British Snakes* John Baker, London

ARNOLD, E. N. & BURTON, J. A. (1978) *A Field Guide to the Reptiles and Amphibians of Europe* Collins, London

BELLAIRS, A. (1969) *The Life of Reptiles* 2 vols, Weidenfeld & Nicolson, London

BROADLEY, D. G. (1971) 'The Reptiles and Amphibians of Zambia' *The Puku* Occ. Papers, Dept of Wildlife, Fisheries, and National Parks, Zambia. No. 6

BROADLEY, D. G. & COCK, E. V. (1975) *Snakes of Rhodesia* Bundu Series, Longman, Rhodesia

BROWN, J. H. (1973) *Toxicology and Pharmacology of Venoms from Poisonous Snakes* Charles C. Thomas, Springfield, Illinois, USA

BUCHERL, W., BUCKLEY, E., DEULOFEU, V. (1968) *Venomous Animals and Their Venoms* 3 vols, Academic Press, New York, London

BURCHFIELD, P. M. (1977) 'An Experimental Artificial Diet for Captive Snakes' *International Zoo Year Book* 172–173, Zoological Society of London

BURKETT, R. D. (1966) *Natural History of Cottonmouth Moccasin* University of Kansas Publications, Museum of Natural History, Vol. 17, No. 9, 435–491

CAZALY, W. H. (1914) *The Common Snakes of India and Burma and how to Recognise Them* Alahabad, The Pioneer Press

COGGER, H. G. (1975) *The Reptiles and Amphibians of Australia* A. H. & A. W. Reed, Sydney, Wellington, London

CONANT, R. (1975) *A Field Guide to Reptiles and Amphibians of Eastern and Central North America* 2nd Ed., Houghton Mifflin Company, Boston, USA

COOPER, J. E. (1973) 'Veterinary Aspects of Recently Captured Snakes' *British Journal of Herpetology* Vol. 5, No. 1, 368–374

COOPER, J. E. (1974) 'Parasites from Reptiles in Kenya with Notes on their Significance and Control' *British Journal of Herpetology* Vol. 5, No. 3, 431–438

DITMARS, R. L. (1960) *Snakes of the World* The Macmillan Company, New York

FITCH, H. S. (1960) *Autecology of the Copperhead* University of Kansas Publications, Museum of Natural History, Vol. 13, No. 4, 85–288

FITZSIMMONS, V. F. M. (1970) *A Field Guide to the Snakes of Southern African* Collins, London

GHARPUREY, K. G. (1935) *The Snakes of India* Popular Book Depot, Bombay

HOOFIEN, J. H. (1972) *Reptiles of Israel* Dept of Zoology, Tel-Aviv University

ISEMONGER, R. M. (1962) *Snakes of Africa* Thomas Nelson & Sons (Africa) (Pty) Ltd

KLAUBER, L. M. (1972) *Rattlesnakes. Their Habits, Life Histories, and Inffuence on Mankind* 2nd Ed., University of California Press

KOCHVA, E. & GANS, C. (1967) 'The Structure of the Venom Glands and Secretion of Venom in Viperid Snakes' *Animal Toxins* Pergamon Press, Oxford & New York

MINTON, A. & MINTON, R. M. (1971) *Venomous Reptiles* George Allen & Unwin, London

PAWLEY, R. (1971) 'A Convenient System for Housing "Off Exhibit" Reptiles in Brookfield Zoo, Chicago' *British Journal of Herpetology* Vol. 4, No. 8, 210–214

PHELPS, T. E. (1978) 'Aspects of Studying Wild Snake Populations' *Report of the Cotswold Herpetological Symposium* England, 16–20

PHELPS, T. E. (1978) 'Seasonal Movements of the Snakes *Coronella austriaca, Vipera berus,* and *Natrix natrix*, in Southern England' *British Journal of Herpetology* Vol. 5, No. 11, 755–761

PITMAN, C. R. S. (1974) *A Guide to the Snakes of Uganda* Rev. Ed., Wheldon & Wesley, Ltd

PRESTT, I. (1971) 'An Ecological Study of the Viper, *Vipera berus*, in Southern Britain' *Journal of Zoology* 164, 373–418

REID, H. A. (1978) 'Bites by Foreign Venomous Snakes in Britain' *British Medical Journal* 17th June, 1598–1600

REID, H. A. & THEAKSTON, D. G. (1978) 'Changes in Coagulation Effects by Venoms of *Crotalus Atrox* as Snakes Age' *American Journal of Tropical and Medical Hygiene* 27 (5), 1053–1057

RICHES, R. J. (1976) *Breeding Snakes in Captivity* The Palmetto Publishing Company, Florida

STEBBINS, R. C. (1966) *A Field Guide to Western Reptiles and Amphibians* Houghton Mifflin Company, Boston, USA

STEWARD, J. W. (1971) *The Snakes of Europe* David & Charles, Newton Abbot, Devon

SWAROOP, S. & GRAB, B. (1954) 'Snakebite Mortality in the World' *Bulletin of the World Health Organisation* 35–76

SWEENEY, R. C. H. (1971) *Snakes of Nyasaland* (Rep. Ed.), Asher & Co., Amsterdam

TWEEDIE, M. W. F. (1961) *The Snakes of Malaya* Government Printing Office, Singapore

UNDERWOOD, G. (1967) *A Contribution to the Classification of Snakes* Brit. Mus. (Nat. Hist.), London

US Navy Bureau of Medicine and Surgery (1968) *Poisonous Snakes of the World* US Government Printing Office, Washington, DC

WALL, F. (1913) *The Poisonous Terrestrial Snakes of our British Indian Dominions (Including Ceylon) and How to recognise them with Symptoms of Snake Poisoning and Treatment* Bombay Natural History Society

WARRELL, D. A. & ARNETT, C. (1976) 'The Importance of Bites by the Saw-Scaled or Carpet Viper *(Echis carinatus)*: Epidemiological Studies in Nigeria and a Review of the World Literature' *Acta Tropica Separtum* Vol. 33, No. 4, 307–341

WRIGHT, A. H. & WRIGHT, A. A. (1957) *Handbook of Snakes* 2 vols., Cornell University Press, New York

Index

Figures in bold refer to colour plates. Those in italics refer to page numbers of black and white illustrations.

226